THE NEURAL BASIS OF RELIGIOUS COGNITION

The Neural Basis of Religious Cognition brings together leading researchers from psychology, neuroscience, and religious studies to identify the neural circuits underlying various aspects of religious behavior and cognition. This book presents cutting-edge research in the cognitive neuroscience of religion, demonstrating how brain research techniques can illuminate the puzzles and complexities of religious experience.

Understanding the neural foundations of religious cognition holds both historical significance and contemporary relevance for human understanding, potentially revealing insights into uniquely human aspects of social brain functioning. Through in-depth explorations of diverse topics, including prayer, psychedelic experiences, and the impact of neurodegenerative disorders on religious cognition, this book provides extensive coverage of this emerging interdisciplinary field. The research presented offers valuable knowledge about how the brain processes religious thoughts, emotions, and behaviors, contributing to broader understanding of human consciousness and spirituality.

This book provides in-depth explorations of various topics within the cognitive neuroscience of religion, including prayer, psychedelics, and the impact of neurodegenerative disorders, making it a must-read for all researchers of the psychology of religion.

Jordan Grafman is Director of Brain Injury Research at the Shirley Ryan AbilityLab in Chicago, IL, USA, and Professor of Physical Medicine and Rehabilitation at Northwestern University, Chicago, IL, USA. Co-PI Cognitive Neuroscience of Religious Cognition (CNRC) Project (cognitiveneuroscienceofreligion.org).

Patrick McNamara is Professor of Psychology at National University, San Diego, California, USA, and Associate Professor of Neurology at Boston University, Boston, MA, USA. Co-PI CNRC Project (cognitiveneuroscienceofreligion.org).

THE NEURAL BASIS OF RELIGIOUS COGNITION

Edited by
Jordan Grafman and Patrick McNamara

Routledge
Taylor & Francis Group
NEW YORK AND LONDON

Designed cover image: Getty Images

First published 2026
by Routledge
605 Third Avenue, New York, NY 10158

and by Routledge
4 Park Square, Milton Park, Abingdon, Oxon, OX14 4RN

Routledge is an imprint of the Taylor & Francis Group, an informa business

ISBN: 9780367744991 (hbk)
ISBN: 9780367744984 (pbk)
ISBN: 9781003158189 (ebk)

DOI: 10.4324/9781003158189

Typeset in Times New Roman
by codeMantra

CONTENTS

PREFACE

The past three decades have witnessed the birth and rapid maturation of a field that once seemed almost paradoxical: the cognitive neuroscience of religion. In the wake of functional neuroimaging, lesion studies, computational modeling, and new approaches to longitudinal clinical data, the once ineffable domain of religious experience has become tractable to scientific analysis. Far from reducing or dismissing religion, these studies have revealed it to be a profound window into the very architecture of human cognition, affect, and social skills. Religious beliefs and practices turn out to be deeply enmeshed with the same neural systems that support empathy, attachment, self-regulation, and meaning-making. The study of religion through the lens of neuroscience is not only about understanding religion itself but also about uncovering fundamental principles of brain–mind function.

This volume, brings together a set of essays that exemplify the best of this interdisciplinary effort. The contributors include leading researchers in cognitive neuroscience, psychology, and neurology, each of whom tackles religion not as a cultural curiosity but as a central and indispensable aspect of human life. The chapters in this book range from lesion-mapping studies of traumatic brain injury to qualitative analyses of spirituality in Parkinson's disease to broader theoretical integrations of emotional, social, and cognitive dimensions of faith. What unites them is a shared conviction: that the religious mind is neither an anomaly nor a vestige, but a crucial dimension of what it means to be human.

In what follows, we introduce each chapter in turn, highlighting its core contributions, the conceptual advances it brings, and the questions it leaves for future exploration. In weaving these together, we aim to provide not merely a summary but also a sense of trajectory—where the field has come from, and where it might go next.

The opening chapter (Chapter 1), by Cristofori, Cohen-Zimerman, Abderrahmane, Gordon, Krueger, McNamara, and Grafman, takes as its starting point one of the most intimate dimensions of religious life: the emotional connection to God. Drawing on the Vietnam Head Injury Study, the authors explore how emotional intelligence—defined as the ability to perceive, regulate, and use emotions—relates to reported closeness to God in veterans with penetrating traumatic brain injury (pTBI).

The results are striking. Among healthy controls, higher emotional intelligence was paradoxically associated with *weaker* connection to God, suggesting that those less adept at managing emotions may turn to God as a compensatory figure of regulation and support. Among pTBI patients, by contrast, no correlation was found; indeed, prior lesion studies suggest that neural damage to prefrontal regions may itself increase reported closeness to God, bypassing typical emotional regulation networks.

The strength of this chapter lies in its causal inference. By combining lesion-mapping with psychometric measures, the authors illuminate how specific neural circuits constrain or potentiate religious experience. They also complicate prevailing assumptions; rather than simply supporting religiosity, emotional intelligence may, in some contexts, *inhibit* it.

The limitations are equally instructive. The sample included only male veterans, constraining generalizability, and the null results for the pTBI group leave open many possible interpretations. Future research should extend these analyses to more diverse populations, examine gender effects, and incorporate measures of attachment and social support. Longitudinal designs could clarify whether lowered emotional intelligence predisposes to religious attachment, or whether strong reliance on divine connection itself alters emotional competencies over time.

The second chapter (Chapter 2), authored by Goodin, Hubbard, Barrett, Schwartz, Levey, and Spaulding, offers a qualitative exploration of religious and spiritual attachment in Parkinson's disease (PD). With 78 participants at baseline and 62 at one-year follow-up, the study uses Granqvist's religion-as-attachment framework to parse how side of disease onset—left (LOPD) versus right (ROPD)—shapes the quality of spiritual connection.

The findings reveal a subtle but consistent pattern. LOPD patients, with right-hemispheric involvement, tend toward cognitively anchored and role-focused attachments: God as a Secure Base supporting continuity, identity, and responsibility. ROPD patients, with left-hemispheric involvement, emphasize emotionally expressive, vulnerable connections: God as a Safe Haven for comfort, intimacy, and relational support. Over time, LOPD participants exhibited more fluidity of attachment and more variance in their God representations, whereas ROPD attachments remained affectively intense.

This chapter's strength is its depth of phenomenological insight. Through careful thematic coding, the authors show how neurodegeneration sculpts not only motor and cognitive functions but also the texture of religious life. The study situates religion as both refuge and orientation during neurodegenerative decline.

Future work should integrate neuroimaging markers of dopaminergic decline with attachment measures and assess whether targeted spiritual care interventions can bolster coping, resilience, and meaning-making in PD. The possibility that religiosity itself might modulate disease risk or progression, hinted at by emerging epidemiological findings, warrants urgent replication.

In Chapter 3, Johnstone, Cohen, and Dennison describe the problem of selflessness and its relation to transcendent religious experiences, grounding these phenomena in the functioning of the right inferior parietal lobe (RIPL). The authors argue that the RIPL serves as a neuropsychological hub for integrating multiple streams of information related to bodily boundaries, cognition, and spatial awareness, such that degradation in its functioning may loosen the integrity of the self. In their studies, the Judgment of Line Orientation task was used as an indirect but tractable measure of RIPL functioning, and its relationship with selflessness and spirituality was examined across both concurrent and longitudinal designs.

The findings were provocative. In cross-sectional analyses, decreased RIPL functioning correlated with greater reported selflessness and with measures of spiritual transcendence. More importantly, longitudinal data gathered from individuals with acquired brain injury or multiple sclerosis revealed that declines in RIPL performance over time predicted subsequent increases in selflessness, which in turn were tied to enhanced experiences of transcendence. The results suggested that generalized forms of disintegration—such as disintegrated bodily sensations, cognition, and contextual awareness—were more powerfully associated with transcendence than narrower, domain-specific disintegrations such as those involving taste or smell. A follow-up functional neuroimaging study, though unpublished, further supported the connection by identifying correlations between specific indices of selflessness and distinct sub-networks within the RIPL.

This chapter is significant because it provides some of the first empirical evidence linking subjective experiences of losing the self to measurable neural substrates. It advances the idea that selflessness can be treated as a neuropsychological construct suitable for systematic scientific study, thereby opening a door for productive collaborations between neuroscientists and scholars of spirituality. Yet this chapter also acknowledges its limitations. Reliance on an indirect proxy measure of RIPL functioning may not capture the full range of processes involved, and the relatively small samples of patients and imaging participants constrain the generalizability of the conclusions. This chapter's results nonetheless raise fertile questions for future research: Could neuromodulation techniques directly targeting the RIPL modulate experiences of transcendence? Might cultural or religious context shape the way in which selflessness is expressed and interpreted? And how can researchers distinguish adaptive forms of selflessness, associated with spiritual meaning, from maladaptive dissociation? In raising these issues, the authors make a compelling case for the RIPL as a neuroanatomical bridge between the dissolution of self and the heights of spiritual experience.

In Chapter 4, Cosimo Urgesi deepens the theme of embodiment by embedding spirituality within the predictive processing framework. He proposes that spirituality, and especially experiences of self-transcendence, arise through altered weighting of bodily prediction errors, a process that changes how the brain integrates and interprets interoceptive signals. In this sense, spirituality is portrayed less as a cognitive endorsement of religious belief and more as a dynamic alteration in how the brain models its own body. Urgesi identifies evidence from neuroimaging, brain stimulation, and behavioral paradigms to support this perspective. Temporoparietal deactivation has been shown to amplify self-transcendent experiences, while stimulation of the vagus nerve can dampen implicit associations with spirituality. Experimental tasks manipulating predictive priors in interoceptive contexts revealed that when participants were led to expect particular bodily states, their implicit spirituality scores increased, even though their explicit religiosity remained unchanged. Other manipulations of prediction error reliability affected interoceptive accuracy but did not alter spiritual or religious self-representations, pointing to a dissociation between spirituality and interoceptive precision. The theoretical advance here is the computational distinction drawn between spirituality and religiosity. Whereas religiosity appears to be sustained by more stable, culturally scaffolded belief systems, spirituality emerges from the fluid and embodied modulation of interoceptive models of the self. By grounding spirituality in the predictive regulation of the body, this chapter gives neuroscientists a testable framework that moves beyond phenomenology to mechanism.

At the same time, Urgesi's account is not without limitations. The predictive coding framework, while powerful, can sometimes become all-encompassing, risking the collapse of complex phenomena into abstract computational terms. Moreover, many of the empirical findings reviewed come from small samples and preliminary studies that require replication. Nevertheless, by situating spirituality in the embodied regulation of bodily signals, Urgesi provides both a conceptual and methodological roadmap for future investigations, suggesting that interventions altering bodily states may have profound consequences for spiritual experience.

In Chapter 5, McNamara turns to the narrative psychology of religion by examining *redemptive turning points* and their relationship to the cognitive process of decentering. McNamara analyzed transcripts of interviews on spiritual life histories of 120 participants using Dan McAdams's life story model, where turning points are conceived as pivotal autobiographical events—moments of crisis, opportunity, or transformation that restructure the self's trajectory. These events are not mere occurrences but interpretive constructions, invested with meaning that helps narrators explain who they have become. Within this framework, two contrasting narrative arcs are distinguished. Redemptive arcs transform suffering into growth and lead to positive resolution, while contaminated arcs portray good beginnings that are spoiled, resulting in disillusionment or despair. The central finding from analysis of the interviews is that decentering—the four-step process of agency down-regulation, liminality, model updating, and reintegration—serves as the cognitive/neuropsychological engine by which people reframe turning points into redemptive or contaminated stories.

To test this idea, McNamara analyzed 247 turning-point narratives drawn from McAdams-style life story interviews with over 120 participants. Each transcript was coded for a variety of markers of the four steps of decentering. The results showed that these markers occurred in the majority of narratives, with 18 narratives containing all four steps in sequence, strongly suggesting a structured cognitive process at work. A key empirical finding was that intense decentering—defined as the presence of four or more markers—was significantly more common in contaminated arcs (about 31%) than in redemptive arcs (about 12%). This suggests that contamination narratives often involve unresolved or excessive decentering, i.e. attempted at decentering, leaving individuals suspended in liminality and unable to integrate the experience into a coherent and hopeful life story. Redemptive arcs, by contrast, typically involved moderate levels of decentering, which seemed sufficient to promote perspective shifting and eventual narrative integration. Participants who achieved redemption often described distancing from the immediate self, entering liminal states of reflection, drawing upon cultural or spiritual frameworks, and ultimately binding their new sense of self into an enriched and coherent identity. In many cases, religious language, references to God, or appeals to transcendent meaning played a pivotal role in this integrative process.

The implications are twofold. First, the findings support narrative identity theory by demonstrating that redemption is not a simple positive reappraisal but a complex, multistep transformation of the self, with decentering at its core. Second, the study underscores the deep entanglement between spirituality and life story construction: when people invoke the transcendent, it is often as part of an effort to metabolize suffering into growth. At the same time, the fact that contaminated arcs were saturated with repeated attempts at decentering suggests that spiritual or therapeutic interventions may be especially helpful at these junctures, providing resources to complete the integrative arc. McNamara proposes that future research should test whether practices that facilitate decentering—such as mindfulness, guided autobiography, or even psychedelic interventions—could increase the likelihood of constructing *redemptive* narratives. In short, Chapter 5 demonstrates that redemptive turning points are a natural laboratory for studying how spiritual and cognitive processes intersect in the making of meaningful lives.

Chapter 6, authored by Bernard Crespi, Nancy Yang, and Sam Doesburg, proposes a bold and mechanistic account of spirituality and religion: that their neurocognitive foundations lie in the serotonin 2A receptor (HT2A). The authors begin by noting that no unique "God module" has been found in the brain. Instead, they advance the *God receptor hypothesis*, arguing that because HT2A receptors are distributed widely across perception, cognition, and emotion systems, their activation—especially in states of hyper-activation—produces the core phenomenology of religious and spiritual experience.

This chapter draws on multiple converging lines of evidence. Lesion and fMRI studies of spiritual cognition show that no single region suffices to explain experiences of God or the sacred, yet patterns of activation align with known sites of HT2A density. Psychedelic studies provide especially striking parallels: LSD, psilocybin, and related substances induce states of awe, insight, ego-dissolution, and communion with a larger reality, all mediated by 2A receptor agonism. Historical and anthropological research on entheogenic rituals further supports the notion that psychedelics may have seeded early religious forms, their visionary effects providing raw material for gods, myths, and ritual practices.

The authors extend this framework beyond psychedelics to psychotic-affective disorders. Schizophrenia, mania, and related conditions often involve auditory hallucinations, delusions of grandeur, and encounters with divine or persecutory agents. These states, too, can be explained by hyper-activation of HT2A systems, interacting with predictive coding machinery that constructs meaning, narrative, and self-world models. Stress provides a third route of induction: fasting, isolation, and physiological challenge—all common in religious ascetic practices—are potent triggers of serotonin 2A activity. Thus, naturalistic, psychotic, and entheogenic pathways converge on the same receptor-level mechanism, suggesting a unified biological basis for the origins of religious thought.

The phenomenology produced by HT2A hyper-activation is described with precision. Three key experiences are highlighted: first, a conviction of profound insight, grounded in lowered thresholds for inference-making; second, awe, understood as extreme prediction-error surprise, which intensifies belief in the reality of the experience; and third, ego-dissolution and a sense of oneness, arising from the relaxation of self-related priors in the brain's default mode network, claustrum, and periaqueductal gray. These core features—insight, awe, and oneness—are then culturally interpreted as encounters with gods, spirits, or ultimate reality, and become institutionalized in religious traditions.

The authors further outline a developmental and evolutionary trajectory. First, novel visionary experiences emerge through entheogenic, psychotic, or stress-related HT2A activation. Second, imagination and narrative scaffold these experiences into culturally resonant frameworks populated by supernatural agents. Third, participation in such frameworks yields fitness advantages through enhanced group cooperation, social cohesion, and shared meaning. In this view, spirituality and religion are emergent products of a receptor system that evolved for adaptive stress responses and predictive coding, but under conditions of hyper-activation gave rise to humanity's gods and myths.

This chapter concludes by situating the God receptor hypothesis within current neuroscience of religion. It is parsimonious, mechanistic, and integrative, drawing together data from psychedelics, psychiatry, stress physiology, and predictive coding. Yet the authors acknowledge its limitations: HT2A activation is not the sole determinant of religious experience, but rather a central trigger interacting with broader neural and cultural systems. Future research is called for in three directions: mapping HT2A-related predictive coding more precisely across brain networks; distinguishing adaptive from maladaptive hyper-activation (e.g., mystical ecstasy vs. persecutory delusion); and testing whether cultural-religious practices exploit receptor-level mechanisms intentionally or incidentally.

In sum, this chapter presents a receptor-based theory of religion's neurocognitive roots. By linking the phenomenology of awe, oneness, and revelation to serotonin 2A hyper-activation, Crespi and colleagues offer a framework that unites naturalistic stress responses, psychotic disorders, and psychedelic rituals under a common mechanistic banner, suggesting that the genesis of gods may be traced to the very receptors that mediate imagination, meaning, and transcendence.

In Chapter 7, Carr and Robertson position dreaming as one of the most enduring and fertile arenas for the interplay between cognition and religion. From the Mesopotamian dream of King Dumuzi, interpreted as a divine warning, to scriptural accounts across Judaism, Christianity, Islam, Hinduism, and Buddhism, dreams have been regarded as authoritative messages from otherworldly agents and as sources of guidance, prophecy, and affirmation.

The authors argue that dreams function as "natural laboratories" for the study of religious cognition, precisely because they regularly generate experiences of agency attribution, meaning-making, and encounters with beings that are not available to the waking self. The theoretical backdrop is the continuity hypothesis of dreaming, which holds that dream content reflects waking concerns, beliefs, and practices. Religious cognition in dreams, then, mirrors the dreamer's cultural and theological framework. Yet dreaming also stretches these frameworks by producing unexpected content, compelling dreamers to grapple with the sacred in new guises. Neurocognitive models support this interpretation: during REM sleep, diminished frontal executive control and altered predictive coding enhance the likelihood of attributing agency to spontaneously generated dream figures, imbuing them with intentionality and significance.

Lucid dreaming occupies a special place in this framework. Lucidity entails awareness of dreaming while the dream unfolds, allowing volitional influence. The authors report qualitative case studies of expert lucid dreamers who intentionally invoked spiritual agents during lucidity. One Christian participant experienced divine reassurance through dream imagery that echoed scripture, reinforcing their devotional faith. Another participant, shaped by eclectic spiritual and meditative practices, encountered what he called the "Magical Personality"—a higher aspect of self-conceived as multidimensional consciousness. Though they deliberately sought these encounters, the dream figures did not act as passive projections of the dreamer's will. Instead, they displayed autonomy, unpredictability, and novel behaviors, which the dreamers themselves described as a "dance between the dreamer and the dream."

From these vignettes, the authors draw several conclusions. First, religious experiences in dreams cannot be disentangled from the dreamer's pre-existing beliefs. Faith traditions, spiritual practices, and personal theology shape both the content of dream encounters and the interpretation of dream figures as divine or transcendent. Second, lucidity adds a unique dimension to religious cognition by blending volition with surprise. Dreamers can intentionally invite spiritual agents, but the agents often exceed expectation, displaying their own quasi-autonomy. This suggests that lucid dreaming may simulate interpersonal or divine relationships more directly than non-lucid dreaming. Third, these findings lend support to the view that dreaming sustains religious cognition not merely through memory consolidation or symbolic replay but by actively generating novel experiences of agency and meaning.

This chapter closes by emphasizing that dreams have always stood at the intersection of science and religion. While theology has treated them as revelations of the sacred, neuroscience shows that the mechanisms of REM sleep—particularly diminished self-agency and heightened generation of surprising content—make dreams a natural source of supernatural experience. Lucid dreaming provides a platform where intention, expectation, and the brain's spontaneous creativity converge to produce experiences of the divine. The authors propose that future work should examine how different kinds of agency attribution operate in lucid versus non-lucid dreams, and how cultural-religious frameworks modulate these experiences across populations.

Ultimately, Carr and Robertson present dreaming as a crucible where cognitive neuroscience and religious phenomenology converge. By attributing agency and meaning to dream figures, humans have the opportunity to engage with the sacred.

In Chapter 8, McNamara continues the focus on the association of REM sleep and dreams with religion and spirituality. This chapter makes the case that REM sleep—and the dreaming states it generates—constitutes a foundational neurobiological substrate for religious and spiritual experience. McNamara begins with the historical record: from Jacob's ladder to Joseph's dream announcing the birth of Jesus, from Islamic accounts of Muhammad's night journey to Buddhist and Hindu dream-visions, religions have long treated dreams as revelations of the sacred. Anthropological studies confirm this continuity, showing that across cultures, dreams have been central to the formation of myths, rituals, doctrines, and systems of belief. Yet despite this long-standing evidence, modern cognitive and neuroscience explorations of religion have rarely considered REM sleep as a generative mechanism for religious cognition.

McNamara argues that REM's neurobiology makes it uniquely suited to produce the phenomenology of the sacred. During REM, the dorsolateral prefrontal cortex deactivates, diminishing executive control and reflective awareness, while limbic and paralimbic regions such as the amygdala and medial prefrontal cortex become hyperactive. This produces states rich in emotional arousal, vivid imagery, and salience attribution. At the same time, serotonergic tone decreases while dopaminergic and cholinergic activity increase, loosening cognitive boundaries and enhancing receptivity to improbable or anomalous experiences. The effect is a fertile cognitive landscape in which figures, voices, or presences are easily imbued with agency, meaning, and spiritual significance.

Dream figures, McNamara explains, are not typically experienced as under the dreamer's control. Because agency is diminished in REM, dreamers often externalize intention, treating dream characters as independent beings. When these figures display surprising but not wholly implausible behaviors—such as offering moral guidance, issuing warnings, or emanating awe—they may be interpreted as supernatural agents. The strong emotional tone of such encounters ensures their memorability and transmissibility. In nightmares, such agents appear demonic; in uplifting dreams, they may appear divine.

This chapter also highlights parallels between REM dreaming and other altered states that produce religious experiences. Psychedelic states, which also act through serotonin 2A receptors, generate a similar phenomenology of ego-dissolution, awe, and sacred presence. This convergence suggests that REM sleep may be the most common, naturally recurring platform for experiences that cultures interpret as spiritual or religious.

McNamara concludes by noting both the theoretical and empirical implications of this framework. Theoretically, it reframes religion not as an epiphenomenon of belief systems but as rooted in recurring neurocognitive states that humans universally experience. Empirically, it calls for systematic studies of dream content in relation to measures of religiosity, spirituality, and neural function. The neglected field of REM dreams and spirituality, he suggests, could provide essential insights into how religions arise, why they persist, and how individual experiences of the sacred are generated and sustained.

In Chapter 9, Cristofori and colleagues argue that we embody the representation of the divine. This is because faith can be viewed as a mental construct that is fundamentally rooted in memory, social cognition, affective processing, and the body. Thus, our beliefs, particularly when practiced, force us to communicate with God using all the resources we have available, including interoception. Of course, different religions may have different profiles of embodiment. For example, depictions of the face of God that are designed to engage our emotions are common in Christianity, but such physical depictions of God are rejected by Muslims and Jews. Cristofori et al. suggest that a key neural pathway for sensing embodiment is the vagal nerve that conveys bodily sensations to the brain, and in return, those bodily sensations are influenced by cortical and subcortical processes such as emotion, mood, and thought. If so, then applying vagal nerve stimulation should modulate our representations of the divine. A fascinating proposal that requires further study.

Summary

A recurring theme across chapters is that religion is an extension of core social-cognitive systems. Studies of theory of mind reveal that perceiving God's intentions recruits the same temporoparietal and medial prefrontal networks used for human mind-reading. Work on empathy shows overlap between neural responses to suffering others and the experience of divine compassion. Computational models illustrate how Bayesian prediction and error-minimization frameworks can be extended to ritual, prayer, and belief updating.

The strengths of these contributions lie in their integration: religion is not treated as a sui generis module but as a natural elaboration of evolved systems for attachment, empathy, and predictive control. The limitations, however, are evident in the relative paucity of longitudinal and developmental data. We still know little about how these neural–cognitive–religious links evolve across the lifespan, or how they differ across traditions and cultural ecologies. Future work must extend beyond WEIRD samples, incorporate comparative and cross-cultural neuroscience, and embrace multimodal methods combining lesion studies, neuroimaging, computational modeling, and ethnographic depth.

The strength of this collection is its refusal to reduce religion to any single factor—neither an illusion of hyper-active agency detection, nor a by-product of attachment insecurity, nor a mere cultural epiphenomenon. Instead, it reveals religious belief as multiply determined, neurally instantiated, and psychologically indispensable.

Future Directions

For cognitive neuroscientists, this volume encourages several new research directions. First, the need for developmental trajectories: How do religious attachments and cognitions unfold across childhood, adolescence, and aging, and how are they shaped by neural plasticity? Second, the imperative for cultural breadth: most existing studies focus on Christian or Western samples, yet the neural underpinnings of religious cognition may differ across traditions with varying emphases on ritual, doctrine, or mysticism. Third, the promise of clinical integration: as the Parkinson's chapter shows, spiritual care is not an optional supplement but may offer significant benefit for resilience, identity, and emotional regulation. Fourth, the opportunity for computational modeling: Bayesian and network models can formalize how beliefs are updated, rituals stabilize expectations, and spiritual agents are simulated. To complement these research efforts, we believe that the field must embrace longitudinal and causal designs, from lesion studies to neuromodulation, to move beyond correlational maps toward a mechanistic understanding.

Finally, with the rise of artificial intelligence (AI), seeking spiritual aids and religious communities involves joining online communities that may alter how humans have historically sought and benefited from religious meaningfulness and comfort. Incorporating the use of AI in the context of cognitive neuroscience research on religion is an inevitability.

Concluding Reflections

To open the black box of religious cognition is not to diminish its mystery but to point the centraility of the human brain in mediating that mystery. Religion is revealed here as both fragile and robust: fragile in its dependence on specific neural circuits and cognitive capacities, robust in its persistence even amid injury, degeneration, and loss. For cognitive neuroscience, religion is no longer peripheral but central to the study of the brain, offering a lens onto how brains create worlds of meaning, bind communities, and sustain hope in the face of mortality.

This book is thus both a report and a provocation. It reports on the state of the art, with empirical richness and theoretical nuance. But it also provokes us to ask more: to probe the boundaries of attachment, to trace the pathways of meaning, to integrate neural data with lived experience, and to recognize that in studying religion we study the very conditions of human consciousness.

Jordan Grafman, Ph.D. and
Patrick McNamara, Ph.D.

1

EMOTIONAL INTELLIGENCE AND THE EMOTIONAL CONNECTION TO GOD

Insights from Traumatic Brain Injury Research

Irene Cristofori, Shira Cohen-Zimerman, Alya Abderrahmane, Barry Gordon, Frank Krueger, Patrick McNamara, and Jordan Grafman

Introduction

Religious and spiritual experiences are deeply intertwined with human cognition, affect, and neurobiology. A central feature of many religious traditions is the notion of forming a personal relationship with a divine being. This Connection to God (CTG) is not only a matter of belief but also an affective experience that shapes one's sense of meaning, support, and belonging. Studies on traumatic brain injury patients have shown that lesions in the ventromedial prefrontal cortex (Cohen-Zimerman et al. 2020; Cristofori et al. 2021) and the right orbitofrontal cortex (Cohen-Zimerman et al. 2025) can increase a person's perceived relationship/connection with God. These findings suggest that neural damage to emotional and social regulation networks may increase spiritual connectedness.

Emotions play a crucial role in influencing cognition and behavior and may be critical in fostering this kind of connection. Among the different emotional constructs, emotional intelligence—the capacity to perceive, understand, regulate, and use emotions—has been linked to many facets of social and psychological functioning (Mayer, Salovey, and Caruso 2008). It has been hypothesized that emotional intelligence may contribute to the capacity to nurture and sustain an emotional CTG.

This chapter examines the relationship between emotional intelligence and emotional CTG, drawing on unique evidence from Vietnam War veterans with penetrating traumatic brain injuries (pTBIs) (Raymont et al. 2011; Cristofori et al. 2024).

DOI: 10.4324/9781003158189-1

Emotional Intelligence and Religious Experience

Cognitive neuroscience evidence has long suggested that emotional intelligence supports prosociality, empathy, and social bonding, and relies on the functionality of an integrated neural network involving the frontal, temporal, and parietal cortex (Frith and Frith 2007; Blakemore 2008; Krueger et al. 2009; Hogeveen, Salvi, and Grafman 2016; He et al. 2018). These same mechanisms and brain structures are often invoked in the context of religiosity. For example, individuals with higher emotional intelligence are more engaged in religious practice, adopt intrinsic religious orientations, and report deeper religious experiences (Paek, 2006; Liu, 2010). The relationship between religious beliefs and emotional intelligence has also been supported by studies on the theory of mind (ToM). ToM has been identified as a prerequisite for religious beliefs, since individuals often conceptualize deities as intentional agents with mental states (Waytz et al. 2010; Gervais and Norenzayan 2012; Willard and Norenzayan 2013). Neuroimaging studies supported these findings and associated religious beliefs (particularly when judging God's perceived emotion) with ToM neural network, including the middle temporal and frontal gyrus (Kapogiannis et al. 2009). ToM ability is also positively associated with emotional intelligence (Barlow, Qualter, and Stylianou 2010; Ferguson and Austin 2010), and individuals with impaired ToM, such as those suffering from autism, tend to report lower levels of belief in God (Norenzayan, Gervais, and Trzesniewski 2012). These findings further support a potential link between religiosity and emotional intelligence.

Altogether, this evidence provides a potential bridge between emotional intelligence and spiritual connectedness.

Brain Injury as a Window into Spirituality

Lesion studies have revealed that damage to specific areas of the prefrontal cortex—particularly the ventromedial and orbitofrontal regions—can increase reported closeness to God (Cohen-Zimerman et al. 2020). These findings suggest that neural systems typically involved in regulating emotion and social cognition may also constrain or shape spiritual experiences. Studying individuals suffering from brain injuries provides a rare opportunity to causally investigate the intersection of neurobiology, emotional processing, and spirituality.

The Vietnam Head Injury Study

The Vietnam Head Injury Study (VHIS; Raymont et al., 2011) is a large, long-term project following American veterans with combat-related brain injuries. In phase 4 (relevant to this chapter), over 100 veterans with pTBI and more than 30 combat-experienced but non-injured controls were assessed 45 after injury. Participants were assessed from 2009 to 2012 at the National Institutes of Health in Bethesda,

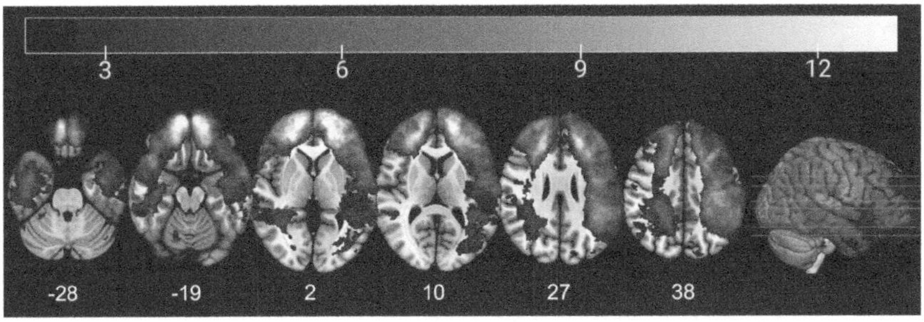

FIGURE 1.1 Overlay Density Map of Traumatic Brain Injury Lesions (pTBI Group). Images are in Radiological Space (i.e., Right Is Left). Z Values from Left to Right: −28, −19, −10, 2, 10, 27, 38.

Maryland, over a five-to-seven-day period with tests that measured a wide variety of neuropsychological functions, including memory, language, executive functioning, and social cognition. See Figure 1.1 for lesion overlay in the pTBI group.

For the study reported in this chapter, two core measures were used:

- Emotional Connection to God (CTG): A 15-item composite scale capturing intimacy, awareness, and reliance on God. More specifically, the items focused on one's relationship with God, regardless of their specific religious affiliation. Items included five items from the Religious Experience Questionnaire (Geffner and Gross, 1984), 8 from the God Image Inventory (Lawrence, 1997), and 2 from the Religiosity Measure Questionnaire (Rohrbaugh and Jessor 1975).
- Mayer-Salovey-Caruso Emotional Intelligence Test (MSCEIT; (Mayer, Salovey, and Caruso 2008)]): A 141-item standardized ability-based assessment of emotional perception, understanding, and regulation. The test measures emotional intelligence and two main components of emotional intelligence: Strategic and Experiential. Strategic emotional intelligence refers to the ability to understand and manage emotions, whereas experiential emotional intelligence is the ability to perceive and use emotions. Higher scores on the test indicate greater emotional intelligence.

Findings

Contrary to expectations, emotional intelligence was not positively associated with emotional CTG. Across the full sample, the study found no evidence of an association between emotional intelligence and CTG (see Figure 1.2, left side).

When considering the results in pTBI group, no significant correlations emerged (see Figure 1.2, right side, black and grey color); while in the healthy control group only, higher emotional intelligence and experiential emotional intelligence were linked to a lower CTG (see Figure 1.2, right side, black or grey color).

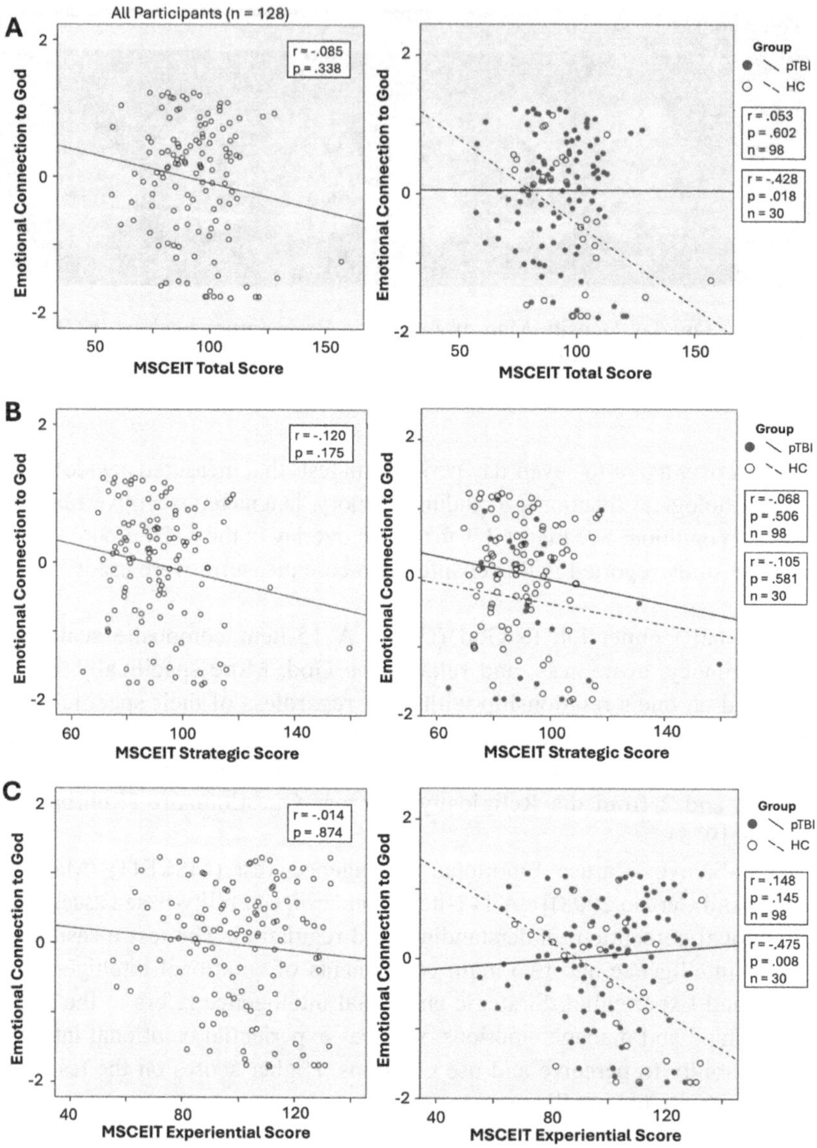

FIGURE 1.2 Correlation Between CTG z-Scores and MSCEIT Scores (Total, Strategic, Experiential). Correlation Between the Emotional CTG z-Score and the MSCEIT Total (a), Strategic (b), and Experiential (c) z-Score for all the Sample (Left) and the pTBI and HC Groups (Right).

Interpretation

These findings diverge from earlier research suggesting a positive link between emotional intelligence and religiosity. Instead, they point toward a more complex dynamic:

1 **Alternative Neural Pathways in Traumatic Brain Injury**: For individuals with brain injury, spirituality may be sustained by mechanisms independent of emotional intelligence, possibly through compensatory neural networks. Previous lesion studies have shown that damage to areas such as the ventromedial prefrontal cortex and right orbitofrontal cortex can lead to an enhanced CTG (Cohen-Zimerman et al., 2020; Cristofori et al., 2021), especially in individuals with a secure attachment (Cohen-Zimerman et al., 2025). This suggests that in cases of neural damage, spirituality may arise or be maintained through alternate, potentially compensatory, pathways not directly dependent on traditional emotional intelligence networks. It is important to note that a null finding does not necessarily indicate the absence of an association; rather, it reflects that no statistically significant relationship was detected under the specific conditions, measures, and sample used in this study. This result may be due to a true lack of association or other factors.

2 **Compensatory Hypothesis in Healthy Controls**: Among healthy individuals, those with lower emotional sensitivity may turn to God as an alternative source of emotional regulation and connection. Individuals with lower experiential emotional intelligence may seek emotional support or regulation through a spiritual connection, thus forming a stronger Emotional CTG. This interpretation aligns with the compensatory model proposed by Schnitker et al. (2012), where insecure attachment or emotional deficits prompt individuals to seek divine connection as a substitute for interpersonal emotional bonds.

   An important factor, warranting consideration, is gender. Studies have consistently shown that women tend to score higher than men in emotional intelligence and empathy (Brackett et al., 2004; Śmieja et al., 2014), and also tend to report stronger religious involvement (Felty and Poloma, 1991).

3 **Gender Considerations:** The sample included only male participants, which may limit the generalizability of these findings and may have influenced the lack of significant emotional intelligence–Emotional CTG correlations. Future studies should incorporate gender-balanced samples to explore potential moderating effects.

In sum, these findings suggest that emotional intelligence, as measured by the MSCEIT, is not positively associated with a CTG in male veterans, especially those with pTBIs. These results invite a re-evaluation of the cognitive and emotional foundations of religious experience, suggesting a greater role for relational and affective mechanisms over abstract emotional competencies (Cristofori et al., 2021). It could also be possible that emotional attachment (the feeling of closeness and affection that helps sustain significant relations over time), rather than emotional competence, guides the closeness and attachment to God. Attachment processes, self-regulation, and broader psychosocial factors may be more central in fostering a CTG.

These findings have theoretical and clinical implications. Theoretically, they suggest re-evaluating models linking emotional intelligence and religiosity. Clinically, they encourage a focus on relational and attachment-based interventions when working with those suffering from traumatic brain injury.

Conclusion

Emotional intelligence, as measured by standardized assessments, does not appear to strengthen an individual's emotional CTG in the context of traumatic brain injury. On the contrary, in healthy individuals (in this specific population of veterans), a strong CTG may serve as a compensatory mechanism when emotional intelligence is lower. The study underscores the need for a broader framework that incorporates emotional attachment, compensatory strategies, and neurobiological variability in understanding the foundations of religious and spiritual experience.

Acknowledgments

This research was supported by a John F. Templeton Foundation (JTF) grant (J. Grafman and P. McNamara) and the Therapeutic Cognitive Neuroscience Fund (B. Gordon). The funders had no role in study design, data collection and analysis, publication decisions, or manuscript preparation. The authors thank all the Vietnam veterans who participated in this study and the National Naval Medical Center and the National Institute of Neurological Disorders and Stroke for providing their facilities and supporting this research. We thank V. Raymont, S. Bonifant, B. Cheon, C. Ngo, A. Greathouse, K. Reding, G. Tasick, S. Bonifant, M. Tierney, L. Glass, L. Yozawitz, C. Noury, V. Tsen, and A. Leopold for testing participants and organizing the study.

References

Barlow, Alexandra, Pamela Qualter, and Maria Stylianou. 2010. "Relationships between Machiavellianism, Emotional Intelligence and Theory of Mind in Children." *Personality and Individual Differences* 48 (1): 78–82. https://doi.org/10.1016/j.paid.2009.08.021.

Blakemore, Sarah-Jayne. 2008. "The Social Brain in Adolescence." *Nature Reviews. Neuroscience* 9 (4): 267–277. https://doi.org/10.1038/nrn2353.

Brackett, Marc A., John D. Mayer, and Rebecca M. Warner. 2004. "Emotional intelligence and its relation to everyday behaviour." *Personality and Individual differences* 36,(6): 1387–1402. https://doi.org/10.1016/S0191-8869(03)00236-8

Cohen-Zimerman, Shira, Irene Cristofori, Patrick McNamara, Frank Krueger, Barry Gordon, and Jordan Grafman. 2025. "Attachment Style and Its Impact on Connection to God in Individuals with Brain Injury: Behavioral and Lesion-Based Findings." *Frontiers in Neurology* 16 (April): 1488890. https://doi.org/10.3389/fneur.2025.1488890.

Cohen-Zimerman, Shira, Irene Cristofori, Wanting Zhong, Joseph Bulbulia, Frank Krueger, Barry Gordon, and Jordan Grafman. 2020. "Neural Underpinning of a Personal Relationship with God and Sense of Control: A Lesion-Mapping Study." *Cognitive, Affective, & Behavioral Neuroscience* 20 (3): 575–587. https://doi.org/10.3758/s13415-020-00787-4.

Cristofori, Irene, Shira Cohen-Zimerman, Frank Krueger, Roxana Jabbarinejad, Ekaterina Delikishkina, Barry Gordon, Pierre-Aurélien Beuriat, and Jordan Grafman. 2024. "Studying the Social Mind: An Updated Summary of Findings from the Vietnam Head Injury Study." *Cortex* 174 (May): 164–188. https://doi.org/10.1016/j.cortex.2024.03.002.

Cristofori, Irene, Wanting Zhong, Shira Cohen-Zimerman, Joseph Bulbulia, Barry Gordon, Frank Krueger, and Jordan Grafman. 2021. "Brain Networks Involved in the Influence of Religion on Empathy in Male Vietnam War Veterans." *Scientific Reports* 11 (1): 1–13.

Feltey, Kathryn M., and Margaret M. Poloma. 1991. "From sex differences to gender role beliefs: Exploring effects on six dimensions of religiosity." *Sex roles* 25(3): 181–193.

Ferguson, Fiona J., and Elizabeth J. Austin. 2010. "Associations of Trait and Ability Emotional Intelligence with Performance on Theory of Mind Tasks in an Adult Sample." *Personality and Individual Differences* 49 (5): 414–418. https://doi.org/10.1016/j.paid.2010.04.009.

Frith, Chris D., and Uta Frith. 2007. "Social Cognition in Humans." *Current Biology: CB* 17 (16): R724–R732. https://doi.org/10.1016/j.cub.2007.05.068.

Geffner, Robert, and Madeleine M. Gross. 1984. "Sex-role behavior and obedience to authority: A field study." *Sex Roles* 10(11): 973–985. https://doi.org/10.1007/BF00288518.

Gervais, Will M., and Ara Norenzayan. 2012. "Analytic Thinking Promotes Religious Disbelief." *Science (New York, N.Y.)* 336 (6080): 493–496. https://doi.org/10.1126/science.1215647.

He, Li, Yu Mao, Jiangzhou Sun, Kaixiang Zhuang, Xingxing Zhu, Jiang Qiu, and Xiaoyi Chen. 2018. "Examining Brain Structures Associated With Emotional Intelligence and the Mediated Effect on Trait Creativity in Young Adults." *Frontiers in Psychology* 9 (June): 925. https://doi.org/10.3389/fpsyg.2018.00925.

Hogeveen, Jeremy, Carola, Salvi, and Jordan, Grafman. 2016. "'Emotional Intelligence': Lessons from Lesions." *Trends in Neurosciences* 39 (10): 694–705. https://doi.org/10.1016/j.tins.2016.08.007.

Kapogiannis, Dimitrios, Aron K. Barbey, Michael Su, Giovanna Zamboni, Frank Krueger, and Jordan Grafman. 2009. "Cognitive and neural foundations of religious belief." *Proceedings of the National Academy of Sciences* 106(12): 4876–4881.

Krueger, Frank, Aron K. Barbey, Kevin McCabe, Maren Strenziok, Giovanna Zamboni, Jeffrey Solomon, Vanessa Raymont, and Jordan Grafman. 2009. "The Neural Bases of Key Competencies of Emotional Intelligence." *Proceedings of the National Academy of Sciences of the United States of America* 106 (52): 22486–22491. https://doi.org/10.1073/pnas.0912568106.

Lawrence, Richard T. 1997. "Measuring the image of God: The God image inventory and the God image scales." *Journal of Psychology and theology* 25(2): 214–226. https://doi.org/10.1177/009164719702500206.

Liu, Chung-Chu. 2010. "The Relationship between Personal Religious Orientation and Emotional Intelligence." *Social Behavior and Personality: An International Journal* 38 (4): 461–467. https://doi.org/10.2224/sbp.2010.38.4.461.

Mayer, John D., Peter Salovey, and David R. Caruso. 2008. "Emotional Intelligence: New Ability or Eclectic Traits?" *The American Psychologist* 63 (6): 503–517. https://doi.org/10.1037/0003-066X.63.6.503.

Norenzayan, Ara, Will M. Gervais, and Kali H. Trzesniewski. 2012. "Mentalizing Deficits Constrain Belief in a Personal God." *PLoS One* 7 (5): e36880. https://doi.org/10.1371/journal.pone.0036880.

Paek, Ellen. 2006. "Religiosity and Perceived Emotional Intelligence among Christians." *Personality and Individual Differences* 41 (3): 479–490. https://doi.org/10.1016/j.paid.2006.01.016.

Raymont, Vanessa, Andres M. Salazar, Frank Krueger, and Jordan Grafman. 2011. "'Studying Injured Minds' – The Vietnam Head Injury Study and 40 Years of Brain Injury Research." *Frontiers in Neurology* 2 (March): 15. https://doi.org/10.3389/fneur.2011.00015.

Rohrbaugh, John, and Richard Jessor. 1975. "Religiosity in youth: A personal control against deviant behavior?." *Journal of Personality* 43:136–155. https://doi.org/10.1111/j.1467-6494.1975.tb00577.x.

Schnitker, Sarah A., Tenelle J. Porter, Robert A. Emmons, and Justin L. Barrett. 2012. "Attachment predicts adolescent conversions at Young Life religious summer camps." *International Journal for the Psychology of Religion* 22(3): 198–215. https://doi.org/10.1080/10508619.2012.670024

Śmieja, Magdalena, Jarosław Orzechowski, and Maciej S. Stolarski. 2014. «TIE: An ability test of emotional intelligence.» *PLoS One* 9(7): e103484. https://doi.org/10.1371/journal.pone.0103484

Waytz, Adam, Kurt Gray, Nicholas Epley, and Daniel M. Wegner. 2010. "Causes and Consequences of Mind Perception." *Trends in Cognitive Sciences* 14 (8): 383–388. https://doi.org/10.1016/j.tics.2010.05.006.

Willard, Aiyana K., and Ara Norenzayan. 2013. "Cognitive Biases Explain Religious Belief, Paranormal Belief, and Belief in Life's Purpose." *Cognition* 129 (2): 379–391. https://doi.org/10.1016/j.cognition.2013.07.016.

2

RELIGION AND SPIRITUALITY IN PARKINSON'S DISEASE

A Qualitative Evaluation

Joel B. Goodin, Eric Hubbard, Kourtney Barrett, Rebecca E. Schwartz, Brian P. Levey, and Nancy Spaulding

Introduction

Parkinson's disease (PD) is a progressive neurodegenerative disorder affecting multiple physical and psychological systems. These are characterized by both motor and non-motor deficits, which are due, in part, to degeneration of dopaminergic neurons in the striatal and mesolimbic-prefrontal dopaminergic systems (Hoehn & Yahr, 1967; Jankovic, 2008; Weintraub et al., 2022). By 2021, PD had emerged as the fastest-growing neurological disorder globally, by some estimates, having affected over approximately 11.5 million patients and steadily increasing (6.5 million in 2017), especially with the growing population of older adults aged 65 or older (Atterling Brolin et al., 2025; Feigin et al., 2017; Ghourchian et al., 2023). In most patients, PD increases in severity over a time span of 10–30 years before reaching its later stages. As symptoms evolve, PD impacts multiple aspects of daily functioning and requires sustained clinical management. PD is characterized by bradykinesia (slowness or paucity in movement and cognition) in addition to at least one of the following core features: postural instability, rigidity, resting tremor, and/or gait disturbances, in addition to a host of non-motor physiologic and neuropsychiatric symptoms. In left-onset Parkinson's disease (LOPD), as opposed to right-onset Parkinson's disease (ROPD), initial symptoms typically present on the left side of the body, consistent with contralateral neurodegeneration affecting right-hemispheric pathways (Haaxma et al., 2010; Steinbach et al., 2023). PD is further associated with pathological reduction in brain dopaminergic activity that can be temporarily treated with levodopa replacement or agonist therapy. Over time, however, these treatments may become associated with further motor and neuropsychiatric complications (Thanvi & Lo, 2004). At present, there is no cure for PD and no effective method to prevent the progression of the disease.

DOI: 10.4324/9781003158189-2

With respect to religious cognition, depression is present in 50–90% of patients with PD (Cong et al., 2022; Hermanns et al., 2012), which may be considered a sufficient reason for turning to spirituality and religion. Given that one out of every three people in the United States seeks alternative treatment (Barnes et al., 2004, 2008), spirituality and religious practices can be considered as an alternative approach within "mind-body practice" (Alwhaibi et al., 2015; Rajendran et al., 2001; Tirgari et al., 2022). Therefore, these issues should be investigated in terms of coping mechanisms and social support (Yang et al., 2024). A healthier mental state seems to be possible if there is meaning and value in life (Czekierda et al., 2017). Depression affects approximately 38%–40% of patients with PD, making it one of the most common non-motor symptoms (Shi et al., 2024). Globally, approximately 84%–85% of the population identifies with a religious tradition, representing over 6 billion individuals worldwide, with religious affiliation remaining prevalent through 2020 (Pew Research Center, 2025; World Population Review, 2024). Decades of work in the social sciences have found that religious or spiritual beliefs and practices can improve people's health and well-being, increase social cohesion, empathy, and altruistic behavior, and protect people against cognitive decline or substance abuse (Koenig, 2012; Koenig et al., 2023). Religion and spirituality are resources that may assist the patient and his or her family in dealing with the isolation and stigma caused by the motor (movement) limitation that develops in addition to the depression seen in PD.

Religion benefits health by providing a sense of coherence and meaning that enables people to understand their role in the universe, the purpose of life, and develop the courage to endure suffering (George et al., 2000; Jeserich et al., 2023). Sense of coherence (see Antonovsky, 1979) is one of many constructs identified by resource theories of stress that address opportunities to respond to suffering and stress with social support (Schwarzer & Leppin, 1991; Lin, 2025), self-efficacy (Bandura, 1977), optimism (Luo et al., 2023; Scheier & Carver, 1992), and hardiness (Kobasa, 1979; Senewiratne et al., 2025). Coping with changes, especially those that are negative, arouses some level of awareness and potential reaction, which relates to the amount of attention given to the stressor or change (Goodin & D'Brot, 2014; Krohne, 2002; Plamann et al., 2021). According to Krohne (2002), coping in the form of blunting (i.e., avoiding) is typically only adaptive with uncontrollable or unavoidable change or stress, whereas monitoring (i.e., information-seeking) forms of coping are more adaptive to stressors with which an individual might gain a greater sense of control over their situation through information. Religious coping appears to be a unique method that does not involve information-gathering but may still provide individuals with a greater sense of control, even in situations that are subjectively uncontrollable. Approaches to palliative care have continued to promote spiritual well-being as a core value in the support provided to patients with significant health issues, including those with PD (Bock et al., 2022). Spiritual well-being is a key factor associated with improvements in patients' overall outcomes and quality of life (Bock et al., 2022). Spirituality appears to provide patients with another source of social support, while improving their tools and techniques to address disease symptoms and stressors as well as grief management. Yet, spirituality, to date, is not an emphasis in neurology training, resulting in an unmet need and opportunity (Bock et al., 2022).

Therefore, spirituality may be a possible coping resource for people with PD in its late stages to combat prolonged grief and non-motor symptoms (Prizer et al., 2020). Non-motor symptoms are increasingly recognized as key features of PD that require routine assessment and management and form an integral part of standard treatment. Spiritual care is as important as physical care and is fundamental to the provision of holistic care. As PD is a movement disorder, healthcare professionals should consider integrating these psychospiritual components into routine physical rehabilitation programs to support patients' coping, symptom management, and holistic well-being. Spirituality improves mental health and quality of life but is also associated with improved overall health and well-being; one study even suggests that spirituality supports adaptation to illness and accelerates recovery (Wade, 2016).

Although PD ultimately involves bilateral symptomology, during the disease progression, the initial side of onset predominantly affects one hemisphere more than the other, thus displaying more acute neuropsychiatric and cognitive symptoms associated with the hemisphere contralateral to the side of onset. Patients with LOPD have shown more substantial neuropathology in right-sided nigro-striatal and meso-cortical dopaminergic systems as well as right-sided neural networks associated with the "social brain," theory of mind processing, and social affective processing (Narayanan & Albin, 2022; Porcelli et al., 2019). Among the non-motor deficits of PD, automatic access to religious representations may be slowed relative to controls, particularly in LOPD patients (Butler et al., 2010, 2011a, 2011b; Giaquinto et al., 2011; McNamara, 2006; Modestino et al., 2017; Morgan et al., 2016). These patients also report fewer religious experiences and engage in fewer religious/spiritual (R/S) practices than controls, although beliefs remain unchanged (Butler et al., 2010, 2011a, 2011b; Giaquinto et al., 2011; McNamara, 2006; Modestino et al., 2017; Morgan et al., 2016). Using the Brief Multidimensional Measure of Religiousness/Spirituality (BMMRS; Fetzer Institute, 1999), Butler et al. (2011a) demonstrated that those with PD ($n = 71$) were significantly lower in overall religiosity than age-matched controls ($n = 75$), with LOPD patients showing the greatest impairment with regard to private spiritual practices and positive spiritual experience but not overall belief or congregational support. Similarly, Giaquinto et al. (2011), in a study with 83 PD patients, showed a significant difference between controls ($n = 79$) and LOPD ($n = 31$), with controls scoring higher across various subscales of experiential religiosity but not belief using the Royal Free Interview of religious attitudes and practices. It also appears that PD impacts an individual's ability to fluently access doctrinal versus experiential religious cognitions (Butler et al., 2010, 2011a, 2011b; Morgan et al., 2016). Using a semantic priming task, Butler et al. (2010) demonstrated that individuals with LOPD had impaired activation of religious cognitive networks. Modestino et al. (2017) reported that LOPD individuals, when off-dopaminergic medication, comprehended scholar-defined experiential phrases with significantly more difficulty than ROPD individuals. Morgan et al. (2016) showed that the more religious the neurotypical controls were, the more quickly they responded under the religious priming condition than the neutral condition, while the participants with PD showed no significant interactions between their religiosity and differences in reaction times under the two priming conditions.

These findings have recently been extended via examination of longitudinal relationships between R/S and PD onset. Otaiku (2022 used multivariate logistic regression modeling on two longitudinal datasets to assess PD-R/S associations across time. Analyses revealed that low religiosity at baseline was associated with a remarkable tenfold increase in risk of developing PD many years later relative to individuals who reported higher religiosity at baseline. There was also evidence for a dose-response relation between religiosity level at baseline and later risk for PD. Although the author employed a variety of sensitivity analyses, as well as a two-year time lag analysis and other modeling adjustment procedures, the result has not yet been replicated, was based on a relatively small number of incident PD cases ($n = 73$), and offered no insights into potential mechanisms. Given that this is a potentially major finding for the PD community, commentary on the result in the *Journal of Religion and Health* called for additional studies to establish reliability and possible mechanisms to account for the finding (Paal et al., 2023).

Most of the other known risk factors for PD (except age), such as hyposmia, cognitive deficits, exposure to pesticides, genetic variants (LRRK2), REM Behavior Disorder, and dopaminergic deficit (via SPECTDAT scan), are more difficult to measure than religiosity and may not provide any easy-to-implement clinical interventions to slow the progression of PD. If the Otaiku finding is replicated, R/S practices like regular meditation may conceivably ameliorate some aspects of PD. For example, Smart et al. (2016) presented the case of a 78-year-old male who was diagnosed with PD 16 years prior to their study. He initially presented with left-hand tremor, stooped posture, shuffling gait, and frequent falls, which eventually progressed to bilateral motor symptoms after three years. Twelve years after his initial diagnosis, his symptoms and signs almost completely remitted, and he stopped all pharmacotherapy for that time. The accuracy of the initial PD diagnosis was supported by an appropriate clinical presentation, history of positive response to Sinemet, and an abnormal SPECTDAT scan. Thus, this case suggests the possibility of remission of symptoms in some patients. The authors proposed that the patient's long history of meditation practice may have been one contributing factor to his improvement, as meditation has been shown to release dopamine in the striatum. Given these and previously documented cross-sectional R/S associations with PD, the most probable causal explanation is that R/S practices such as prayer and meditation stimulate midbrain dopaminergic activity and related synaptic proliferation. Consistent with that hypothesis, several studies have demonstrated enhanced dopaminergic activity or brain volume in striatum and limbic dopaminergic sites associated with R/S practices and mindfulness meditation (Blum, 2025; Perez-Díaz et al., 2025; Tang et al., 2015), combined with exercise (Garner, 2023).

In this chapter, we describe the study's thematic analyses of a set of interviews focused on the religious and spiritual life histories of a group of individuals who have PD. This was a longitudinal, mixed-method study, with 78 participants in Time 1 (T1) and 62 in Time 2 (T2), designated as LOPD, ROPD, or undetermined side of onset (UPD). These individuals shared their stories related to their emotional-social sense of attachment to God compared to ordinary but significant others in structured video or telephonic interviews. The intent of this research was to contribute to current studies related to changes in religious attachment to God among left versus right onset PD (LOPD/ROPD) over 12 months. The study emphasizes the neural basis of loss and of acquisition or enhancement of access to affective and relational representations of belief in God. By emphasizing attachment to God among PD patients with comparison by side of onset, the study implicitly addresses the development of and constraints on cognitive forms of relational religious belief.

As noted above, our qualitative data, especially in our T1 dataset, was driven by Granqvist's (2012) idea that interaction with God is founded on the way a person feels attached to God as a non-corporeal being. Research to date has provided minimal understanding of what restriction of access to religious thought includes (e.g., feelings of attachment, doctrinal knowledge). Further understanding of how left-onset and right-onset PD participants explain their attachment and interactive experiences and perceptions with God may provide a better understanding of how restrictions on access to religious cognitions influence experiences and vice versa. To be clear, the word "God" is used in this study to represent any spiritual agent (e.g., including energies, forces, or deities from any formal or informal religion or belief system).

Attachment to God and Internal Working Models

Bowlby's (1982) attachment theory posits that humans innately possess psychobiological needs that he referred to as the attachment behavioral system. The attachment behavioral system motivates humans to identify and engage with supportive others (attachment figures), especially in response to stressors and needs for protection, safety, and comfort. According to Ainsworth (1978), humans either connect or attach in response to distress or a need for comfort in order to find "a *Safe Haven*" or they attach to a *Secure Base* that seems to serve as a home from which they can leave, explore, learn, prosper, and then return as needed. Attachment theory emphasizes variation in attachment systems and how they function (Ainsworth, 1978) in response to the unique experiences that each person may have with attachment figures. Each individual forms a mental representation of themselves and others, which are referred to as internal working models (IWMs) (Bowlby, 1973).

Positive IWMs of self (i.e., self-worth) and others' (e.g., attachment figures) benevolence are built and developed by interactions with sensitive and responsive attachment figures like parents and caregivers (Pietromonaco & Barrett, 2000). These positive interactions increase feelings of attachment security, wherein a person develops expectations that they will have the support of their attachment figure when needed. In contrast, attachment insecurity can result from unreliable sensitivity and responsiveness, leading to more negative IWMs (Thompson et al., 2022). Attachment theorists suggest that attachment begins to be developed with sensitive and responsive caregiving and culminates in the formation of secure attachments (Feeney, 2016; Mikulincer & Shaver, 2016). As they become formalized, secure attachments promote growth and buffer against anxiety.

The religion-as-attachment model (Granqvist, 2020) suggests that religion can explain beliefs, behaviors, and experiences for individuals as they interact in society. The model conceptualizes God(s) or deities (singular or plural) as non-corporeal attachment figures. Prominent monotheistic faith traditions espouse a conceptualization of a deity that is a source of love and comfort and a powerful, supportive ally (i.e., a *Safe Haven* or *Secure Base*), such that believers or followers of those faith traditions can form a relationship (i.e., an attachment bond) with the deity (Cherniak et al., 2021; Kirkpatrick & Shaver, 1992). The doctrinal and experiential-affective representation of a deity (e.g., God) as an attachment figure is present in religion and spirituality (Davis et al., 2021). Various representations of human attachment to God have been supported by neuroscientific research (Schjoedtet al., 2009), such as the relational conversational experience that can occur during personal prayer. Over time, as children develop the cognitive maturity to attach to others (e.g., parents) when they are not physically present by depending on internal sources of security, they are increasingly able to conceptualize, represent, and become attached to non-corporeal entities such as God (Granqvist, 2020).

There is consistent empirical support that believers are motivated to attach to God as a *Safe Haven* and *Secure Base* (Granqvist, 2020). For example, Hood et al. (2018) identified explicit pleas and requests for protection among prayers (e.g., petitionary prayer) and rituals (e.g., closing one's eyes). For instance, the conceptualization of attachment as a *Secure Base* has been supported by Birgegårdand Granqvist's (2004) findings that adults and children increased their closeness to God in response to attachment-related threat primes (e.g., separation). Threat primes (e.g., failure) have also been found to increase believers' cognitive access to God-related concepts (Granqvist et al., 2012). Further, Granqvist et al. (2012) found that a "God" prime increased positive affective responses to neutral stimuli and more access to positive wording suggestive of a *Secure Base* function. In keeping with the God-as-a-secure-base conceptualization, a God prime made people more willing to explore and take risks, especially among believers with a secure attachment to God (Kupor et al., 2015). The *Secure Base* conceptualization of attachment to God was further supported by findings that individuals securely attached to God had higher tolerance of opposing or alternative views and were more open to theological/existential exploration, despite remaining firm in their beliefs (Beck, 2006; Leow et al., 2024).

Pathways to Religion Based on Attachment-Related Experiences

Attachment-related experiences are hypothesized to lead to theistic forms of cognition in two ways (Granqvist & Kirkpatrick, 2016; Kirkpatrick & Shaver, 1992). The *correspondence hypothesis* suggests that interpersonal IWMs and experiences generalize to the development of IWMs of God. Whereas positive interpersonal IWMs promote representations of a benevolent God, negative interpersonal IWMs can produce more negative or inconsistent representations of God, such as mythological representations of mercurial Greek gods. The correspondence hypothesis further suggests that the sensitivity and responsiveness of a parent or caregiver and the subsequent secure attachment orientation enable social learning from the attachment figure (e.g., parent), which cultivates parent-offspring similarity in religion (i.e., socialized correspondence) and shared spiritual culture. The *compensation hypothesis* simply suggests that religious experiences may be used by believers to compensate for their own lack of secure, interpersonal attachments. Both hypotheses have been well-supported by research findings (Granqvist, 2020). Secure close relationships and experiences with sensitive and responsive caregivers are associated with IWMs of a loving God (Cassibba et al., 2008; Granqvist, 2002; Granqvist et al., 2020; Pietromonaco & Barrett, 2000; Thompson et al., 2022). Estimates of sensitive and responsive interpersonal caregiving were found to predict believers' coherent depiction of and ascribed benevolence of God three years later (Zarzycka, 2018).

In research on IWM correspondence, childhood attachment (Birgegård & Granqvist, 2004; Granqvist et al., 2007) and adult attachment style (Granqvist et al., 2012) were associated with increased closeness to God and access to God concepts in response to threat primes. An intergenerational link reminiscent of the correspondence hypothesis is suggested by findings that children of securely attached mothers felt closer to God than did children of mothers with insecure attachments (Cassibba et al., 2013), which is similar to an intergenerational transmission of religion found by Granqvist (2002) and Granqvist and Hagekull (1999). Emphasizing a *Secure Base* motive, the correspondence hypothesis was supported by research suggesting that higher attachment security was associated with more thorough exploration of religious ideas and alternatives (Greenwald et al., 2018). In interviews about religious exploration, participants with secure attachment to close others were more likely to mention secure-based themes (e.g., optimism, confidence, perceived security) (Kimball et al., 2013).

Within the context of high parental religiosity, individuals who experienced responsive caregiving scored higher on religious variables than those who experienced less responsive caregiving (Granqvist, 1998; Granqvist et al., 2020; Kirkpatrick & Shaver, 1990; Thompson et al., 2022). Similarly, attachment-secure adults experienced religious change aligned with their parents' religiosity during childhood (Greenwald et al., 2018). In contrast, Greenwald et al. (2018) found that attachment anxiety has been linked to sudden religious changes, rejection of parents' religiosity, and more emotional compensation themes. Attachment avoidance was linked to less religious exploration and socialization themes. During adolescent religious development, secure attachment to parents predicted alignment with the parents' faith (Schnitker et al., 2012; Thompson et al., 2022).

The compensation hypothesis is mostly supported by research on religious conversion. Attachment insecurity and insensitive caregiving have been linked to religious instability, especially with regard to sudden, dramatic religious conversions in times of crisis and turmoil (Granqvist & Kirkpatrick, 2004; Zarzycka et al., 2024). Religious instability has also been associated with attachment insecurity by adults recalling their attachment to parents (Pirutinsky, 2009; Zarzycka, 2018) and in the context of current romantic attachment (Greenwald et al., 2018). Moreover, the links between attachment insecurity and religious instability have been found across faiths and cultural contexts (Greenwald et al., 2018; Zarzycka, 2018) and in cross-sectional and longitudinal studies (Kirkpatrick, 1997, 1998). Cherniak et al. (2021) suggested that attachment-insecure individuals can earn a sense of security over time in a compensational relationship with God, despite the difficulty of overcoming negative IWMs that tend to linger.

Religion-As-Attachment and Neuropsychiatric Function in PD

The religion-as-attachment model suggests a religion-mental health link (Granqvist, 2020), which could have implications for PD patients pertaining to resilience and persistence in the face of obstacles, crises, or chronic illness. Contextual factors that influence proximity-seeking (e.g., stress) increase the association of religion and mental health. Just as mental health issues may be attenuated by what religion may offer in the form of a *Safe Haven* (e.g., freedom from worry) or a *Secure Base* (e.g., personal control), religion is consistently linked to mental health when it involves secure attachment to a benevolent God (Henderson & Kent, 2021; Hill & Pargament, 2008). In two Christian samples, secure attachment to God has been associated with reduced psychological distress and emotional problems (Ellison et al., 2014; Hiebler-Ragger et al., 2016). Research among Muslims (Miner et al., 2014) and Jews (Pirutinsky, 2019) has produced similar findings. While similar associations were found, relationships with Allah (i.e., God) were described as less personal (Miner et al., 2014), and Judaism was described as more behavioral/ritual than emotional/relational (Pirutinsky, 2019). Secure attachment to God has predicted mental health better than intrinsic religiosity, social support, or interpersonal attachment styles (Ellison et al., 2014; Hiebler-Ragger et al., 2016; Miner et al., 2014; Pirutinsky, 2019).

Another study found that religious and spiritual struggles predicted more negative experiences with God (i.e., insecure attachment) six months later, which were predictive of more negative doctrinal views of God after another year (Van Tongeren et al., 2019). Using a sample of 531, Calvert (2010) found that insecure attachment to God linked to diminishing health over time with significance and effect greater than interpersonal attachment. In contrast, secure attachment to God prospectively predicted optimism (Bradshaw & Kent, 2018) and transformative sacred moments (e.g., transcendence and interconnectedness) after six months, resulting in increased resilience and spiritual growth (Beck, 2019). Such increased optimism and resilience, among other factors, could be noteworthy in better understanding how religious cognition and attachment to God may differentially benefit those who may experience decreased relationship to God (e.g., LOPD patients).

We have described in detail methods of our study in a separate publication. The qualitative longitudinal, comparative case study of 78 (T1) and 62 (T2) Parkinson's patients assessed differences in neuropsychological function, theistic beliefs, IWMs of relationship and commitment to God, and religious experiences and practices between LOPD and ROPD patients. The LOPD and ROPD participants were compared to one another with regard to their human and their Spiritual and Religious (R/S) attachments. RQ1: "How do individuals with PD (LOPD and/vs. ROPD) describe their relationships with and perceived access to God as an attachment figure (content, quality, and intensity)?" The interviews were coded and scored by the PI, the qualitative data analyst, and the research assistant team of four coders for relevant themes. In keeping with standardized Adult Attachment Interview (George et al., 1996) manualized methods, coding was validated via independent scoring of at least 20% of randomly selected transcripts until inter-rater reliability of at least 90% was reached. Qualitative data were thematically analyzed by stages described by Braun and Clarke (2006).

Human and Spiritual Attachment Distinctions

In the context of this analysis, "spiritual attachment" is a relatively novel application of attachment theory that has previously focused on humans (e.g., Secure, Insecure). Whereas human attachment focuses on connection and engagement with humans, spiritual attachment refers to participants' descriptions of their perceived relationship with or orientation toward a divine presence (e.g., God, Jesus, the Holy Spirit), transcendent force, or religious reality that goes beyond institutional affiliation. While many participants referenced traditional religious language (e.g., prayer, scripture, worship), "spiritual" attachment was distinguished from purely doctrinal or behavioral religiosity by its relational, affective, and often experiential content. Participants described God as an emotional companion, helper, healer, or moral guide, signaling an attachment bond that paralleled, if not sometimes replaced, interpersonal human relationships.

Spiritual attachment was often conveyed through verbs of emotional interaction ("talk," "listen," "cry out," "feel"), suggesting an active, dynamic connection. For example, participants spoke of "having a conversation with God," "whining to Him," or feeling "wrapped in His arms." Some emphasized God's constancy amid life changes or illness progression, aligning closely with Granqvist's (2020) description of attachment to God as either a *Safe Haven* (relief in distress) or a *Secure Base* (confidence to explore or endure). Importantly, many participants framed this spiritual bond as evolving, deepening after diagnosis, or becoming more emotionally intimate over time.

Finally, the "spiritual" dimension also encompassed themes of mystical union, gratitude, surrender, and comfort beyond the boundaries of organized religion. Some individuals who rejected institutional religion nonetheless spoke of a personal or experiential connection to a divine force. Thus, "spiritual" across these 78 cases signifies both formal theistic relationships and broader affective/spiritual experiences of attachment, agency, and support rooted in a transcendent source.

Prelude, Religious and Spiritual Attachment Importance

With regard to *Religious or Spiritual (R/S) Attachment Importance* from T1 interview responses, the categories of *Foundational, Present, and Perfunctory* emerged, describing the centrality of R/S connection and motivation of R/S cognition and behavior in participants' lives. The category, *Foundational*, was used when a participant's faith was described as a core part of one's identity or worldview, deeply rooted and long-standing, though not always actively practiced or emotionally expressive. The second category, *Present*, was used to characterize R/S engagement that was current and active in daily life, often referenced as meaningful, supportive, or integrated into coping, even if not dramatic or theologically complex. The third category, *Perfunctory*, applied when religious or spiritual engagement was present but minimal, often driven by habit, social expectations, or residual upbringing rather than emotional conviction or intentional practice. Overall, participants' statements about the importance of their R/S attachments showed the

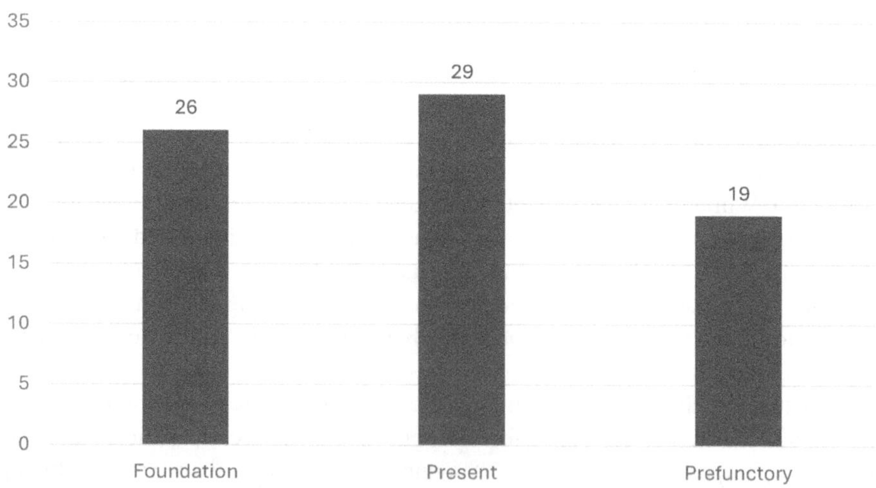

FIGURE 2.1 Religious/Spiritual Attachment Importance Groupings.

most to least frequency and volume in the *Foundation* category (*n* = 26; 35%), the *Present* category (*n* = 29; 39%), and the *Perfunctory* category (*n* = 19; 26%), respectively (see Figure 2.1).

Religious/Spiritual Attachment Importance by Gender

With regard to *Religious/Spiritual Attachment Importance* characterizations by gender, males are most represented among the *Foundation* category (*n* = 17), the *Present* category (*n* = 12), and the *Perfunctory* category (*n* = 11), respectively. In contrast, females were most represented among the *Present* category (*n* = 17), with almost equal representations among the *Foundation* and *Perfunctory* categorizations (*n* = 9 and *n* = 8, respectively).

Religious/Spiritual Attachment Importance by Side of Onset

R/S Attachment Importance for the three categories differed by onset, as seen in Figure 2.2. LOPD participants were most represented among the *Present* category (*n* = 17; 45%), whereas their representations among the *Foundation* and *Perfunctory* categories were somewhat equivalent (*n* = 10 or 26% and *n* = 11 or 29%, respectively). In contrast, ROPD participants were most represented among the *Foundation* category (*n* = 14; 44%), followed by *Present* (*n* = 11; 34%), and *Perfunctory* (*n* = 7; 22%) categories. UPD was represented in each category (*n* = 2 or 50%, *n* = 1 or 25%, and *n* = 1 or 25%, respectively), slightly more elevated than *Foundation*, comparatively.

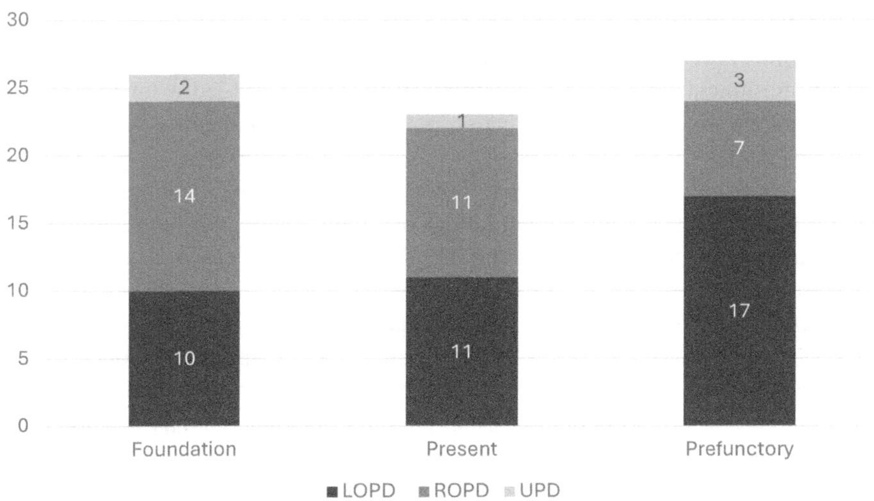

FIGURE 2.2 Religious/Spiritual Attachment Importance by Side of Onset.

Within the categories of *Foundation*, *Present*, and *Perfunctory*, the findings of coding yielded six cross-sectional dimensions used to characterize the data: *Ritual and Routine*, *Emotional Comfort*, *Community and Fellowship*, *Service and Outreach*, *Transformation/Turning Point*, and *Existential Meaning*. Just as *Foundation*, *Present*, and *Perfunctory* lie along a continuum of depth of R/S engagement, these subthemes trace an arc from everyday practice through social connection and purposeful action to deeper self-reflection. They give a more granular, "*en vivo*" (i.e., in the moment) view of how participants experience and describe their faith.

- *Ritual and Routine* emerged from any mention of regular religious practices (traditional R/S activities, daily prayer, weekly Mass or devotional study, and other habits of worship). For example, participants spoke of "Bible study" and "prayer." These repeated acts seemed to anchor participants' faith in the rhythm of their everyday lives.
- *Emotional Comfort* captured statements about peace, hope, relief, or reassurance derived from faith (e.g., *He cares for me and will comfort me*). This dimension appeared when the tenor of comments focused less on what participants did and more on how their beliefs steadied them emotionally.
- *Community and Fellowship* reflected participants' references to human connections, such as small groups, congregations, spouses, or friends as fellow sojourners in faith. Phrases such as "I am a part of a small group" typified this subtheme, highlighting faith as a shared, social experience.
- *Service and Outreach* denoted active expressions of faith through helping others, often through volunteering, mission work, or support ministries. Even brief notes like "Just repurposed by God to help others" signaled participants' conviction that faith should translate into tangible service.
- *Transformation/Turning Point* encompasses pivotal moments of conversion, recommitment, or life-changing realization ("I've changed a lot of things"). These narratives mark the inflection points when participants' spiritual trajectories shifted.
- *Existential Meaning* arose from reflections on purpose, calling, or destiny afforded by faith. "Life is fragile and precious." Such statements go beyond ritual or comfort to articulate the broader "why" of their lives as shaped by spiritual belief.
- *Relationship/Closeness* referred to personal, relational language used to describe one's connection with God or a higher power. Participants often spoke of "talking with God, feeling close to Him," or "having a relationship with Jesus," framing faith not only as belief but as an ongoing, intimate companionship. These statements suggested that spiritual engagement was not distant or abstract but deeply interpersonal, rooted in a sense of being known, heard, and cared for by a divine presence.

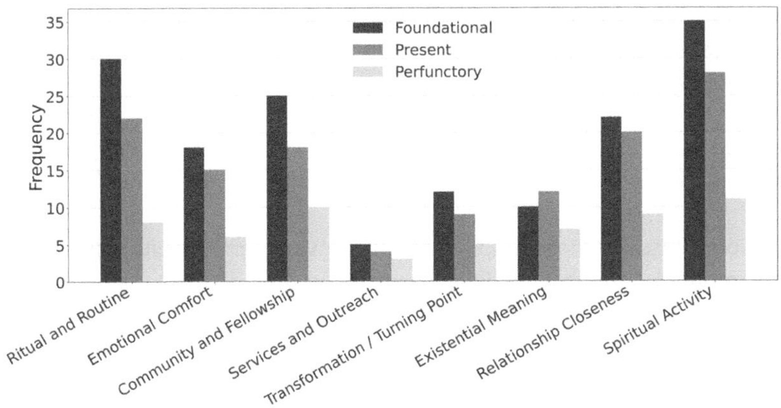

FIGURE 2.3 Religious/Spiritual Attachment Importance Categories and Dimensions.

- *Spiritual Activity* encompassed broader expressions of religious or spiritual engagement beyond formal ritual. This included reading religious texts, listening to faith-based podcasts or music (*filling my mind with [good things]*), attending retreats, or using apps for meditation or reflection. Quotes in this dimension conveyed a commitment to staying spiritually nourished through a variety of practices tailored to personal needs and preferences, showing how participants actively sought spiritual connection in both structured and flexible ways.

These eight dimensions will now be used to provide a more meaningful, but concise snapshot of how the importance of participants' R/S attachments was represented across participants and their statements within the *Foundation*, *Present*, and *Perfunctory* categories (see Figure 2.3). Rather than presenting quotes characterized by singular categories, all quotes will be grouped in relation to multiple subthemes, which provide a more multifaceted, layered characterization of each participant's response.

Prelude, Religious/Spiritual Attachment Importance, Category 3: *Foundational*

In the *Prelude*, the first of three categories of *R/S Attachment Importance* to emerge was *Foundational*. Participants in this category demonstrated deeply ingrained spiritual practices that served as a steady anchor throughout their lives, reflecting the central role faith plays in their emotional and spiritual well-being. P50 (M71-UPD-T1) shared a lifelong journey that ultimately led him to recognize his spiritual purpose:

> We go back and think about it. I could see His hand at work throughout my life, both in a spiritual way, in a more practical ways. I actually committed myself to

> Christ in when I was 21, but the background means everything to me, but I'm not sure where it starts sometimes. I've got, I've been around 71 years, and so it's a lot of, lot of life. It was a big thing I worked for the big parties where they bought a lot of alcohol. And in the meantime, I discovered God or He just, He pointed out to me, And I began to pray for people, and they were getting healed. And, and I saw I was supposed to do something with this. There's a purpose.

This quote illustrates how his faith evolved over time, transitioning from a less certain, more sporadic connection to a profound, foundational commitment. P50's reference to discovering God and realizing his life's purpose marks a significant *Transformation/Turning Point*, illustrating the maturation of his faith into something central to his existence. His awareness of God's influence in his life and the healing he witnessed underscore the *Existential Meaning* subtheme, highlighting how his spiritual journey now shapes his broader sense of purpose.

P62 (M65-LOPD-T2) also illustrated this theme through his reflections on his deeply ingrained religious practices, emphasizing *Ritual and Routine* and *Spiritual Activity*. He shared,

> Daily Bible reading has always been a part of my life, and I think it forms a foundation for walking through Parkinson's at this time. Fellowship or being part of the church body is very important and has been, has become more important.

His commitment to daily Bible reading and the increasing importance of communal worship underscore the *Ritual and Routine* and *Community and Fellowship* subthemes. These practices are not only foundational but also serve as an anchor for him during life's challenges, illustrating the stability and consistency of his faith.

P69 (M64-LOPD-T1) remarked on his faith, saying, "It's taken forefront…It's become more important for, and it has been my backbone. It's been my foundation." This statement clearly exemplifies both *Ritual and Routine* and *Emotional Comfort*. He views his faith as the central pillar of his life, providing him with emotional and spiritual grounding. His declaration that faith has become his "backbone" and "foundation" directly reflects the *Foundational* categorization, indicating the deep, stabilizing effect of his spiritual beliefs. This emotional resonance underscores a profound *Spiritual Activity* that supports him in everyday life.

P63 (F72-UPD-T2) shared,

> I didn't understand who God was until about 35, but now I figured out how much He loves me. And when I met [Current Husband], I got really better about going to church every time I could. Before that, if I hadn't felt real well or something, I didn't have any enthusiasm that [he had] to get up and go. So he's improved me a lot, and I hope I have his life, but spirituality/religion very important in my life now.

This quote embodies *Ritual and Routine*, as she describes how church attendance became a regular and vital part of her life, particularly after her husband's influence. Her words highlight the *Community and Fellowship* subtheme, as her relationship with her husband played a key role in deepening her connection to faith. The emotional comfort she now feels through a better understanding of God's love points to *Emotional Comfort*, while her active engagement in *Spiritual Activity* reflects the growing importance of spirituality in her life.

For several individuals, faith had always been an integral part of their lives, shaping both identity and response to hardship. P65 (F58-ROPD-T1) shared, "My grandfather was the pastor of our church, and so I grew up in church. I mean, from the very beginning, I mean, I was there three times a week." One LOPD participant (P56, M71-LOPD-T2) echoed this same lifelong spiritual grounding, stating, "Prayer is just what I do. I've done it since I was a kid, and I still pray every morning and night. That routine keeps me grounded."

Others framed their foundation in more existential terms, "God's been there from the beginning, even when I didn't notice. Looking back, I can see a pattern. I know He's had a purpose for me" (P50, M71-LOPD-T1). A few spoke to more recent rediscovery, as one woman explained, "I didn't used to be very spiritual, but after my diagnosis, I felt pulled back to my roots. Now my faith gives me strength every day" (P67, F72-ROPD-T2). These reflections collectively illustrate how foundational faith, whether lifelong or rediscovered, served a *Secure Base* function, providing structure, meaning, and continuity amid the challenges of PD.

The experiences of these participants reflect the *Foundational* nature of their faith, where their spiritual practices and beliefs have served as anchors throughout their lives. The transformation from less certain or sporadic engagement to a deeply rooted, consistent connection with faith illustrates the development of *Foundational Attachment*, a theme that emphasizes the importance of ongoing spiritual practices, communal connections, and personal transformation over time. These accounts, drawn from both LOPD and UPD participants, reflected *Secure Base* functioning, where God provided structure, purpose, and identity across time. Notably, the emotional tone was generally steady and reflective rather than affectively intense, especially in LOPD narratives. This contrasts with themes that follow, where *Safe Haven* dynamics and more affective expressions begin to emerge, especially among ROPD participants.

Prelude, Religious and Spiritual Attachment Importance, Category 2: *Present*

In the *Prelude*, the second category of *R/S Attachment Importance* to emerge was *Present*. Participants in this category reflected ongoing commitment and re-engagement rather than dramatic conversion or emotion-driven experiences. P30 (F52-LOPD-T2) emphasized her dual roles as educator and parent within her church, reflecting *Ritual and Routine* and *Spiritual Activity*. She shared, "Still very,

very involved in the Catholic Church. I teach religious ed classes; all of my kids have been confirmed. My beliefs are exceptionally important to me and make me a better person." Her description of daily teaching responsibilities and family faith milestones illustrates how established routines ("teach religious ed classes") and active participation ("all of my kids have been confirmed") reinforced both her personal devotion and her family's spiritual growth.

P5 (F78-LOPD-T2) spoke about his R/S engagement in a way that we characterized as Present. He said, "God and I've got a close relationship. I just talk to him a few times a day. Relationship with God hasn't changed much but pretty much constant." His statement reflects a steady, consistent connection with God, emphasizing the *Present theme*. The routine of talking to God daily shows an active engagement with faith. Despite the lack of major changes in his spiritual life, the connection remains foundational and continuous, signifying a *Relationship/Closeness* that is maintained regularly without dramatic shifts.

P20 (M65-LOPD-T1) shared his spiritual journey, which we also categorized within the *Present* theme. He reflected,

> Accepted Christ when I was 16 years old, and I didn't walk with Christ for a number of years. Um, but in my mid-twenties, I came back to the standard and I've been following ever since. There have been times where I've been a lot closer than I am now. There've been times where I've been farther away than I am now. Um, so it's an ongoing positioning kind of thing where if I'm, if I'm faithful, not at doing, but in communicating, then I'm in a much better place.

This narrative highlights the fluidity of his spiritual connection, emphasizing the ongoing nature of his relationship with God, which is defined by continuous *Transformation/Turning Point* and *Emotional Comfort*.

P2 (F67-ROPD-T1) discussed how her understanding of faith had shifted, reflecting the *Present* theme. She mentioned,

> I still believe in those things, but I have a much more open, diverse view of religion now because I don't think—I don't think if someone doesn't accept Jesus Christ as their Lord and Savior, they'll be barbecued in the next life; that doesn't make any sense.

Her belief in God remains intact, but there is a clear shift in her Cognitive Religious Attachment, indicating that her faith is evolving such that her present-day beliefs remain grounded in early faith but have broadened over time.

P10 (F61-ROPD-T1) spoke about how her faith had grown over time and what brought her closer to God, fitting into the *Present* category. She shared about focusing more on the Bible and the Old Testament in particular because she did study that growing up. During a time of exploration and some distancing from her original faith roots:

> [I] took a lot of classes in religious studies, and some are more eastern religions...like Buddhism and, and Hinduism and stuff like that. So I, I've got, for a while, I tried meditation and that kind of stuff, you know. And that didn't really do anything for me.

She got re-involved

> in the church. And I've kinda slacked off that VFW some because they drink and they party and they fight with each other, and I don't think they're carrying out the mission that I want to carry out. You know?

P10's journey from exploring other religions to recommitting to her faith reflects an ongoing *Transformation/Turning Point* and *Spiritual Activity*, demonstrating an active and deepening connection to her spiritual life.

Several participants described a *Present*-tense connection to God that, while not always overtly emotional, remained consistent or quietly adaptive. P11 (F70-ROPD-T1) shared about her consistent faith since childhood, saying,

> Faith has stayed pretty consistent since childhood. I am very spiritual. I don't necessarily, even though I'm a Catholic, I don't necessarily go to church all the time... My faith in God and... teachings of Christ... that's what the faith is about, not necessarily about what man does with his, what he thinks he knows.

Her reflections convey a *Cognitive Attachment*, sustained across time, even as her formal religious practice became more flexible.

Others described spiritual persistence despite disillusionment or shifting institutional loyalties. P77 (M75-UPD-T1), a former church elder, shared how his spiritual engagement changed during the pandemic, noting that he began attending a different church that emphasized scripture more centrally as his current church "seemed to be going... toward wokeness." He expressed discomfort with his old church's political shift and found renewed commitment in a more focused setting by "going to other churches and listening to other speakers outside the Church of Christ that are more in tune with scripture." In T2, however, he faced physical limitations:

> We're not able to go to church on Sunday mornings, which I miss that tremendously. But we're able to tune in to some worship services online. And my wife and I watch two or three worship services. So we go to church even though we're shut-ins, and we hear some funny inspirational sermons and worship experiences.

His account exemplifies a *Cognitive Secure Base*, sustained over time through *reappraisal and adaptive alignment* with his personal beliefs. His T1 reflections highlighted a principled shift toward scripture-centered worship, while his T2 comments revealed continuity in faith practice despite physical limitations, facilitated by virtual engagement.

A similar return to familiar foundations emerged in P23 (F70-LOPD-T1), who described her faith as once shaken by illness and personal losses. She explored other faiths, saying, "We explored different religions, and we always ended up coming back to Catholic [church]," although she now reports practicing with less rigidity and more acceptance. Despite the challenges, her attachment to God remained a quiet source of strength, highlighting an ongoing *Cognitive Secure Base* orientation.

P29 (M76-LOPD-T1) described his faith journey as gradual and unremarkable in outward drama, but deeply meaningful. After attending a church retreat, he found himself becoming more faithful and involved, even though he noted no moment that changed everything, but reported experience that "just kinda made me at look at everything a little bit differently…That since even in my personal faith journey, if you wanna call it that, has just continued to grow." His experience demonstrates *Secure Base functioning* that developed slowly through consistent exposure, reflection, and steady personal engagement.

These accounts broaden our understanding of the *Present* attachment (Category 2). They illustrate how a connection to God can remain steady despite institutional shifts, cognitive re-evaluation, or lived losses. The *Present* theme, then, reveals faith as a durable inner compass, especially among LOPD individuals, whose affective language tended to be more subdued. In contrast, upcoming themes highlight more explicitly *Safe Haven* dynamics and emotional language, particularly among ROPD participants. Overall, participants described a *Present*-tense connection with God marked by spiritual consistency, daily ritual, or quiet but steady reflection. For many, especially those interviewed at T2 (e.g., P30, P78), this involved *Secure Base* functioning through structured routines, family milestones, or educational roles. Several LOPD participants, including P20 and P52, conveyed a calm, grounded emotional tone in their reflections, suggesting that their *Present* attachments were cognitively anchored and affectively stable. Others, like P5 and P10, noted emotional shifts or renewed commitment through life disruptions, indicating mild *Safe Haven* dynamics. Overall, *Present Attachment* emerged as a midpoint between static tradition and adaptive continuity, showing that even without dramatic change, participants sustained meaningful spiritual connection over time.

Prelude, Religious and Spiritual Attachment Importance, Category 3: *Perfunctory*

In the *Prelude*, the last category of *R/S Attachment Importance* to emerge was *Perfunctory* (Category 3). These participants described their relationship with God in more detached or routine ways, often out of habit or upbringing rather than deep emotional connection. P30 (F64-LOPD-T2) noted that she believes in God but does not actively pursue religious practices, stating, "I believe, but I don't go to church much anymore. I used to." Similarly, P25 (M66-ROPD-T2) explained that he "grew up going to church," but does not currently attend. P17 (F68-ROPD-T1) said that she believes in God but was clear that she doesn't "get into prayer" or read religious material.

P22 (F72-ROPD-T1) reflected on faith beyond formal practice and its comforting presence, capturing *Community* and *Fellowship, Spiritual Activity*, and *Emotional Comfort*. She said:

> And in between time, I did leave the Catholic church when I got divorced, and then I went with Unity Church. I was with them for quite a few years. And then, most recently with the Episcopal Church, I'd go to both, Unity, Episcopal, but I've always been spiritual. Well, I've always believed that God is all loving, all knowing. He's a good person. He's a good God. He's not an angry God and that He protected me, and that the blessed Mother protected me and kept me safe. And I think without them, I would be much worse off today. And, um, brought me a lot of peace.

Her account shows that while her church attendance fluctuated, her belief in divine love and protection remained constant, offering emotional reassurance and a sense of connection to God. However, her focus on affective comfort over theological engagement suggests that her spiritual attachment may be more perfunctory than deeply relational. Her engagement centered less on active seeking or commitment, and more on sustaining emotional ease.

P24 (F73-LOPD-T1) described a rejection of her religious affiliation, a period of religious experimentation, and then a renewed commitment, illustrating *Community* and *Fellowship, Spiritual Activity*, and *Existential Meaning.* She shared:

> I stopped going to church because I didn't think the Catholic Church gave me anything...I started going to different churches to see what was going on... I took sociology of religion...very curious about it...I stayed in non-denominational churches until, actually, I got diagnosed with Parkinson's.

After some disengagement from the church, she became involved again:

> I was looking for a church and tried a couple of different ones feeling I needed to start going to church. And I met some friends... they go to the Episcopal church nearby. So, I just recently started back into going to church... trying to make a habit out of it. The only time I could see my friends on Sundays. So, that's one of why I didn't go to church for a long time, part of the reason.

Her narrative illustrates how intellectual curiosity and social connection, rather than a deep emotional or theological bond, guided her re-engagement with religious practice, ultimately restoring a sense of routine and community more than personal devotion.

P37 (F71-LOPD-T1) described her difficulties with church attendance amid PD-related physical limitations. Still, she seemed to find reassurance through faith, discussing aspects of *Ritual and Routine, Spiritual Activity, and Emotional Comfort*. She explained:

> And I just continue going to Baptist Church. Why are my children in the Baptist Church? And I don't know that there's a significant difference except in the last few years. I just don't have the energy to go to church. So I'd changed more to, uh, modern church service where they stand most of the time, and I just can't do that anymore. Some positive experiences confirms and reaffirms that he [God] is real, and he is there. Is God punishing [me with] PD? I didn't really think of it as a punishment. I think that it is a life story that sometimes bad things happen, and we have to get through it.

Her reflection seems to illustrate that perfunctory attendance could potentially be the result of PD-related life restrictions.

P43 (F72-LOPD-T1) articulated a faith identity independent of church buildings, exemplifying *Relationship/Closeness*, *Emotional Comfort*, and *Existential Meaning*. She shared her account:

> [I] stopped going to church at 46 when middle son was ostracized by priest for being gay. And the, the changes, being the good Catholic girl still even though I was 46, I was very concerned about [Son's Name], not feeling like he was a child of God. There's so much cruelty out there towards gay people…I told him, I said, you are a child of God.

She went with him as he came out to the priest as gay, to see if he could get help, but it went poorly. Her son ran to her crying and she vowed to disengage with church. She reflected on her new stance, explaining, "I will not claim religiousness, but I will claim faithfulness. I will come, claim spirituality. I will claim love of my Maker. I will claim that I know my Maker loves me, but I don't go to the building." Her reflection suggests that while her engagement with church has diminished, her faith remains intact and functions as a quiet, cognitive anchor. The perceived "perfunctory" nature of her religious life may reflect not spiritual detachment, but practical limitations imposed by PD.

P3 (M76-LOPD-T1) described returning to church after marriage "because [I] thought it would be good for business," a statement that highlights the role of practical incentives over personal belief. P24 (F73-LOPD-T2) reported drifting away from the Catholic Church and re-entering religious spaces later in life, primarily due to social engagement: "I just recently started back into going to church… trying to make a habit out of it. The only time I could see my friends on Sundays."

Her remarks suggest that faith functioned more as a social activity than a deeply spiritual one during this phase of her journey. P30 (F68-LOPD-T1) also captured a faith rooted in familiarity rather than fervor, explaining that she "didn't really get into studying or anything like that," but "always knew He was there." Her passive phrasing signals an enduring yet distant relationship with God.

These participants reflected *Perfunctory* faith, marked by low emotional intensity but sustained through habit, social norms, or cognitive continuity. Their religious practices remained present more out of routine than deep relational connection. Most were LOPD cases interviewed at T1, suggesting this pattern may emerge early in the disease and reflect a more cognitively oriented approach to R/S coping. Rather than offering a *Safe Haven*, these attachments functioned as a *Secure Base*, not through intimacy with God, but through the structure and familiarity of religious practice.

With regard to the categories of *Religious/Spiritual Attachment Importance*, three primary categories each reflected a different orientation to spiritual identity: *Foundational*, *Present*, and *Perfunctory*. These three trajectories reflected variation in the centrality of R/S belief, ranging from deeply embedded faith to more passive or habitual belief systems.

Cross-Cutting Dimensions of Religious/Spiritual Attachment

Within each of these three overarching categories, six cross-cutting dimensions also emerged through the coding process. These dimensions included *Ritual and Routine*, *Emotional Comfort*, *Community and Fellowship*, *Communication with God*, *Identity and Purpose*, and *Agency and Coping*. Characterizing the content across these dimensions provided texture and depth to the ways participants articulated spiritual importance. Together, these structures revealed meaningful differences in affective tone, attachment function, and possible associations with side of onset.

The *Foundational* category reflected narratives from participants who expressed long-standing, deeply integrated religious or spiritual beliefs. These individuals conveyed a spiritual identity that was consistent over time and closely tied to their self-understanding. Their faith was often established early in life and had either remained steady or intensified in response to PD. Spirituality was described not only as important but as indispensable. Participants in this group often engaged regularly in religious practices such as prayer, Bible reading, or church attendance, indicating the prominence of *Ritual and Routine* as a stabilizing factor. They frequently described their beliefs in confident, matter-of-fact terms and tended to emphasize the protective, guiding, and grounding role of faith in their lives. For these participants, religious belief functioned primarily as a *Secure Base*, offering cognitive and emotional stability from which they approached life's uncertainties.

For example, one participant shared that he grew closer to God through the act of praying for others and witnessing their healing. Another stated that he had become more serious in his faith following his diagnosis and had since begun praying with his wife every night. These accounts suggested a shift toward more conscious dependence on spiritual practices, even among those whose faith had long been a part of their lives. A woman in this group described God as being "with her" through every phase of life, noting that she had seen divine protection in retrospect. Others conveyed that faith was something they never abandoned and that their belief system offered a stable moral and emotional structure across changing life circumstances.

Across the *Foundational* category, the dimension of *Identity and Purpose* was particularly salient. Participants saw their faith as something that defined them and gave their lives direction. *Ritual and Routine* reinforced this orientation, serving as a container for both personal and collective meaning. *Communication with God* was described as ongoing and sincere, even if not always emotional. Although *Emotional Comfort* was sometimes present, it often took a secondary role to the grounding function of faith. *Secure Base* dynamics were clearly dominant here, with spirituality offering both structure and existential coherence. *Safe Haven* functioning was less frequently emphasized, but not absent. Some participants did refer to prayer or divine presence as providing comfort during moments of fear, pain, or isolation, suggesting that both attachment functions could coexist, even if one was more salient.

Side of onset appeared to influence both the content and tone of these narratives. Participants with LOPD were more heavily represented in this group and tended to frame their religious identity through structured, cognitively grounded language. They often spoke about discipline, routine, and moral clarity. Their faith was embedded in systems of thought and behavior, with less overt affective expression. By contrast, participants with ROPD, while less common in this group, expressed their beliefs in more emotionally descriptive terms when present. These ROPD participants sometimes emphasized relational closeness with God or divine comfort, adding a more *Safe Haven* functionality to their accounts.

The *Present* category represented participants who were spiritually engaged at T1 but described their beliefs as adaptive, changing, or recently renewed. Faith was meaningful, but it was often in the process of being redefined. These individuals described how adult experiences, shifts in worldview, or personal crises had shaped their current spiritual orientation. In this group, belief was still central but more exploratory and dynamic than among *Foundational* participants. The tone of these narratives was often reflective, questioning, or open to complexity. Unlike the unshaken certainty found in the *Foundational* group, the *Present* group often conveyed a process of spiritual negotiation or transformation.

One woman shared that she had shifted her theological perspective to be more open-minded, believing that salvation extended beyond rigid denominational lines. Another participant discussed having explored Eastern religions before ultimately recommitting to Christianity, while still holding on to broader spiritual values. Others in this group described the importance of religious community as a site of moral accountability and belonging, even when traditional beliefs had been challenged or reshaped. There were also references to life events, such as divorce or illness, that had deepened or reoriented spiritual priorities.

The six dimensions appeared prominently in this group, particularly *Identity and Purpose*, *Emotional Comfort*, and *Communication with God*. Participants often described God as an active conversation partner, especially in times of uncertainty or grief. *Emotional Comfort* was present in descriptions of God as listener, protector, or stabilizer. *Agency and Coping* was also relevant, as participants described how spirituality helped them navigate the disruptions of PD or frame their condition within a broader theological narrative. *Ritual and Routine* was still practiced by many but often in modified or personally tailored ways. *Community and Fellowship* was described as supportive but was sometimes the site of disappointment or disillusionment as well.

Safe Haven dynamics were more clearly present in this group than in the *Foundational* group. Many participants described turning to God for relief, reassurance, or emotional regulation during moments of personal suffering. These expressions often involved affective language and described a personal, intimate connection with the divine. At the same time, *Secure Base* functioning remained active, particularly in the ways participants used faith to maintain perspective or derive strength in the face of progressive illness.

Both LOPD and ROPD participant exemplars appeared in this group. LOPD individuals tended to emphasize cognitive and theological restructuring, reflecting on belief systems or spiritual roles with deliberation. ROPD participants more often emphasized emotional closeness or experiential depth, suggesting that right-hemispheric involvement may be associated with more relational or affect-laden expressions of faith, which could explain dampened emotionality in LOPD participants' discussions of closeness. ROPD participants thus reflected a rich intersection of both attachment functions, with individual variation shaped by temperament, life history, and possibly neurological profile.

The *Perfunctory* category included participants for whom spiritual belief was present but minimally engaged. These individuals expressed belief in God or alignment with religious identity but did not describe active spiritual practice or deep emotional involvement. Often, their religious orientation had been shaped in childhood or through cultural norms and had remained in the background of their adult lives. For some, health limitations or disillusionment with religious institutions contributed to their current distance from organized religion. In this group, belief often took the form of implicit trust or quiet reassurance rather than active pursuit.

Some participants stated that they had stopped attending church due to mobility issues or fatigue. Others cited frustration with organized religion but maintained a private sense of faith. One woman described feeling spiritually supported by God and the Virgin Mary but did not engage in prayer or formal worship. Another participant noted that while he no longer regularly attended church, he still believed in God and found comfort in occasional online sermons or memories of spiritual teachings from earlier in life.

In this group, the cross-sectional dimensions appeared in a more diluted or past-tense form. *Ritual and Routine* was often described in terms of what used to be done. *Emotional Comfort* was occasionally referenced but usually in general or habitual terms. *Identity and Purpose* were less often articulated, though some participants did describe faith as a quiet part of their upbringing or cultural background. *Communication with God*, when mentioned, was framed as sporadic or internal rather than dialogic or relational. *Agency and Coping* appeared in occasional references to fate, perspective, or quiet resilience, but these were not dominant themes.

Secure Base functioning was still modestly present, particularly in how participants used faith as a quiet anchor during periods of reflection or loss. *Safe Haven* functioning was minimal but occasionally surfaced in language describing God as a protector or comforting presence. The dominant tone was one of passive belief or cultural continuity rather than active relational attachment.

Perfunctory accounts were more common among LOPD participants at T1, consistent with the broader pattern of cognitive structuring and emotional neutrality observed in the broader data set. These individuals often conveyed a residual connection to faith through belief rather than felt experience. ROPD participants were less represented here, though when present, their accounts tended to include slightly more emotional content, even when their religious engagement was limited.

Taken together, these three categories reflect a spectrum of religious and spiritual attachment importance, from deeply embedded and active commitment to quiet, background-level belief. Each was characterized not only by differences in content but also by affective tone, cognitive framing, and attachment function. The six dimensions that appeared across these categories provided additional layers of meaning, illustrating how participants relied on rituals, drew emotional strength, maintained spiritual dialogue, found meaning in identity, and used faith to support coping.

Side of onset differences were evident across the data. LOPD participants more frequently described structured, cognitively grounded forms of spiritual engagement and were overrepresented in both the *Foundational* and *Perfunctory* groups. Their narratives tended to reflect *Secure Base* functioning through stability, moral orientation, and perspective taking. ROPD participants, while fewer in number, tended to use more affectively expressive language and relational metaphors, particularly in the *Present* group. Their narratives more often reflected *Safe Haven* dynamics, with faith functioning as an emotionally responsive refuge during uncertainty or distress.

In sum, the T1 data represented in the *Religious/Spiritual Attachment Importance* categorizations across the various dimensions characterize religious or spiritual attachment as an important, though variably expressed, aspect of life for many individuals living with PD. For some, faith is foundational and unshaken, deeply woven into their identity and way of coping. For others, it is present and adaptive, responsive to life transitions and evolving beliefs. For still others, it remains perfunctory, quiet, or passive, yet still available as a source of cultural continuity or personal reflection. These findings underscore the importance of attending not only to the presence or absence of religious belief, but to the functional and emotional ways it supports individuals facing chronic illness. They also suggest that side of onset and attachment function may intersect in meaningful ways that shape how spirituality is felt, expressed, and utilized over time.

Coding Framework: Groupings, Themes, and Functional Labels

Given the understanding gleaned from evaluating the data with the initial categories and dimensions, we then proceeded to code subthemes and themes developed for RQ1. Although informed by our initial categorical and dimensional evaluation, the primary coding structure for themes and subthemes was ultimately driven by a modified attachment theory framework integrating Granqvist's (2020) spiritual attachment taxonomy and Mikulincer and Shaver's (2007) concepts of *Safe Haven* and *Secure Base*. The primary domains of attachment were *Spiritual* and *Human*, each analyzed for its qualitative configuration, functional purpose, and emotional valence. Every quote or sub-quote was assigned an *attachment configuration*, a *functional label*, and a *valence rating* (*Positive*, *Negative*, or *Neutral*). To be clear, this modified attachment theory was our original plan. Still, we gained extensive foundational knowledge of the participants and their narratives from our initial evaluation. Although not emphasized throughout, those categorizations and dimensions were used throughout all analyses to provide a more nuanced and textured understanding of the data, especially as we considered subtle differences in R/S attachment engagements.

Thus, based on the modified attachment framework, we began to identify attachment configurations, including five primary types (*Priority*, *Complementary*, *Oneness*, *Togetherness*, and *Change*). *Priority* refers to a hierarchical attachment (e.g., "God comes first" or "my family is my center"), whereas *Complementary* indicates a parallel or coexisting attachment system (e.g., "My wife and my faith get me through"). *Oneness*, however, suggests a mystical or dependent fusion with God or a human other (e.g., "vanishing into God," "couldn't survive without her"). Similar in sentiment, but practically more divided, *Togetherness* refers to a mutual partnership, either spiritual (e.g., praying with a spouse) or interpersonal (e.g., feeling loved and supported). Finally, *Change*, for present purposes, indicates marked shifts from T1 to T2 in either content, intensity, or orientation of attachment. Thus, between *Spiritual* and *Human* attachments, there were various subdivided combinations of attachment, such as *Spiritual-Priority*, *Human-Priority*, *Spiritual-Complementary*, *Human-Complementary*, *Oneness-Spiritual*, *Oneness-Human*, *Togetherness-Spiritual*, *Togetherness-Human*, and *Balanced* (used when quotes blended elements of both without a clear preference).

Classic attachment theory offered useful functional labels such as *Safe Haven, Secure Base*, and *Ambivalent Safe Haven.* The label of *Safe Haven* is used when the attachment figure (God or a human) was relied upon to soothe distress or provide comfort. *Secure Base* indicated that an attachment figure provided support to grow, explore, or face adversity with confidence. A third label, *Ambivalent Safe Haven*, was not relevant to any exemplars, but would have characterized participants who turned to God or others inconsistently or with emotional conflict (e.g., "I'm angry with God, but I still talk to Him").

These labels helped distinguish whether the relationship primarily functioned as an emotional refuge or a source of existential stability and growth. For example, one participant noted, "God gives me peace, but I also feel Him pushing me forward," which was classified as a *Secure Base* with *Priority–Spiritual* configuration. Finally, valence coding reflected the emotional tone of each quote to characterize each as *Positive* (e.g., comfort, gratitude, love), *Negative* (e.g., anger, confusion, disappointment), or *Neutral or Mixed* (e.g., questioning, ambiguity without clear distress). Together, this coding system enabled robust and nuanced categorization of attachment language, capturing both the *structure* and *function* of each participant's spiritual and human connections across time points and onset types. Single-point Cases (T1 or T2 only—Not both) are presented below with relevant themes, categories, codes, and commentary. Note that some cases had missing data or insufficient data from which to draw conclusions about change over time. Although intact (T1 and T2) cases were explored in the *Epilogue* (*Supplementary Analyses and Discussion)*, cases with one time point were still considered as they provided unique insights and context.

Research Question 1: Parkinson's Disease and Attachment with God

To address RQ1, *How do individuals with Parkinson's Disease (LOPD and/ vs ROPD) describe their relationships with and perceived access to God as an attachment figure (content, quality, intensity)*?, data analysis of both T1 and T2 data resulted in themes, *Belief in God Since PD Onset*, *Emotional Connection in Spiritual/Religious Practices Since PD Onset*, and *Change in Importance of God/ Spirituality Since PD Onset by Side of Onset,* related subthemes, categories, and dimensions. Each theme will be addressed in the paragraphs below with subthemes provided when relevant. Figure 2.4 provides an overall representation of frequency and volume of participants and their responses that were characterized by each theme. Most participants' responses ($n = 36$, 42%) were all or partially characterized by Theme 1 (*Belief in God Since PD Onset*). The representation of participants and their responses in Theme 2 (*Emotional Connection in Spiritual/Religious Practices Since PD Onset)* was a bit smaller ($n = 30$, 35%), whereas Theme 3 (*Change in Importance of God/Spirituality Since PD Onset)* was represented by a smaller subset of participants ($n = 20$; 23%). Note that some participant responses were characterized by multiple themes.

Figure 2.5 shows *Dispersion of Participants Thematic Representation by Side of Onset.* Notably, there were no substantial differences in representation by themes

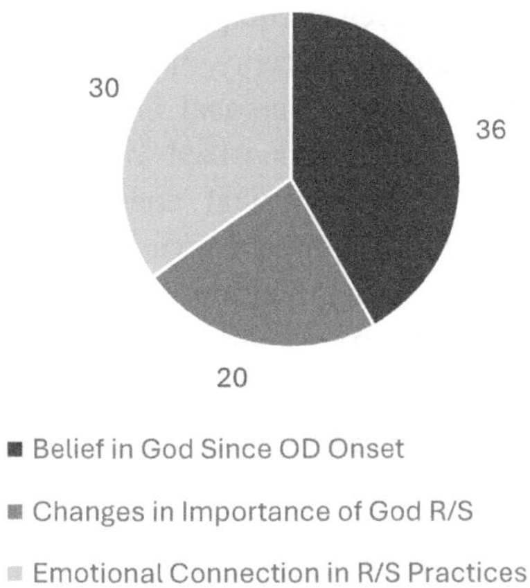

FIGURE 2.4 Overall Thematic Representation in Response to RQ1.

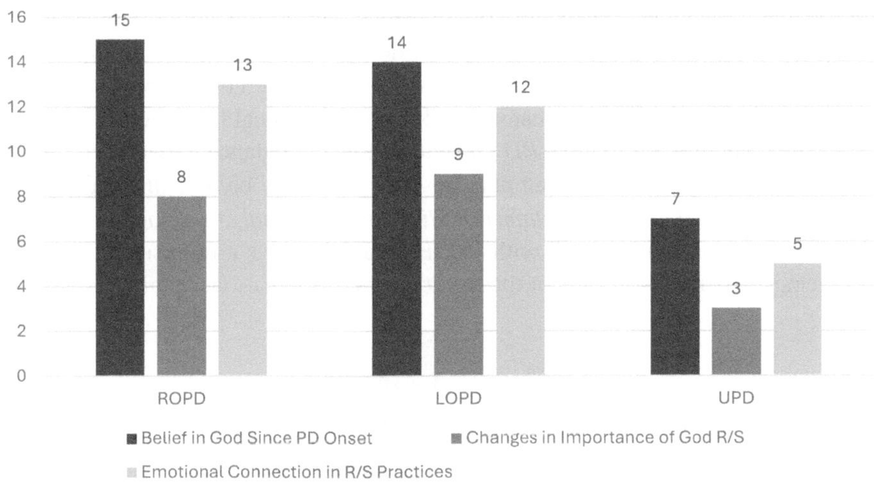

FIGURE 2.5 Participants' Thematic Representation by Side of Onset.

when considering side of onset for LOPD and ROPD individuals. The UPD group seemed to show a bit more diversity, potentially due to the smaller subsample size.

RQ1, Theme 1: Belief in God Since PD Onset

The first theme to address RQ1, *Belief in God Since PD Onset* was developed through a close, inductive thematic analysis of participants' narratives regarding how their belief in God had changed, remained stable, or evolved since the onset of PD. The overarching theme, *Belief in God Since PD Onset*, reflects how individuals navigate belief amid the uncertainties and challenges of a progressive neurodegenerative disease. Sixteen participants (n = 16) described continuity in belief alongside changes in religious activity, often emphasizing a shift from organized religious participation to more personal or emotionally grounded spiritual practice. Another subset (n = 11) emphasized intentionality and effort in maintaining religious behaviors despite physical, cognitive, or emotional challenges, suggesting that sustaining faith required active *resilience*. In contrast, a smaller subset (n = 9) expressed a loosening of emotional or personal significance in their spiritual lives. Some within this group continued attending services or engaging in prayer but described the experience as "routine" or emotionally distant, while others described a more pronounced sense of spiritual detachment or absence of felt connection.

Rather than presenting belief as either fully retained or entirely lost, this theme reveals a broad spectrum of spiritual responses to PD, including sustaining, growth, adaptation, reaffirmation, emotional disengagement, and ongoing struggle. The varied accounts offer understanding of the dynamic nature of belief systems under the strain of chronic illness, involving systems that are simultaneously stable and responsive to changes in capacity, relationships, and life meaning. However, the data do not suggest mass deconversion or widespread loss of faith. Instead, the data suggest a complex reorientation of spiritual identity shaped by personal resilience, support systems, theological meaning-making, and physical limitations.

In sum, *Belief in God Since PD Onset* captures the balance between continuity and change in religious life. It emphasizes how faith may be reconfigured through quiet *Persistence, Cognitive Reinterpretation*, or *Emotional Disengagement* as participants age and adjust to life with PD. Figure 2.6 shows a representation of the subthemes, wherein over half of the participants' responses were fully or partially

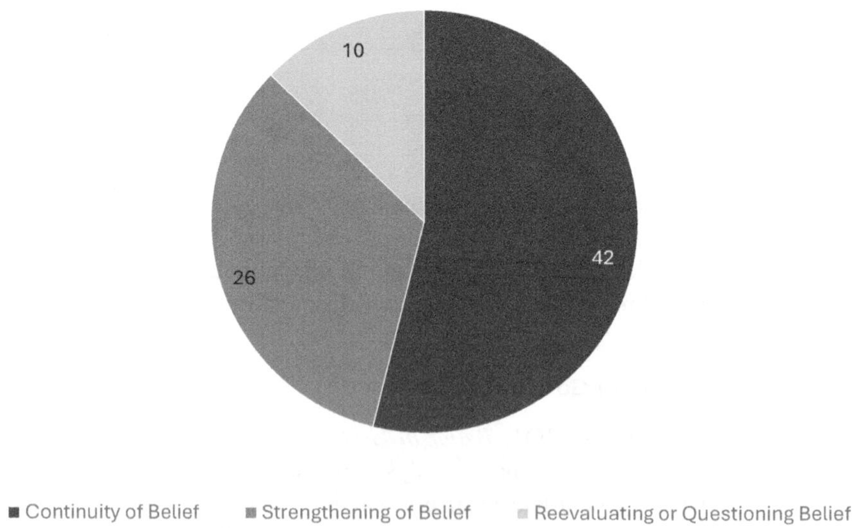

FIGURE 2.6 Themes of Belief in God Since PD Onset.

characterized by *Continuity of Belief* (*n* = 42, 54%). A third were characterized by a *Strengthening of Belief* (*n* = 26, 33%), and a small subset was characterized by *Re-evaluating or Questioning Belief* (*n* = 10, 13%).

RQ1, Theme 1, Subtheme 1: Continuity of Belief

> The Continuity of Belief subtheme characterized 42 participants (54%) whose statements reflected consistent or enduring spirituality. P4 (M63-LOPD-T2) recalled lifelong spiritual conditioning and demonstrated unwavering faith despite PD:
>
> I've always felt that as I grew up, everybody said God has to be number one in your life. Your family is number two. And so, I've always had that drummed into me. So, I still believe that God is number one. And things have not changed at all with that because it was so ingrained in me.

P4's statement emphasized how his belief was "drummed into" him, suggesting deep internalization of religious priorities. This is a clear representation of *Continuity*, in which PD did not disrupt foundational beliefs.

Another participant we characterized as reflecting *Continuity*, P23 (F70-LOPD-T2), described her spirituality as unchanged, with a subtle increase in devotional behavior. She shared, "Just having more of the same outlook, but just praying more." Her emphasis on constancy with a shift in R/S practice suggested that her belief remained stable while behavior adapted slightly, highlighting her personal grounding in belief.

P12 (F52-ROPD-T2) acknowledged change in her interpretive depth rather than belief itself, marking a nuanced form of *Continuity*. She explained, "It's always been very important to me, but I guess it's important in a different way now. Like, when I read scriptures, it speaks differently to me now, if that makes sense." For P12, this evolving engagement with scripture (speaking "differently") reflected a deepening, rather than a departure from her long-standing belief system.

In Subtheme 1, *Continuity of Belief*, participants described their spirituality as stable or enduring despite the challenges of PD. Among the exemplars, LOPD participants (such as P4 and P23) tended to portray belief systems as deeply ingrained and largely unaffected by the illness. P4 emphasized that placing God first had been "drummed into" him since childhood, and P23 noted no significant change in her outlook, although she now prays more. This suggests a slight increase in devotional behavior without cognitive or emotional reprocessing. These accounts may reflect a *Secure Base* function, in which spirituality serves as a stable foundation amid physical decline. In contrast, the ROPD exemplar (P12) described continuity with interpretive evolution, noting that scriptures "speak differently" to her now. This may reflect a *Safe Haven* function, where spiritual engagement offers emotional processing or reappraisal without disrupting core beliefs. Although based on a small set of exemplars, this contrast suggests a possible side-of-onset distinction in *emotional-spiritual* connection, with LOPD participants describing spiritually steady ground with minimal emotional shift, and ROPD participants showing greater emotional engagement or interpretive depth in maintaining continuity.

RQ1, Theme 1, Subtheme 2: Strengthening of Belief

The *Strengthening of Belief* subtheme characterized 26 participants and their statements (33%), partially or completely. These narratives reflected not only sustained faith post-diagnosis, but a deepened sense of meaning, purpose, or reliance on R/S belief systems in the face of chronic illness. For many, PD catalyzed an intensified attachment to God as a *Safe Haven* or *Secure Base*, either providing emotional refuge during uncertainty or guiding their daily meaning-making and moral direction. One example of *Strengthening of Belief*, P13 (F49-LOPD-T2) attributed her resilience to her faith, highlighting its amplified centrality post-diagnosis. She noted, “My faith is the only reason why I'm probably the way I am now because I'd probably be down in the dumps and probably be... deteriorated if I didn't have my faith.” Her comment frames faith as a primary source of strength, signifying a *protective factor* against psychological decline, playing a *functional* and *emotional* role. The emphasis on “only reason” suggests that her belief system provides both existential grounding and emotional insulation, a *Safe Haven* in the face of vulnerability. P27 (M75-LOPD-T2) articulated a more active spiritual surrender post-diagnosis, in which PD facilitated an active reorientation toward divine trust:

> When I do get in a situation where I really feel moved to pray. I'm just asking God to be with me and show me the way. And I'm happy to be led. I've been thankful that I'm not in charge.

This narrative underscores the *Secure Base* function of faith, allowing the participant to relinquish control while finding direction and comfort through spiritual reliance. His gratitude in “not being in charge” marks a cognitive realignment that emphasizes surrender and prioritizes faith-led coping.

P52 (M74-LOPD-T2) reflected on a subtle yet transformative improvement in his spiritual perception, explaining, “It's improved. My connection with watching God work in my life is very much better. But how many times do you take it for granted that the miracles have happened to you every day?” Here, *Spiritual Strengthening* is defined not by new behavior but by heightened awareness of divine presence. His recognition of “daily miracles” reflects both increased *Cognitive Salience* and *Emotional Receptivity*, signaling a shift in interpretive lens toward *Spiritual Mindfulness*.

P19 (M68-ROPD-T1) described increased dialogue with God, marking a shift toward more regular, relational engagement. He said, “God speaks to me through my wife and other people more.” His account, though succinct, signals both

Behavioral Increase and *Affective Engagement.* It exemplifies *Strengthening of Belief* and draws a contrast with his prior state, suggesting an intensification of practice.

P10 (F61-ROPD-T1) discussed a transformative return to faith, prompted by caregiving experiences and social nudges. She explained [Paraphrase]:

> Even though [I] strayed from church, [I] didn't stop believing. Took religious studies in college and explored Eastern religions. And one of the hospice nurses told me. 'God has a purpose for you. You're gonna go through some changes, and you're gonna end up doing things to help people.'… I feel like I am closer to the Lord than I have ever been before. It's just amazing.

Her journey from *Spiritual Exploration* to *Renewed Commitment* suggests a dynamic, affective evolution of belief. This quote spans emotional, cognitive, and behavioral elements of *Attachment to God* and highlights how PD-related caregiving interactions can reactivate spiritual purpose and perceived calling.

In Subtheme 2, *Strengthening of Belief*, participants described how their spirituality not only persisted after PD diagnosis but deepened in meaning, reliance, or emotional engagement. Among the exemplars, LOPD participants (P13, P27, P52) emphasized a cognitively mediated form of spiritual growth, including deliberate trust in God, reinterpretation of everyday experiences as spiritually significant, and increased mindfulness of divine presence. Their accounts often reflected *Secure Base* or *Safe Haven* dynamics, such as P27's gratitude in "not being in charge," which suggested spiritual surrender and faith-led coping. In contrast, the ROPD participants (P19, P10) described a more emotionally rich or relational pathway to belief strengthening, marked by conversational intimacy with God and affective renewal through caregiving experiences. These cases suggest that while PD can catalyze stronger attachment to faith across the board, the emotional and cognitive contours of that growth may vary by side of onset. As with all exemplar-based interpretations, these observations are not conclusive but provide insight into how spiritual intensification may reflect diverse coping trajectories grounded in both belief and attachment.

RQ1, Theme 1, Subtheme 3: Re-evaluating or Questioning Belief

The *Re-evaluating or Questioning Belief* subtheme characterized ten participants and their statements (13%), partially or completely. For instance, P60 (M77-LOPD-T2) expressed spiritual liminality, positioned between belief and detachment. He said, "I'm kind of disengaged with the religious side right now. I can't tell you why. I'm not a nonbeliever, but I'm kind of in between an agnostic and a borderline not going to church kind of guy." His uncertainty and passive withdrawal suggest emotional distance without complete rejection.

In another instance of *Re-evaluating or Questioning Belief*, P24 (F73-LOPD-T2) noted a marked R/S disengagement post-diagnosis, suggesting a reduction in

Spiritual Salience. She explained, "Once I had [PD] diagnosed, I don't think I was involved at all. I stopped listening to the YouTube preachers. I haven't done that in quite a while." Her abandonment of once-regular religious media signals a *Re-evaluation* of faith's importance. P64 (M58-ROPD-T2) maintained emotional R/S ties but signaled a potentially disrupted routine and spontaneity. He reported, "There's emotion involved. I don't pray automatically." His quote could imply that his faith is less reflexive, perhaps reflecting spiritual change, but not necessarily detachment. His quote represents altered engagement rhythms.

These accounts reveal a quieter but meaningful pattern in which PD prompted some participants to re-evaluate or shift their spiritual engagement, often without total detachment. The LOPD participants (e.g., P60, P24) in this subtheme typically described more cognitive forms of distancing, such as decreased participation in spiritual media or a liminal stance between belief and unbelief, suggesting internal negotiation around faith salience. In contrast, the one ROPD exemplar (P64) retained emotional ties to spirituality but described disrupted routines, possibly reflecting affectively aware disengagement rather than disinterest. This contrast echoes the hemispheric split observed in other subthemes, wherein LOPD narratives more often emphasized internalized belief reassessment or apathy, whereas ROPD voices trended toward relational or emotional disconnection. Although none of these cases directly rejected belief, their accounts reflect diminished access to either *Safe Haven* or *Secure Base* functions of spiritual attachment. The *Re-evaluation* theme thus captures an undercurrent of spiritual ambivalence or detachment that rounds out the broader pattern of belief continuity and strengthening seen in the larger sample.

In Subtheme 3, *Re-evaluating or Questioning Belief*, a small group of participants (13%) described shifts in their spiritual engagement following PD diagnosis. Rather than outright rejection, these narratives reflected subtle forms of disengagement, uncertainty, or reassessment. Among LOPD participants, P60 expressed spiritual liminality, identifying as "in between" belief and agnosticism, while P24 described a decline in spiritual behavior, such as no longer following religious media. These accounts suggest cognitive distancing and reduced spiritual salience. The sole ROPD exemplar, P64, noted that he no longer prayed reflexively, though he retained emotional ties to God, indicating a disruption in spiritual rhythm rather than detachment. These examples reflect diminished access to traditional *Safe Haven* or *Secure Base* functions of faith, suggesting that for some individuals, PD may prompt a quiet spiritual reappraisal rather than reinforcement. While based on a small number of cases, this subtheme highlights the variability in spiritual response and rounds out the broader Theme 1 pattern in which belief most often persisted or deepened but occasionally gave way to disengagement or uncertainty.

RQ1, Theme 1: Summary

Across Theme 1, participants described how their spirituality provided emotional support and existential grounding as they navigated the challenges of PD. Some found comfort and stability in daily routines such as prayer, worship, and devotional music, with LOPD participants often emphasizing structure and cognitive regulation, and ROPD participants describing relational warmth and divine companionship. Others recounted more direct, personal experiences of connection with God, marked by emotional intensity and spiritual intimacy. These encounters frequently took place outside of institutional settings and reflected *Safe Haven* dynamics, especially among ROPD participants, who tended to articulate stronger affective immediacy. For a smaller group, faith became a lifeline during moments of acute hardship such as illness progression, medical crises, or personal loss. In these cases, participants described a deepening reliance on God for peace, endurance, or daily survival. While both *Safe Haven* and *Secure Base* functions were evident across accounts, their form and emphasis appeared to vary by side of onset. ROPD narratives more often featured emotional closeness and experiential expressions of spiritual attachment, whereas LOPD accounts reflected steadier, cognitively grounded approaches to faith. Though drawn from exemplar cases and not generalizable (i.e., not transferable), these patterns suggest that spirituality served not only as a background belief system, but as an active and emotionally adaptive tool in coping with PD.

RQ1, Theme 2: Emotional Connection in Spiritual/Religious Practices Since PD Onset

The second theme to emerge in response to RQ1, *Emotional Connection in Spiritual/Religious Practices Since PD Onset*, was developed through inductive thematic analysis of participants' reflections on how they experience spirituality or religion (R/S) in emotional terms following their PD. Codes clustered around *Affective Reassurance*, *Spiritual Intimacy*, *Ritual Stability*, and *Emotional Resilience*. Unlike themes focused on belief or theological orientation, the *Emotional Connection in Spiritual/Religious Practices Since PD Onset* theme highlights how *Spiritual Engagement* becomes an emotional coping resource amid illness-related vulnerability. Three distinct subthemes emerged from this data: *Emotional Fulfillment through Routine Practices* ($n = 18$, 47.37%), *Personal Experiences of Divine Connection* ($n = 11$, 28.94%), and *Faith as a Lifeline During Hardship* ($n = 9$, 23.68%).

Figure 2.7 displays the proportion of participants whose responses were characterized by each of these subthemes.

The first subtheme, *Emotional Fulfillment Through Routine Practices*, highlights the calming and grounding effects of *Spiritual Routine*. Participants described prayer, devotional reading, or worship music as *Stabilizing Forces* that helped them manage daily frustrations and uncertainty. The second subtheme, *Personal Experiences of Divine Connection*, reflects deeply personal, often non-verbal or mystical, encounters with the divine, which typically occur during solitary reflection, time in nature, or moments of intense emotional clarity. The third subtheme,

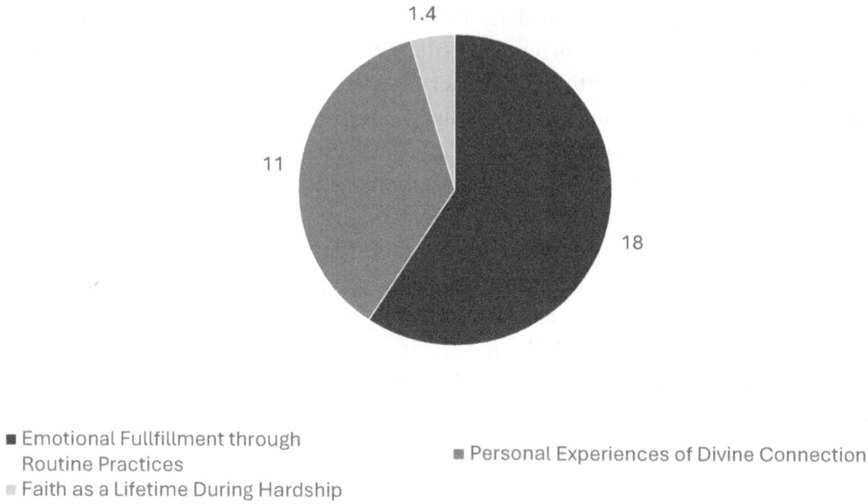

FIGURE 2.7 Subthemes for Emotional Connection in Spiritual/Religious Practices Since PD Onset.

Faith as a Lifeline During Hardship, focuses on experiences of emotional and spiritual survival during episodes of acute hardship such as bereavement, health crises, or isolation.

Collectively, these subthemes describe prominent affective roles that R/S engagement can play during life with PD. Rather than being diminished by illness, *Emotional Engagement* with R/S appears in many cases to deepen or intensify, serving as a scaffold for psychological resilience and meaning-making. Participants' accounts point to spirituality not just as *Doctrine*, but as *Felt Experience* and an *Emotional Resource* that anchor them amid decline and uncertainty.

RQ1, Theme 2, Subtheme 1: Emotional Fulfillment through Routine Practices

This subtheme, *Emotional Fulfillment through Routine Practices,* included 18 participants (23.08%) who described finding emotional comfort, calm, or joy through consistent *Spiritual Routines* such as prayer, attending worship, or listening to religious music. Such *Rituals* offered *Emotional Grounding* in the face of PD-related distress and uncertainty. P30 (F52-LOPD-T2) described how daily *Spiritual Routines* gave her a sense of calm and supported her emotional regulation. She reported, "And I pray before I go to bed every night and that usually has meaning because it's a reflection on my day… reminding me that God's in the control of all this." Her practice of prayer reflects the anchoring and calming effect of Spiritual Discipline in managing stress and health challenges associated with PD.

P64 (M58-ROPD-T2) reflected on the emotional comfort and perceived companionship experienced during *Spiritual Engagement* (e.g., prayer). He explained, "So I find comfort and peace with God, through Christ, knowing that I'm going to go, knowing that He's with me all the time, knowing He never leaves me or forsakes me." His language suggests that his prayer transcends mere *Ritual* and becomes an *Emotionally Sustaining* and *Relationally Fulfilling Relational Experience.*

P9 (F41-ROPD-T2) offered a musical dimension to routine *Spiritual Practice*, showing that emotional uplift can come from listening as well as active participation in *Routines and Rituals*. She explained her priorities, saying, "It's time in scripture. It's time praying. It's the music you listen to, listening to the praise and worship…I think there's a deeper appreciation for what God does for me." P9's use of gospel or worship music as a daily emotional reset reinforces the idea that *Spiritual Routines* serve affective needs.

In Subtheme 1, *Emotional Fulfillment through Routine Practices*, participants described how consistent spiritual activities such as prayer, devotional reading, worship attendance, and religious music provided emotional comfort, grounding, or uplift in the context of PD. LOPD participants, such as P30, often emphasized structure and repetition, highlighting how daily routines like prayer and scripture reading offered a sense of calm and supported emotional regulation. This may reflect a loosely aligned *Secure Base* function, in which spirituality serves as a stable anchor for navigating daily challenges, though relational dynamics were less foregrounded. In contrast, ROPD participants, including P64 and P9, more frequently described these routines as emotionally rich or relationally meaningful. P64's emphasis on God's constant presence and unwavering support suggests a clear *Safe Haven* function, with spirituality providing emotional refuge and perceived companionship. P9's reference to a "deeper appreciation for what God does" also hints at relational connection, suggesting that music and prayer served as both expressive and sustaining. These patterns tentatively reflect side-of-onset differences, with LOPD narratives leaning toward structured, self-regulatory practices, and ROPD accounts emphasizing affective connection. While these distinctions are based on exemplars and should be interpreted cautiously, they may align with broader theories of hemispheric lateralization in spiritual cognition and emotional expression.

RQ1, Theme 2, Subtheme 2: Personal Experiences of Divine Connection

Personal Experiences of Divine Connection characterized 11 participants (14.10%) and their full or partial responses as they described moments of direct *Spiritual Intimacy*, often outside formal religion. These experiences included sensing God's presence during solitary reflection or becoming overwhelmed emotionally in moments of connection with nature or music. For example, P48 (M79-LOPD-T2) described a deeply emotional moment, stating, "I'm more emotional about all those sort of things. I don't know if that's the Parkinson's or not, but I certainly am more emotional. Feel more connected to God." His account, which is both unstructured and rooted in *Personal Reflection* rather than *Institutional Practices*, underscores the affective and existential qualities of experience *Divine Presence,* but may also be influenced by PD or demographic factors (e.g., age). It illustrates how a *Felt Sense of Connection* to God can emerge in emotionally charged experiences that may be more frequent during a chronic illness like PD.

Similarly, P35 (F71-ROPD-T1) shared a subtle yet emotionally vivid account of *Divine Presence* experienced during human isolation. She explained:

> I felt like I was being, like, enveloped in his [God's] arms, but there was just this tiny little sheer something that kept me from, like, vanishing into Him, if that makes any sense at all...Excited to be in his presence... It's unbelievable that He wants to love me and has always loved me.

Her account evokes a deeply personal experience of *Spiritual Intimacy* that transcends structured prayer or religious observance. As with P48 (above), her reflections illustrate a sustained *Emotional Connection* to the divine, emphasizing how faith continues to meet *Psychological and Existential Needs* (i.e., *Safe Haven*) even amid the *Social and Emotional Isolation* that can accompany PD.

P38 (M70-ROPD-T1) also reflected on his dialogue with God and his experiences of *Divine Connection,* which emphasized volume and depth beyond traditional or institutional religious engagement. He shared:

> He's spoken to me in my heart...I was saying, 'Lord, is that you?' And he wouldn't tell me if it was Him or not...in so many different ways, the Lord has spoken to me in my life...in a very more, a clearer way...I even recognize His voice...[Something] I have learned is that God's voice is not a shouting voice. Of course, that's what the Bible says. He speaks in a still small voice.

His reflections underscore how *Spiritual Intimacy* can be cultivated outside of formal settings, highlighting a form of *Relational Closeness* that is experiential, quiet, and deeply personal. This challenges the notion that structured religious practice is necessary for meaningful spiritual encounters.

In Subtheme 2, *Personal Experiences of Divine Connection,* participants described moments of spiritual intimacy that occurred outside the bounds of formal religious practice. These experiences, reported by 11 participants (14.10%), often emerged in solitary or emotionally charged contexts, such as personal reflection, nature, or music, and were marked by a sense of divine presence or communication. P48 (M79-LOPD-T2) reflected, "I certainly am more emotional...more connected to God," suggesting a growing spiritual sensitivity potentially influenced by age or PD. P35 (F71-ROPD-T1) described being enveloped in God's arms, expressing awe that such love was directed toward her. Her vivid language reflected a profound affective bond with the divine, consistent with *Safe Haven* dynamics.

P38 (M70-ROPD-T1) shared his experience of recognizing God's voice as a "still small voice," illustrating a personal and enduring spiritual dialogue that could be seen as a subtle expression of *Secure Base* attachment. While both LOPD and ROPD participants described divine connection, their expressions varied in tone. LOPD participants tended to describe these experiences with reflective or cognitive framing, whereas ROPD participants often conveyed greater emotional immediacy and relational intimacy. Though based on a small number of exemplars, these differences align cautiously with theoretical perspectives on lateralized cognitive and emotional processing. The accounts also suggest that for some individuals, spirituality remains a deeply personal and emotionally sustaining resource even when detached from institutional forms.

In Subtheme 3, *Faith as a Lifeline During Hardship*, participants described how their spiritual beliefs became essential supports during periods of acute difficulty associated with PD, including physical decline, personal loss, and major medical procedures. Rather than functioning as background identity markers, faith practices were framed as lifelines that offered emotional steadiness, peace, and existential grounding. P36 (F75-LOPD-T1) reflected on the unconditional love and guidance of God during a time of divorce and instability, emphasizing that "just to know that God loves you" helped her through. Her narrative illustrates a strong *Safe Haven* dynamic, in which spiritual belief provides emotional rescue during despair. Similarly, P63 (F72-UPD-T1) described feeling unexpectedly calm during a high-risk surgery, attributing her peace to God and collective prayer, despite her typical fearfulness. P58 (F74-LOPD-T2) spoke of relying on God in a deeper way after her diagnosis, describing PD as a completely different set of circumstances that required intensified spiritual dependence. Her account suggests a possible *Secure Base* function in her evolving relationship with faith. Across these examples, participants conveyed faith as a dynamic and emotionally salient resource rather than a passive identity. While *Safe Haven* dynamics were especially prominent, some individuals also described long-term reliance on God for strength and direction in navigating uncertainty. ROPD narratives more frequently emphasized emotional expressiveness and felt closeness to God, while LOPD accounts tended to frame spiritual reliance in more cognitive or disciplined terms. Although these patterns are drawn from a small group of exemplars, they tentatively reflect side-of-onset distinctions in how individuals emotionally and cognitively process spiritual coping. Collectively, this subtheme portrays faith as an active coping tool that provides not only theological meaning but also psychological stability in the context of living with PD.

RQ1, Theme 2: Summary

Theme 2 explored the emotional and relational functions of faith as participants navigated the challenges of PD. Across the subthemes, participants described spirituality not only as a belief system but as an experiential and emotionally sustaining resource. Some found comfort and regulation through routine spiritual practices such as prayer, worship, and music. LOPD participants often emphasized structured and cognitively anchored engagement, while ROPD participants more frequently highlighted relational intimacy and affective resonance. Others described deeply personal and often unstructured moments of divine connection, experienced through stillness, reflection, or emotionally charged encounters. These accounts illustrated *Safe Haven* dynamics, particularly among ROPD participants, where divine presence was described as emotionally responsive and reassuring. A third group portrayed faith as a lifeline during times of acute hardship, including illness progression, personal loss, or medical crisis. In these cases, spirituality served both as an emotional refuge and as a source of resilience and guidance. LOPD participants tended to articulate a more measured and enduring reliance on God, while ROPD participants expressed more vivid emotional closeness. Although these findings are drawn from a small set of exemplars and should not be overgeneralized, they suggest that spiritual coping in PD may reflect distinct affective or cognitive contours that are shaped in part by side of onset. Faith functioned not only as theological belief, but as a lived and adaptive resource that supported emotional stability, meaning-making, and connection.

RQ1, Theme 3: Change in Importance of God/Spirituality Since PD Onset

The third theme, *Change in Importance of God/Spirituality Since PD Onset*, emerged from close inductive coding of participant reflections on whether and how participants' relationships with God or spirituality had shifted in perceived value since being diagnosed with PD. Unlike beliefs themselves, which may remain cognitively consistent, this theme focused on the perceived *Centrality* or *Emotional Importance* of God or spiritual life. Some participants described a heightened reliance on spiritual frameworks to cope with illness and find meaning. Others maintained that the role of God or spirituality in their life remained unchanged, while a smaller group reported a diminished sense of importance or connection.

The overarching *Change in Importance of God/Spirituality Since PD Onset* theme adds depth to the understanding of how spiritual life is not just retained or lost but actively re-evaluated over time. It highlights a dynamic negotiation of meaning in which PD may either intensify, reaffirm, or disrupt the centrality of the R/S engagement in one's daily experience. The data suggest that while increases in importance were relatively common, so too was stability. Such continuity, rather than change, seemed to be the dominant pattern. Nonetheless, a non-negligible minority of participants expressed decreased importance, emphasizing that *Spiritual Disengagement* also warrants attention in understanding the full spectrum of PD-related identity shifts.

Through iterative thematic analysis, three subthemes were developed: (1) *Increased Importance* (n = 26; 33.33%), (2) *Unchanged but Still Important*

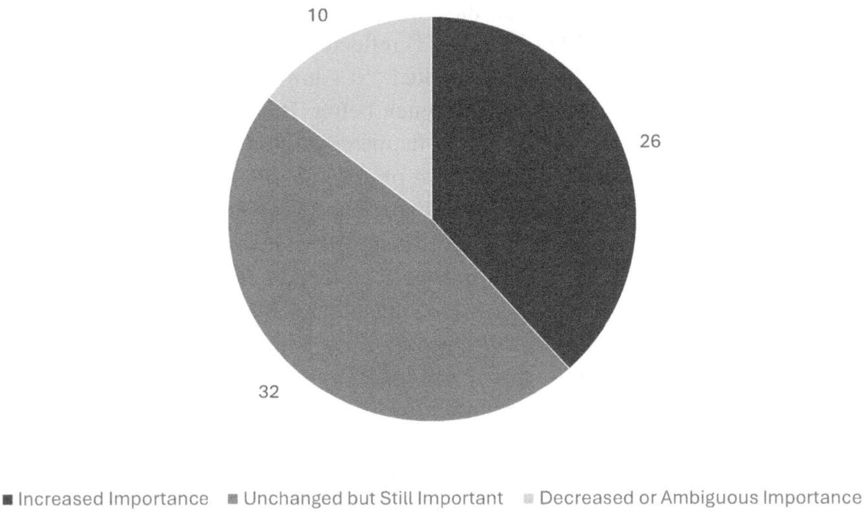

FIGURE 2.8 Change in Importance of God/Spirituality Since PD Onset Subthemes.

(n = 32; 41.03%), and (3) *Decreased or Ambiguous Importance* (n = 10; 12.82%). A small group of participants (n = 10, 12.82%) did not provide interpretable or relevant data on this theme. Figure 2.8 displays the three subthemes and their degree of representation.

RQ1, Theme 3, Subtheme 1: Increased R/S Importance

The *Increased Importance* subtheme captures the experiences of participants (n = 26; 33.33%) who reported a heightened sense of religious or spiritual significance following their PD diagnosis. This often signaled a positive valence shift, where spiritual life became more meaningful or purposeful after diagnosis. An increase in importance is often associated with participants finding greater grounding and meaning through their faith, especially in response to the challenges of living with PD. For many participants, the diagnosis catalyzed a strengthening of their connection to God, often leading to an increase in prayer, spiritual practices, or a reprioritization of spiritual matters (i.e., R/S). These narratives frequently reflect increased dependence on faith for emotional support and perspective, often prompted by a heightened awareness of their own mortality and the impact of PD on their physical and emotional well-being. This intensified connection often served an attachment function, with participants relying on God as a *Safe Haven* during distress or as a *Secure Base* to face PD-related challenges with renewed strength.

In contrast to the neutral or unchanged faith expressed by other participants, those in *Increased Importance* category emphasize growth and development in their spiritual lives, signifying a positive valence shift in the importance of religion or spirituality. Rather than simply enduring hardship, these participants articulate a sense of spiritual fulfillment that has emerged more strongly due to their lived experience with PD. P52 (M74-LOPD-T2) reflected on the *Deepening* of his faith in response to living with PD. He remarked, "It's improved. My connection with watching God work in my life is very much better. But how many times do you take it for granted that the miracles have happened to you every day." Rather than despair, his comments emphasize a sense of spiritual attentiveness and gratitude that has grown stronger with illness. His experience points to a more active awareness of *divine presence* in daily life, portraying PD not solely as a source of suffering but as a catalyst for deeper spiritual connection. The narrative conveys a positive-valence attachment shift in which heightened faith provides both perspective and emotional grounding in the face of chronic decline. Most of the quotes featured in this subtheme come from participants with LOPD, and they often reflect a more cognitively effortful or reframed spiritual stance. By contrast, ROPD narratives in the broader dataset more commonly conveyed emotionally spontaneous, affect-laden expressions of connection to God. This observed pattern may align with lateralization-related differences in how spiritual coping is processed. Notably, LOPD participants leaned on cognitive effort, and ROPD participants expressed more affective engagement. The LOPD participants' thoughtful reinterpretations of spiritual priorities suggested cognitively driven spiritual deepening may be more pronounced than among ROPD.

P44 (M48-LOPD-T2) stated, "The priorities in my life have changed, and I think that has helped me…on my spiritual journey." His quote carries a positive but subtle valence, indicating a shift in focus toward R/S as a result of PD. Although he does not state that his faith dramatically increased, the change in his priorities points toward a gentle yet significant growth in spiritual importance. The mention of a spiritual journey and how the change in life priorities has helped him emphasizes a constructive redirection of energy, but without the deep emotional weight found in quotes of some others. The tone here remains more measured, suggesting the participant's faith has remained steady, but it has gained new importance due to his seemingly evolving perspective on life and illness.

P58 (F74-LOPD-T2) reported increased "prayer life, [and] depending on God more for my peace in my life. I guess, I speak with Him more often than I have [before]." She later went on to add, "I'm relying on God to help me through this. And when I didn't have Parkinson's, I relied on God for certain things, but this is different. This is a completely different set of circumstances." Her remarks reflect a strong positive valence, highlighting an increased dependence on God and deepened reliance on prayer. She acknowledges that her prayer life has grown, emphasizing more frequent communication with God to find peace amid the challenges posed by PD. The follow-up statement intensifies this by marking a clear shift in the role of faith. What was once a routine reliance on God has now evolved into a stronger, more urgent dependence due to the heightened struggles associated with PD. The phrase "this is different" serves as a clear indicator of how PD has reshaped her relationship with spirituality, emphasizing a *Heightened Emotional* and *Spiritual Engagement* that was not previously as present. This demonstrates an active shift in her faith practices, with God becoming more central as she faces her diagnosis, portraying PD as a catalyst for a deeper, more profound connection to her faith.

P77 (M75-UPD-T2) reflected a *Positive* valence in his tone, while emphasizing increased devotion to his faith practices such as prayer and scripture reading. He explained, "As the symptoms began to emerge, I realized that I needed to spend more time in the Word and in prayer." His realization that he needed to spend more time in these activities reflects an intentional effort to prioritize spirituality amid the challenges of PD. His statement implies that his onset of symptoms led to a spiritual awakening or re-engagement, where PD acted as a catalyst for increased *Spiritual Practices*. This reflects a clear *Positive Shift*, where he actively seeks *Spiritual Sustenance*, suggesting a renewed commitment to faith to cope with PD.

P6 (M55-LOPD-T2) remarked, "I was just getting back into it. So, I think the momentum was just to keep going. And so, I think my spiritual journey only deepened as time went on." His statement has a neutral to slightly positive valence. He notes that his spiritual journey deepened over time, though his language is not as emotionally charged as some other quotes. There's a gradual deepening of faith, as opposed to an immediate or intense spiritual transformation. The participant's acknowledgment that his spiritual connection grew steadily over time reflects a consistent reliance on spirituality, though without dramatic emotional shifts. He seemed to convey a stable, ongoing process, highlighting that faith has remained a constant presence, deepening rather than shifting dramatically. This indicates a solid, steady increase in spiritual engagement over time, despite the lack of a sudden emotional awakening.

P72 (F62-LOPD-T1) shared her reflections on her faith journey and how it has evolved over time. She noted, "Faith now is very important." She shared that she wished she had become connected to God earlier in life, but that was not what happened. She became more connected to God within the last four or five years. Her reflection illustrates a late but significant deepening of her *Spiritual Connection*. She reflects a positive valence shift in attachment to God, highlighting how her relationship with faith and spirituality intensified following her PD diagnosis. The quote conveys a sense of growth in her spiritual life, particularly in how she reprioritized her connection to God despite earlier challenges in developing that bond. The quote's valence is positive, focusing on the strength and importance of faith as a central aspect of her current life.

P62 (M80-LOPD-T2) described a strengthening of his foundational faith since the onset of Parkinson's. He explained, "I think it's stronger…Some of the practices have not stayed at the same level of intensity, but they can't…But the basic faith has grown, I think." While acknowledging that certain outward practices had diminished in intensity due to limitations, he emphasized that the core of his spiritual belief had continued to grow. His remarks suggest a resilient, inward deepening of faith despite external constraints.

In Subtheme 1, *Increased R/S Importance*, participants described how their faith or spirituality became more meaningful following their diagnosis of PD. For many, the challenges of illness prompted a reassessment of priorities and a deeper reliance on God for strength, peace, or purpose. These shifts reflected a positive valence in which spirituality provided not only emotional support but also a renewed sense of direction. Several participants described intensified prayer, greater attentiveness to divine presence, or a deliberate return to spiritual routines. For some, this shift was emotionally expressive, conveying strong *Safe Haven* dynamics in which God served as a source of comfort and stability. Others reflected a quieter but steady deepening, with *Secure Base* elements that framed faith as an anchor for re-engaging with daily life. LOPD participants were especially represented in this subtheme and tended to describe faith in more cognitively effortful and disciplined terms. By contrast, ROPD narratives in the broader dataset more commonly featured emotionally spontaneous connections to God, suggesting possible side-of-onset differences in how spiritual change is experienced. Age and gender also appeared to shape how participants framed spiritual growth, with older adults reflecting long-term deepening and women more frequently highlighting relational or emotional expressions of belief. Taken together, these accounts illustrate how PD can catalyze spiritual reorientation, with faith functioning as both an emotional refuge and a source of perspective in the face of ongoing uncertainty.

RQ1, Theme 3, Subtheme 2: Unchanged but Still Important

The subtheme, *Unchanged but Still Important,* represents participants (n = 32, 47.06%) who noted no change in the importance of God or spirituality since PD onset. Most expressed that their religious values had always held a central place in their lives. Instead of indifference or passivity, their responses emphasized consistency and steadfastness. For this group, the onset of PD did not disrupt but reaffirmed a long-standing spiritual foundation. P4 (M63-LOPD-T2) indicated a continuity of his spiritual or religious beliefs post-PD diagnosis. He explained, "Things have not changed at all with that because it was so ingrained in me." Rather than a change in faith or R/S importance, he expressed sustained conviction, rooted in his long-held identity. The stability expressed suggested a form of resilience by being grounded in tradition or upbringing.

P15 (M69-UPD-T2) responded with a straightforward "no-nonsense" neutral valence regarding the potential of a change in his faith:

> I don't believe my faith is any stronger now. I think the difference in this all is because of convenience…It isn't so much that I did not pray before or did not attend mass as regularly as I could. It was all predicated by my working full time and being at work early in the mornings and whatever…So, I think my faith is probably about the same.

While the participant acknowledges logistical shifts post-retirement, his underlying faith remains unchanged. His tone suggests steadfastness rooted in lifelong spiritual values.

P23 (F70-LOPD-T2) reported no change in perspective on her life but noted increased R/S activity in the form of engaging with God through prayer. She reported [Paraphrase]: "Just having more of the same outlook but just praying more." The tenor of her response, signaled by the word "just," seemed to downplay the importance of her sustained faith despite PD onset. Alternatively, she may have been suggesting that her continued faith should not be surprising, meaning "just" as in "of course."

In Subtheme 2, *Unchanged but Still Important*, participants described how the onset of PD did not alter the significance of their spirituality or belief in God. For this group, faith remained a central and steady presence, rooted in long-held values or lifelong religious identity. Rather than signaling disinterest, their responses reflected consistency and resilience, with spirituality continuing to provide quiet support without major emotional shifts. P4 (M63-LOPD-T2) emphasized that nothing had changed in his faith because it had been deeply ingrained from early life, while P15 (M69-UPD-T2) noted that his faith had remained steady and was previously shaped more by work routines than belief. P23 (F70-LOPD-T2) echoed this sentiment, reporting that her spiritual perspective was unchanged, even though she now prayed more frequently. These narratives generally lacked strong *Safe Haven* or *Secure Base* dynamics, instead portraying spirituality as a stable background presence rather than an actively mobilized coping tool. Although a later paragraph in the section referenced participants experiencing spiritual fatigue or disengagement, those reflections are conceptually distinct and may represent a different trajectory not fully aligned with this subtheme. Within this subtheme, the overarching pattern is one of quiet stability, where faith continued to matter, even as its role remained largely unchanged in the face of illness.

RQ1, Theme 3, Subtheme 3: Decreased Importance or Disengagement

Within Theme 3, a distinct subset of participants (n = 10; 12.8%) characterized by the *Decreased Importance or Disengagement subtheme* described a notable decline in the salience of their spiritual or religious commitments following their PD diagnosis. Rather than expressing outright repudiation of belief, these individuals portrayed an erosion of the habitual, affective, and cognitive structures that had previously sustained their faith practices. Emotional detachment diminished cognitive resources, and a growing sense of existential distance converged to render once-automatic rituals effortful or altogether abandoned.

P24 (F73-LOPD-T2) expressed a withdrawal from spiritual content. She reported, "Once I had [PD] diagnosed, I don't think I was involved at all. I stopped listening to the YouTube preachers." The phrase "involved at all" conveys a decisive rupture in her engagement, while "stopped listening" suggests active disengagement from sources of spiritual nourishment, perhaps reflecting both cognitive fatigue and affective distancing.

P60 (M77-LOPD-T2) described more of a mechanical disengagement from R/S connectivity. He characterized his experience as "kind of disengaged with the religious side right now. I can't tell you why." His use of the term "disengaged" evokes the image of a system that has lost its drive, and his inability to articulate a cause could intimate that PD-related cognitive strain may undermine the reflective capacity required for sustained involvement. Alternatively, not knowing why he has disengaged could indicate subconscious distancing and existential confusion common in grieving patterns.

In Subtheme 3, *Decreased Importance or Disengagement*, a small group of participants described a notable decline in the role of spirituality or religion following their PD diagnosis. Rather than explicitly rejecting their faith, they conveyed a quiet withdrawal, marked by emotional detachment, reduced motivation, or diminished engagement with spiritual practices. P24 (F73-LOPD-T2) reported that she stopped listening to religious content altogether, and P60 (M77-LOPD-T2) described himself as disengaged from the religious side of life without being able to explain why. These reflections suggest a loss of affective and cognitive connection to previously meaningful spiritual routines, possibly reflecting the cumulative strain of illness or neurological changes associated with PD. From an attachment perspective, these participants appeared to have lost access to God as a *Safe Haven* and did not show signs of relying on faith as a *Secure Base*. Although this pattern was relatively uncommon, it occurred more frequently among LOPD participants, raising tentative questions about how the side of onset may influence one's ability to emotionally engage with or sustain spiritual coping strategies. These cases highlight the quiet erosion of religious salience that can occur without overt disavowal, offering a distinct contrast to the deepening or continuity of belief described in other subthemes.

RQ1, Theme 3: Summary

Theme 3 explored how participants experienced changes, or stability, in the personal importance of religion or spirituality, following a diagnosis of PD. Responses varied widely and were grouped into three primary trajectories. One group reported that spirituality became more meaningful after diagnosis, describing a positive shift in their reliance on faith for strength, peace, or perspective. These individuals often increased their prayer life, deepened their spiritual awareness, or returned to previously diminished religious routines. For many in this group, particularly those with LOPD, faith was approached as a structured and cognitively mediated source of grounding. ROPD participants more often conveyed emotionally spontaneous or relational forms of engagement. *Safe Haven* dynamics were evident among those who sought comfort or emotional support from God, and *Secure Base* patterns appeared in narratives where faith helped participants re-engage with daily life under new conditions.

A second group described no meaningful change in their spiritual commitments, emphasizing continuity and stability. These participants often held long-established beliefs before their PD diagnosis and saw no need to reinterpret or intensify their faith. Their responses reflected steady conviction and consistent practice but generally lacked active expressions of attachment. In these accounts, spirituality functioned as a background presence rather than as a resource for emotional regulation or existential reframing.

A third and smaller subset of participants described a decline in spiritual importance or engagement. These individuals did not express outright rejection of belief but conveyed a quiet disengagement marked by emotional distance, reduced motivation, or a fading connection to former practices. Their reflections suggest diminished access to the emotional or relational functions of spirituality, especially the *Safe Haven* role. This pattern was more frequently observed among LOPD participants, which raises tentative questions about how left-onset neurological changes may influence the emotional and motivational aspects of spiritual coping.

Taken together, Theme 3 illustrates the diversity of spiritual responses to PD. While some individuals deepened their connection to faith or drew renewed comfort from religious practices, others maintained a steady baseline or experienced subtle disengagement. These trajectories appear to be shaped by personal history, neurological characteristics such as side of onset, and possibly by age or gender. However, such patterns should be interpreted cautiously, given the exemplar-based nature of the data.

RQ1, Discussion

This section addressed RQ1 which asked, "*How do individuals with Parkinson's Disease (LOPD and/vs ROPD) describe their relationships with and perceived access to God as an attachment figure?*" Across 78 participants, responses revealed varied patterns of spiritual attachment, organized around three primary themes: *Belief in God Since PD Onset, Emotional Connection in R/S, Practices Since PD Onset, and Change in Importance of God/Spirituality Since PD Onset.* Each theme represents dynamic configurations of participants' IWMs of God, filtered through their lived experience with PD.

Granqvist's (2020) work on attachment and religion provides a theoretical lens for understanding these responses. His framework distinguishes between secure, avoidant, and anxious styles of religious attachment and clarifies how *Safe Haven* and *Secure Base* functions may evolve in the face of adversity. PD, as a progressive neurodegenerative disease, introduces chronic uncertainty, loss of control, and increased dependency, each of which can activate attachment systems. Therefore, we present an application of these concepts to summarize and interpret participants' descriptions of spiritual connection in the wake of PD.

Findings related to belief in God since PD onset reveal how individuals negotiate spiritual belief amid illness-related decline. Most participants described

Continuity or *Strengthening* of belief, with only a small subset expressing *Diminished or Re-evaluated* faith. The range of responses supports Granqvist's notion that religion can function as a compensatory or complementary attachment figure, modulating emotional vulnerability and existential distress.

Those who described a continuity of belief showed internalized, secure God images. Several participants shared that their faith remained steady despite the challenges of PD. For example, P57 (F78-LOPD-T2) said, "I have a cup of coffee with Jesus every morning. And talk to Him and tell Him my thoughts…a quiet time with Him. Daily communion," and P42 (M85-ROPD-T2) stated, "I've tended to say daily prayers and ask for forgiveness and that kind of thing. I still continue to go to church on Sundays." These accounts typify what Granqvist (2020) would call autonomous-secure religious attachment, wherein beliefs are stable, non-coercive, and personally integrated.

Others who described a strengthening of belief experienced a deepened relationship with God following PD diagnosis. P52 (M74-LOPD-T2) shared, "It's improved. My connection with watching God work in my life is very much better." Similarly, P66 (M66-LOPD-T1) noted his "relationship with God…with my creator and with Jesus, his Son, has been very meaningful, um, very significant, and has really directed my path ever since [PD Onset]. There's peace with Parkinson's. All of that is sacred." These statements illustrate the *Safe Haven* function of attachment to God, in which divine connection serves as a source of emotional regulation and strength. This reliance on spiritual support reflects how participants drew comfort and stability from their relationship with the divine in the face of illness.

A smaller group of participants described a transformation in which they became more spiritually open or attentive than before. P71 (F46-ROPD-T2) shared that her faith has increased since PD, saying, "I think it's more important than ever. Yeah. It's very important. Yeah. Because I see my purpose through more spiritual eyes in some ways." This cognitive-emotional shift may reflect a developing *Secure Base* function, wherein participants turned to God not only for comfort but also as a foundation for growth and new meaning-making.

Some participants also reported what appeared to be deeply personal or mystical experiences of God's presence. For instance, P4 (M63-LOPD-T2) said, "I feel emotional because sometimes I feel God's presence when I speak to him and talk to him. And I find it comforting to talk to God." These direct experiences reflect an emotionally immediate sense of God as close, present, and responsive, a characterization consistent with attachment experiences of intimacy and accessibility. Although not all described overt supernatural events, these moments conveyed an affective closeness to God that helped participants manage uncertainty and fear.

Faith also functioned as a stabilizing force in day-to-day practices. P30 (F52-LOPD-T2) noted, "I pray before I go to bed every night and that usually has meaning because it's a reflection on my day." This expression of ritualized connection reflects spiritual consistency, perhaps as a regulatory practice that embeds emotional grounding in routine. Though the emotional intensity varied across accounts, participants consistently described spiritual rituals as sustaining, especially in the face of physical decline.

Findings related to *Change in Importance of God/Spirituality* emphasized shifts in the centrality of participants' faith lives. Some described increasing reliance on God. P19 (M67-ROPD-T2) explained, "I certainly understand a lot more different parts of the Bible because of my Parkinson's than I did before." This shift illustrates a re-engagement or intensification of spiritual meaning-making, consistent with *Secure Base* expansion, in which God becomes a foundation for exploration and cognitive-emotional growth.

Others described no major change but emphasized the continuing significance of their spiritual lives. P12 (F52-ROPD-T2) said,

> [Faith has] always been very important to me, but I guess it's important in a different way now. So, it just, you know, keeps me going. Like, when I read scriptures, it, they, it speaks differently to me now, if that makes sense.

For these individuals, spirituality retained its value through familiarity and internalization, which seems to represent stable IWMs that are resistant to disruption. Few participants reported diminished importance of God or spiritual practice. While a bit more ambivalence or disengagement was predicted based on prior frameworks, the current dataset did not include verified statements clearly describing spiritual withdrawal, fading belief, or detachment from faith routines. Thus, while attachment deactivation or insecurity may occur in PD, no confirmed examples were present in this subset.

Other findings related to RQ1 involved attachment patterns by side of onset (LOPD vs. ROPD). When considered by side of onset, participants with LOPD tended to speak with less affective immediacy, and their descriptions of God often reflected a more effortful or emotionally muted quality as inferred from reduced emotional word density and fewer spontaneous expressions of spiritual comfort. This finding is a proposed interpretation, rather than a measured variable, based on ROPD participants' average of 4.45 emotional words per 1,000 words of speech versus 3.56 (per 1,000 words) in LOPD. In contrast, participants with ROPD tended to report more consistent and affectively rich spiritual experiences. While these differences were not absolute, they echo prior neuropsychological findings suggesting that LOPD is associated with right-hemispheric degeneration, which may compromise emotional processing, social cognition, and fluid access to symbolic religious representations (Butler et al., 2010; Modestino et al., 2017). These functional deficits may disrupt the capacity for perceiving God as a present, emotionally attuned attachment figure.

From an attachment theory perspective, as elaborated by Cherniak et al. (2021), such disruptions may impair believers' ability to experience God as a *Safe Haven* (a reliable source of comfort in distress) or as a *Secure Base* (a foundation from which one can explore and make meaning of illness). Many ROPD participants demonstrated these two functions in action. Their narratives often conveyed an inner sense of stability and emotional security derived from their perceived relationship with God. For instance, comments like "[I get] healing in my prayer" and "He is with me through whatever valley" exemplify normative attachment processes wherein God functions as an internalized caregiver (Cherniak et al., 2021; Granqvist, 2020).

LOPD participants, however, were more likely to exhibit what might be described as attachment deactivation (i.e., muted emotional language, reduced prayer spontaneity, or disengagement from spiritual rituals) or hyper-activation (i.e., anxiety about spiritual distance or frustration with feeling disconnected from God). These findings align with Cherniak and colleagues' discussion of individual differences in attachment functioning, particularly how neurological or interpersonal disruptions can shape people's IWMs of God. If one's capacity to represent relational comfort is neurologically constrained, as may be the case in some LOPD individuals, then their IWM of God may come to feel more emotionally distant, cognitively inaccessible, or effortful to maintain.

Notably, though, several LOPD participants described eventual reconnection or even strengthening of their spiritual life over time, suggesting that earned security (Granqvist, 2020) through religious coping is possible even in the presence of disease-related barriers. These accounts support the compensation hypothesis proposed by Granqvist and Kirkpatrick (2016), which holds that insecure attachment experiences in human relationships, or disruptions such as those caused by chronic illness, may be offset by a compensatory attachment to a divine figure (e.g., God). In these cases, God is not merely a continuation of prior secure relationships (i.e., the correspondence hypothesis) but becomes a reparative source of emotional stability when interpersonal or cognitive capacities are challenged.

Indeed, some participants' experiences may illustrate compensatory dynamics. For example, those who felt isolated, overwhelmed, or emotionally abandoned due to PD often described turning to God in a newly urgent or intimate way. In such cases, spiritual engagement served as a substitute attachment relationship that helped regulate distress, a function well-documented in attachment theory as a response to perceived threat (Cherniak et al., 2021). Others, however, exhibited a correspondence pattern, wherein stable, early-life secure attachments generalized into stable and secure relationships with God despite the presence of disease. These individuals often used language of continuity, calm trust, and enduring faith that did not fluctuate with illness severity.

Overall, these qualitative differences between LOPD and ROPD point to the neuropsychological modulation of attachment to God. While participants across both groups employed spiritual resources, their capacity to experience God as emotionally present, responsive, or relationally reliable may be shaped by their neurological profiles and broader relational histories. As Cherniak et al. (2021) argue, God functions not only as a symbolic referent but as an emotionally loaded attachment figure, whose availability and intimacy are experienced through both cognitive and affective channels. Disruption to these channels via brain pathology or insecure relational templates can therefore complicate spiritual intimacy.

In sum, the RQ1 findings, when situated within the religion-as-attachment framework, highlight the importance of IWMs, the functions of *Safe Haven* and *Secure Base*, and developmental pathways such as correspondence and compensation. These mechanisms offer explanatory depth for the diverse ways participants with PD, especially those with LOPD, described their perceived connection with God. These findings also underscore the clinical relevance of attending to spiritual attachment dynamics in PD care, particularly for patients whose neurological or emotional constraints may obscure or limit their capacity to access spiritual resources that could otherwise enhance psychological resilience and existential well-being.

References

Ainsworth, M. D. S. (1978). *Patterns of attachment: A psychological study of the Strange Situation*. Lawrence Erlbaum Associates.

Alwhaibi, M., Sambamoorthi, U., Madhavan, S., & Kelly, K. M. (2015). Type of multimorbidity and complementary and alternative medicine use among adults. *Evidence-Based Complementary and Alternative Medicine, 2015*, Article 362582. https://doi.org/10.1155/2015/362582

Antonovsky, A. (1979). *Health, stress, and coping*. Jossey-Bass.

Atterling Brolin, K., Schaeffer, E., Kuri, A., Rumrich, I. K., Schumacher Schuh, A. F., Darweesh, S. K., & Noyce, A. J. (2025). Environmental risk factors for Parkinson's disease: A critical review and policy implications. *Movement Disorders, 40*(2), 204–221. https://doi.org/10.1002/mds.30067

Bandura, A. (1977). Self-efficacy: Toward a unifying theory of behavioral change. *Psychological Review, 84*(2), 191–215. https://doi.org/10.1037/0033-295X.84.2.191

Barnes, P. M., Bloom, B., & Nahin, R. L. (2008). *Complementary and alternative medicine use among adults and children: United States, 2007* (National Health Statistics Reports No. 12). National Center for Health Statistics.

Barnes, P. M., Powell-Griner, E., McFann, K., & Nahin, R. L. (2004). *Complementary and alternative medicine use among adults: United States, 2002*. National Center for Health Statistics.

Beck, A. T. (2006). *Depression: Clinical, experimental, and theoretical aspects*. University of Pennsylvania Press.

Beck, B. D. (2019). Sacred moments in guided imagery and music. *Approaches: Music Therapy and Special Education, 11*(1), 1–15.

Birgegård, A., & Granqvist, P. (2004). The correspondence between attachment to parents and God: Three experiments using subliminal separation cues. *Personality and Social Psychology Bulletin, 30*(9), 1122–1135. https://doi.org/10.1177/0146167204264266

Blum, K. (2025). Neurospirituality connectome-role in neurology and reward deficiency syndrome (RDS). *EC Neurology, 17*, 1–25.

Bock, M., Sillau, S. H., Kluger, B. M., & Kutner, J. S. (2022). What's in the sauce? The specific benefits of palliative care for Parkinson's disease. *Journal of Pain and Symptom Management, 63*(6), 1031–1040. https://doi.org/10.1016/j.jpainsymman.2022.01.017

Bowlby, J. (1973). *Attachment and loss: Vol. 2. Separation*. Basic Books.

Bowlby, J. (1982). *Attachment and loss: Vol. 1. Attachment* (2nd ed.). Basic Books.
Bradshaw, M., & Kent, B. V. (2018). Prayer, attachment to God, and changes in psychological well-being in later life. *Journal of Aging and Health, 30*(5), 667–691. https://doi.org/10.1177/0898264316688116
Braun, V., & Clarke, V. (2006). Using thematic analysis in psychology. *Qualitative Research in Psychology*, *3*(2), 77–101.
Butler, P. M., McNamara, P., & Durso, R. (2010). Deficits in the automatic activation of religious concepts in patients with Parkinson's disease. *Journal of the International Neuropsychological Society, 16*(2), 252–261. https://doi.org/10.1017/S1355617709991202
Butler, P. M., McNamara, P., & Durso, R. (2011a). Side of onset in Parkinson's disease and alterations in religiosity: Novel behavioral phenotypes. *Behavioral Neurology, 24*(2), 133–141. https://doi.org/10.3233/BEN-2011-0282
Butler, P. M., McNamara, P., Ghofrani, J., & Durso, R. (2011b). Disease-associated differences in religious cognition in patients with Parkinson's disease. *Journal of Clinical and Experimental Neuropsychology, 33*(8), 917–928. https://doi.org/10.1080/13803395.2011.575768
Calvert, S. L. (2010). Children as consumers: Advertising and marketing. *The Future of Children, 18*(1), 205–234. https://doi.org/10.1353/foc.0.0001
Cassibba, R., Granqvist, P., & Costantini, A. (2013). Mothers' attachment security predicts their children's sense of God's closeness. *Attachment & Human Development, 15*(1), 51–64. https://doi.org/10.1080/14616734.2013.743253
Cassibba, R., Granqvist, P., Costantini, A., & Gatto, S. (2008). Attachment and God representations among lay Catholics, priests, and religious: A matched comparison study based on the Adult Attachment Interview. *Developmental Psychology, 44*(6), 1753–1763.
Cherniak, A. D., Mikulincer, M., Shaver, P. R., & Granqvist, P. (2021). Attachment theory and religion. *Current Opinion in Psychology, 40*, 126–130. https://doi.org/10.1016/j.copsyc.2020.08.020
Cong, S., Xiang, C., Zhang, S., Zhang, T., Wang, H., & Cong, S. (2022). Prevalence and clinical aspects of depression in Parkinson's disease: A systematic review and meta-analysis of 129 studies. *Neuroscience and Biobehavioral Reviews, 141*, 104749. https://doi.org/10.1016/j.neubiorev.2022.104749
Czekierda, K., Banik, A., Park, C. L., & Luszczynska, A. (2017). Meaning in life and physical health: Systematic review and meta-analysis. *Health Psychology Review, 11*(4), 387–418. https://doi.org/10.1080/17437199.2017.1327325
Davis, E. B., Granqvist, P., & Sharp, C. (2021). Theistic relational spirituality: Development, dynamics, health, and transformation. *Psychology of Religion and Spirituality, 13*(4), 401–414.
Ellison, C. G., Bradshaw, M., Flannelly, K. J., & Galek, K. (2014). Prayer, attachment to God, and symptoms of anxiety-related disorders among U.S. adults. *Sociology of Religion, 75*(2), 208–233.
Feeney, J. A. (2016). Adult romantic attachment: Development and dynamics in couple relationships. In J. Cassidy & P. R. Shaver (Eds.), *Handbook of attachment: Theory, research, and clinical applications* (3rd ed., pp. 424–446). Guilford Press.
Feigin, V. L., Nichols, E., Alam, T., Bannick, M. S., Beghi, E., Blake, N., & Vos, T. (2017). Global burden of neurological disorders: A systematic analysis for the global burden of disease Study 2016. *The Lancet Neurology, 16*(11), 877–897. https://doi.org/10.1016/S1474-4422(17)30299-5
Fetzer Institute & National Institute on Aging Working Group. (1999). *Multidimensional measurement of religiousness/spirituality for use in health research: A report of the Fetzer Institute/National Institute on Aging Working Group*. Fetzer Institute.

Garner, C. T. (2023). *The effects of mindfulness and exercise on symptoms of Parkinson's disease: A systematic review*. Western Michigan University.

George, C., Kaplan, N., & Main, M. (1996). *The adult attachment interview protocol*. Unpublished manuscript, University of California, Berkeley.

George, L. K., Ellison, C. G., & Larson, D. B. (2000). Explaining the relationships between religious involvement and health. *Psychological Inquiry, 13*(3), 190–200.

Ghourchian, S., Gruber-Baldini, A. L., Shakya, S., Reich, S. G., von Coelln, R., & Shulman, L. M. (2023). Spirituality in Parkinson's disease within a sample from the USA. *Journal of Religion and Health, 62*(6), 4177–4191. https://doi.org/10.1007/s10943-023-01817-4

Giaquinto, S., Bruti, L., Dall'Armi, V., Palma, E., & Spiridigliozzi, C. (2011). Religious and spiritual beliefs in outpatients suffering from Parkinson's disease. *International Journal of Geriatric Psychiatry, 26*(9), 916–922. https://doi.org/10.1002/gps.2624

Goodin, J. B., & D'Brot, V. M. (2014, March). Aspiring health professionals' career goals and healthcare reform orientations. Presented at the Central Group on Educational Affairs (Association of American Medical Colleges), March 2014.

Granqvist, P. (1998). Religiousness and perceived childhood attachment: On the question of compensation or correspondence. *The Journal for the Scientific Study of Religion, 37*(2), 350–367. https://doi.org/10.2307/1387533

Granqvist, P. (2002). Attachment and religiosity in adolescence: Cross-sectional and longitudinal evaluations. *Personality and Social Psychology Bulletin, 28*(2), 260–270. https://doi.org/10.1177/0146167202282011

Granqvist, P., & Kirkpatrick, L. A. (2004). Religious conversion and perceived childhood attachment: A meta-analysis. International Journal for the Psychology of Religion, 14(4), 223–250. https://doi.org/10.1207/s15327582ijpr1404_1 added to references

Granqvist, P. (2012). Introduction to the special issue: Advancements in the study of attachment and religion/spirituality. *International Journal for the Psychology of Religion, 22*(3), 173–179. https://doi.org/10.1080/10508619.2012.670010

Granqvist, P. (2020). *Attachment in religion and spirituality: A wider view*. Guilford Publications.

Granqvist, P., & Hagekull, B. (1999). Religiousness and perceived childhood attachment: Profiling socialized correspondence and emotional compensation. *Journal for the Scientific Study of Religion, 38*(2), 254–273. https://doi.org/10.2307/1387793

Granqvist, P., & Kirkpatrick, L. A. (2016). Attachment and religious representations and behavior. In J. Cassidy & P. R. Shaver (Eds.), Handbook of attachment: Theory, research, and clinical applications (3rd ed., pp. 507–533). Guilford Press.

Granqvist, P., Ivarsson, T., Broberg, A. G., & Hagekull, B. (2007). Examining the building blocks of faith: A longitudinal study of religiousness in childhood and adolescence. *International Journal for the Psychology of Religion, 17*(2), 89–120.

Granqvist, P., Mikulincer, M., & Shaver, P. R. (2020). An attachment theory perspective on religion and spirituality. In K. E. Vail & C. Routledge (Eds.), *The science of religion, spirituality, and existentialism* (pp. 175–186). Academic Press. https://doi.org/10.1016/b978-0-12-817204-9.00014-7

Granqvist, P., Mikulincer, M., Gewirtz, V., & Shaver, P. R. (2012). Experimental findings on God as an attachment figure: Normative processes and moderating effects of internal working models. *Journal of Personality and Social Psychology, 103*(5), 804–821.

Greenwald, E. A., Cook, K. E., & Finkel, E. J. (2018). Attachment insecurity and religious belief across the lifespan: A meta-analytic review. *Personality and Social Psychology Bulletin, 44*(12), 1756–1771.

Haaxma, C. A., Bloem, B. R., Borm, G. F., Oyen, W. J. G., Leenders, K. L., Eshuis, S., & Horstink, M. W. I. M. (2010). Gender differences in Parkinson's disease. *Journal of Neurology, Neurosurgery & Psychiatry, 78*(8), 819–824. https://doi.org/10.1136/jnnp.2006.103788

Henderson, W. M., & Kent, B. V. (2021). Attachment to God and psychological distress: Evidence of a curvilinear relationship. *Journal for the Scientific Study of Religion, 61*(4), 742–759. https://doi.org/10.1111/jssr.12767

Hermanns, M., Deal, B., & Haas, B. (2012). Biopsychosocial and spiritual aspects of Parkinson disease: an integrative review. *The Journal of neuroscience nursing : journal of the American Association of Neuroscience Nurses, 44*(4), 194–205. https://doi.org/10.1097/JNN.0b013e3182527593

Hiebler-Ragger, M., Kapfhammer, H. P., & Unterrainer, H. F. (2016). Insecure attachment and depression: The mediating role of meaning in life. *Journal of Religion and Health, 55*(3), 1051–1064.

Hill, P. C., & Pargament, K. I. (2008). Advances in the conceptualization and measurement of religion and spirituality: Implications for physical and mental health. *Psychology of Religion and Spirituality, S*(1), 3–17. https://doi.org/10.1037/1941-1022.S.1.3

Hoehn, M. M., & Yahr, M. D. (1967). Parkinsonism: Onset, progression, and mortality. *Neurology, 17*(5), 427–442. https://doi.org/10.1212/wnl.17.5.427

Hood, R. W., Jr., Hill, P. C., & Spilka, B. (2018). *The psychology of religion: An empirical approach* (5th ed.). Guilford Press.

Jankovic, J. (2008). Parkinson's disease: Clinical features and diagnosis. *Journal of Neurology, Neurosurgery & Psychiatry, 79*(4), 368–376. https://doi.org/10.1136/jnnp.2007.131045

Jeserich, F., Klein, C., Brinkhaus, B., & Teut, M. (2023). Sense of coherence and religion/spirituality: A systematic review and meta-analysis based on a methodical classification of instruments measuring religion/spirituality. *PLOS ONE, 18*(8), e0289203. https://doi.org/10.1371/journal.pone.0289203

Kimball, C. N., Boyatzis, C. J., Cook, K. V., Leonard, K. C., & Flanagan, K. S. (2013). Attachment to God: A qualitative exploration of emerging adults' spiritual relationship with God. *Journal of Psychology and Theology, 41*(3), 175–188.

Kirkpatrick, L. A. (1997). A longitudinal study of changes in religious belief and behavior as a function of individual differences in adult attachment style. *Journal for the Scientific Study of Religion, 36*(2), 207–217. https://doi.org/10.2307/1387553

Kirkpatrick, L. A. (1998). God as a substitute attachment figure: A longitudinal study of adult attachment style and religious change in college students. *Personality & Social Psychology Bulletin, 24*(9), 961–973. https://doi.org/10.1177/0146167298249004

Kirkpatrick, L. A., & Shaver, P. R. (1990). Attachment theory and religion: Childhood attachments, religious beliefs, and conversion. *Journal for the Scientific Study of Religion, 29*(3), 315–334. https://doi.org/10.2307/1386461

Kirkpatrick, L. A., & Shaver, P. R. (1992). An attachment-theoretical approach to romantic love and religious belief. *Personality and Social Psychology Bulletin, 18*(3), 266–275. https://doi.org/10.1177/0146167292183002

Kobasa, S. C. (1979). Stressful life events, personality, and health: An inquiry into hardiness. *Journal of Personality and Social Psychology, 37*(1), 1–11. https://doi.org/10.1037/0022-3514.37.1.1

Koenig, H. G. (2012). Religion, spirituality, and health: The research and clinical implications. *ISRN Psychiatry, 2012*, 278730. https://doi.org/10.5402/2012/278730

Koenig, H. G., King, D. E., & Carson, V. B. (Eds.). (2023). *Handbook of religion and health* (3rd ed.). Oxford University Press.

Krohne, H. W. (2002). Stress and coping theories. In R. Fernandez-Ballesteros (Ed.), *Encyclopedia of psychological assessment* (pp. 789–793). Sage.

Kupor, D. M., Laurin, K., & Levav, J. (2015). Anticipating divine protection? Reminders of God can increase nonmoral risk taking. *Psychological Science, 26*(4), 374–384. https://doi.org/10.1177/0956797614563108

Leow, K. L., Wong, M. S. C., & Lim, Y. L. (2024). The role of perceived attachment to God in times of distress on psychological well-being: A mixed-method study. *Sains Humanika, 16*(3), Article 097. https://sainshumanika.utm.my/index.php/sainshumanika/article/view/2097

Lin, J. (2025). Exploring social support theory: Key concepts, current research hotspots and future gaps. *Academic Journal of Humanities & Social Sciences, 8*(7), 34–42. https://doi.org/10.25236/AJHSS.2025.080705

Luo, J., Cao, W., Zhao, J., Zeng, X., & Pan, Y. (2023). The moderating role of optimism between social trauma and depression among Chinese college students: A cross-sectional study. *BMC Psychology, 11*(1), 270.

McNamara, P. (Ed.). (2006). *Where God and science meet* (Vols. 1–3). Praeger Perspectives.

Mikulincer, M., & Shaver, P. R. (2007). Attachment, group–related processes, and psychotherapy. *International Journal of Group Psychotherapy, 57*(2), 233–245.

Mikulincer, M., & Shaver, P. R. (2016). *Attachment in adulthood: Structure, dynamics, and change* (2nd ed.). Guilford Press.

Miner, M., Ghobary, B., Dowson, M., & Proctor, M. T. (2014). Spiritual attachment in Islam and Christianity: Similarities and differences. *Mental Health, Religion & Culture, 17*(1), 79–93.

Modestino, E. J., Amenechi, C., Reinhofer, A., & O'Toole, P. (2017). Side-of-onset of Parkinson's disease in relation to neuropsychological measures. *Brain and Behavior, 7*(1), Article e00590. https://doi.org/10.1002/brb3.590

Morgan, J., Clark, D., Tripodis, Y., Halloran, C. S., Minsky, A., Wildman, W. J., Durso, R., & McNamara, P. (2016). Neuropsychologia impacts of religious semantic priming on an intertemporal discounting task: Response time effects and neural correlates. *Neuropsychologia, 89*, 403–413. https://doi.org/10.1016/j.neuropsychologia.2016.07.020

Narayanan, N., & Albin, R. (2022). *Cognition in Parkinson's disease*. Elsevier.

Otaiku, A. I. (2022). Religiosity and risk of Parkinson's disease in England and the USA. *Journal of Religion and Health, 62*. Advance online publication. https://doi.org/10.1007/s10943-022-01603-8

Paal, P., Avión Martínez, S., Lorenzl, S., & Goldzweig, G. (2023). A rejoinder to *Otaiku: Religiosity and risk of Parkinson's disease in England and the USA — The health determinants of spirituality, religiosity and the need for state-of-the-art research. Journal of Religion and Health, 62*(6), 4209–4214. https://doi.org/10.1007/s10943-022-01726-y

Perez-Díaz, O., Hernández, S. E., Brown, L. L., Xiao, Y., González-Mora, J. L., Rubia, K., & Barros-Loscertales, A. (2025). Striatal functional connectivity associated with Sahaja Yoga meditation. *Scientific Reports, 15*(1), Article 14513. https://doi.org/10.1038/s41598-025-98256-w

Pew Research Center. (2025). How the global religious landscape changed from 2010 to 2020. https://www.pewresearch.org/religion/2025/06/09/how-the-global-religious-landscape-changed-from-2010-to-2020/

Pietromonaco, P. R., & Barrett, L. F. (2000). The internal working models concept: What do we really know about the self in relation to others? *Review of General Psychology, 4*(2), 155–175. https://doi.org/10.1037/1089-2680.4.2.155

Pirutinsky, S. (2009). Conversion and attachment insecurity among Orthodox Jews. *International Journal for the Psychology of Religion, 19*(3), 200–206.

Plamann, K., McCarthy Veach, P., LeRoy, B. S., MacFarlane, I. M., Petzel, S. V., & Zierhut, H. A. (2021). Effects of monitoring versus blunting on the public's preferences for information in a hypothetical cancer diagnosis scenario. *Journal of Genetic Counseling, 30*(1), 132–143.

Porcelli, S., Wee, N. Van Der, Wer, S. Van Der, Aghajani, M., Glennon, C., Heukelum, S. Van, Mogavero, F., Lobo, A., Javier, F., Lobo, E., Posadas, M., Dukart, J., Kozak, R., Arce, E., Ikram, A., Vorstman, J., Bilderbeck, A., Saris, I., Kas, M. J., & Serretti, A. (2019). Social brain, social dysfunction and social withdrawal. *Neuroscience and Biobehavioral Reviews, 97*, 10–33. https://doi.org/10.1016/j.neubiorev.2018.09.012

Prizer, L. P., Gay, J. L., Wilson, M. G., Emerson, K. G., Glass, A. P., Miyasaki, J. M., & Perkins, M. M. (2020). A mixed-methods approach to understanding the palliative needs of Parkinson's patients. *Journal of Applied Gerontology, 39*(8), 834–845.

Rajendran, P. R., Thompson, R. E., & Reich, S. G. (2001). The use of alternative therapies by patients with Parkinson's disease. *Neurology, 57*(5), 790–794. https://doi.org/10.1212/WNL.57.5.790

Scheier, M. F., & Carver, C. S. (1992). Effects of optimism on psychological and physical well-being: Theoretical overview and empirical update. *Cognitive Therapy and Research, 16*(2), 201–228. https://doi.org/10.1007/BF01173489

Schjoedt, U., Stødkilde-Jørgensen, H., Geertz, A. W., & Roepstorff, A. (2009). Highly religious participants recruit areas of social cognition in personal prayer. *Social Cognitive and Affective Neuroscience, 4*(2), 199–207. https://doi.org/10.1093/scan/nsn050

Schnitker, S. A., Felke, T. J., Fernandez, C. E., Redmond, N., & Eccles, J. S. (2012). Attachment and spiritual development in adolescence. *Psychology of Religion and Spirituality, 4*(4), 275–284. https://doi.org/10.1080/10508619.2012.670024

Schwarzer, R., & Leppin, A. (1991). Social support and health: A theoretical and empirical overview. *Journal of Social and Personal Relationships, 8*(1), 99–127. https://doi.org/10.1177/0265407591081005

Senewiratne, S., Sendjaya, S., Gunasekara, A., & Newman, A. (2025). Cognitive hardiness in the workplace: A systematic review and call for future research. *Management Review Quarterly*. Advance online publication. https://doi.org/10.1007/s11301-025-00512-w

Shi, Y., Dobkin, R., Weintraub, D., Cho, H. R., Caspell-Garcia, C., Bock, M., Brown, E., Aarsland, D., & Dahodwala, N. (2024). Association of baseline depression and anxiety with longitudinal health outcomes in Parkinson's disease. *Movement Disorders Clinical Practice, 11*(9), 1103–1112. https://doi.org/10.1002/mdc3.14145

Smart, K., Durso, R., Morgan, J., & McNamara, P. (2016). A potential case of remission of Parkinson's disease. *Journal of Complementary and Integrative Medicine, 13*(3), 311–315. https://doi.org/10.1515/jcim-2016-0019

Steinbach, M. J., Campbell, R. W., DeVore, B. B., & Harrison, D. W. (2023). Laterality in Parkinson's disease: A neuropsychological review. *Applied Neuropsychology: Adult, 30*(1), 126–140.

Tang, Y.-Y., Hölzel, B. K., & Posner, M. I. (2015). The neuroscience of mindfulness meditation. *Nature Reviews Neuroscience, 16*(4), 213–225. https://doi.org/10.1038/nrn3916

Thanvi, B. R., & Lo, T. C. N. (2004). Long term motor complications of levodopa: Clinical features, mechanisms, and management strategies. *Postgraduate Medical Journal, 80*(946), 452–458. https://doi.org/10.1136/pgmj.2003.013912

Thompson, R. A., Simpson, J. A., & Berlin, L. J. (2022). Taking perspective on attachment theory and research: Nine fundamental questions. *Attachment & Human Development, 24*(5), 543–560. https://doi.org/10.1080/14616734.2022.2030132

Tirgari, B., Khaksari, M., Soltani, Z., Mirzaee, M., Saberi, S., & Bashiri, H. (2022). Spiritual well-being in patients with chronic diseases: A systematic review and meta-analysis. *Journal of Religion and Health, 61*(5), 3969–3987. https://doi.org/10.1007/s10943-022-01595-5

Van Tongeren, D. R., Sanders, M., Edwards, M., Davis, E. B., Aten, J. D., Ranter, J. M., Tsarouhis, A., Short, A., Cuthbert, A., Hook, J. N., & Davis, D. E. (2019). Religious and spiritual struggles alter God representations: A longitudinal study of God images and concepts. *Psychology of Religion and Spirituality, 11*(3), 225–232. https://doi.org/10.1037/rel0000173

Wade, D. T. (2016). Rehabilitation – a new approach. Part four: A new paradigm, and its implications. *Clinical Rehabilitation, 30*(2), 109–118. https://doi.org/10.1177/0269215515601177

Weintraub, D., Aarsland, D., Chaudhuri, K. R., Dobkin, R. D., Leentjens, A. F., Rodriguez-Violante, M., & Schrag, A. (2022). The neuropsychiatry of Parkinson's disease: Advances and challenges. *The Lancet Neurology, 21*(1), 89–102.

World Population Review. (2024). Religion by country 2024. https://worldpopulationreview.com/country-rankings/religion-by-country

Yang, M., Xue, J., Kong, X., Liu, W., Wang, Y., Zou, Y., Wang, L., & Dong, C. (2024). Correlation of psychological resilience with social support and coping style in Parkinson's disease: A cross-sectional study. *Journal of Advanced Nursing,* 1–10. https://doi.org/10.1111/jan.16408

Zarzycka, B. (2018). Parental attachment styles and religious and spiritual struggle: A mediating effect of God image. *Journal of Family Issues, 39*(15), 3650–3669. https://doi.org/10.1177/0192513X18813186

Zarzycka, B., Grupa, M., Krok, D., & Rynasiewicz, A. (2024). Parental attachment styles, religiousness, and deconversion processes in adolescence. *Mental Health, Religion & Culture*, *27*(1), 87–100.

3

SELFLESSNESS AS THE NEUROPSYCHOLOGICAL FOUNDATION OF SPIRITUAL TRANSCENDENCE

Brick Johnstone, Daniel Cohen, and Andrew Cullen Dennison

Introduction

There is increased interest in determining the neurological and neuropsychological foundations of religious and spiritual experiences. Although religion and spirituality are now conceptualized and measured as empirically distinct constructs, the need exists to differentiate their neuropsychological foundations (i.e., what is the experiential nature of religious versus spiritual experiences?) and determine where in the brain these processes are mediated. This chapter provides evidence for a universal neuropsychological model to explain the nature of spiritual experiences for individuals from diverse cultures and faith traditions but suggests the need for a novel way of conceptualizing these experiences from a neuropsychological perspective.

To date religion has generally been conceptualized in terms of cognitive (i.e., systems of belief), behavioral (i.e., ritual practices), and affective processes (i.e., awe, wonder), all of which are associated with a broad range of neuroanatomical networks (Cristofori et al., 2022; Grafman et al., 2020; Johnstone & Cohen, 2019; McNamara, 2009; McNamara & Grafman, 2024). Spiritual experiences (defined as experiences of connection with the divine, however so conceived) have been more difficult to conceptualize and understand, as spirituality is more than how we think, feel, and act, as exemplified in individuals who report being spiritual but not religious (i.e., they can have experiences of ultimate connection to the divine without reference to religious beliefs). These difficulties in conceptualizing spirituality have required new neuropsychological models to explain their nature.

This chapter describes our JTF funded study (i.e., *A Longitudinal fMRI Study of Theistic Relational Processing in Individuals with Neurologic Dysfunction*) that sought to demonstrate that spiritual (vs. religious) experiences are best

DOI: 10.4324/9781003158189-3

conceptualized in terms of a neuropsychological process that minimizes the sense of self (i.e., creating experiences of selflessness) that can lead to spiritual transcendence under certain conditions.

Defining Spiritual Transcendence

To identify a universal neuropsychological process to explain spiritual transcendence, it is first necessary to define the construct, although this is not a simple task. For example, spiritually transcendent experiences have been described throughout history by mystics and religious followers in terms of connection with the divine, however so conceived (e.g., Atman/Brahman in Hinduism, Annata in Buddhism, kenosis in Christianity). Spiritually transcendent experiences have also been variably conceptualized and described in the humanities and social sciences in terms of mysticism, experiences of absorption, an undivided unity, universality, flow states, or an infinite/collective/universal consciousness (Canby et al., 2024; James, 1902; Lifshitz et al., 2019; Stace, 1960; Taves, 2020), thereby limiting the scientific study of spiritual transcendence. To further illustrate the difficulties inherent in studying this construct, the American Psychological Association (APA) dictionary defines transcendence as "a state of existence or perception that is *not definable* (italics added) in terms of normal understanding or experience" (APA Dictionary of Psychology, n.d.). These examples explain why many neuroscientists have been reluctant to conduct research in religion or spirituality (McNamara et al., 2024).

For these reasons, our study was guided by the definition of spiritual transcendence proposed over a century ago by William James (1902), who was one of the first psychologists who attempted to scientifically study spiritual experiences. Briefly, James stated that spiritual experiences could be described in terms of four general components, including ineffability (i.e., indescribable), passivity (i.e., not controllable), selflessness (i.e., the loss of the typical experience of a self), and an undivided unity (i.e., a dissolution of boundaries between the self and others). Whereas ineffability, passivity, and an undivided unity are not explainable in existing neuropsychological processes, the neuropsychological nature of the self (and experiences of selflessness) has been conceptualized and studied within the neurosciences.

Evolution of the Neuroscientific Study of Spiritual Transcendence

Early studies in the neurology of religiosity and spiritual experiences were exploratory and generally used neuroimaging (i.e., CT, MRI, fMRI, EEG, SPECT) to assess individuals during (or immediately before and after) religious practices (i.e., prayer, meditation; Aftanas & Golocheikine, 2001; Azari et al., 2001; Herzog, 1990–91; McNamara et al., 2006; Newberg et al., 1997; 2001, 2003; Saver & Rabin, 1997). Although they identified many neurological networks and neurotransmitters associated with measures that often conflated religion and spirituality, they were lacking in their ability to identify a common neuropsychological process to explain these experiences. Other studies used neurostimulation (i.e., to activate or inhibit neural functions) in different parts of the brain to induce spiritual experiences (Urgesi et al., 2010). The concepts of religion and spirituality were not well-defined in many of these early, but very important, foundational studies, and as a result, distinctions could not be made as to their different neuropsychological foundations.

Other research has evaluated the neurology of religiosity and spiritual transcendence by studying individuals with brain dysfunction (based on the premise that if spirituality is brain-based, then variability in brain functioning will be associated with similar variability in self-reported transcendence; Uddin et al. (2006)). For example, our initial studies investigated relationships among measures of transcendence [i.e., Inspirit, Brief Multidimensional Measure of Religiousness/Spirituality (BMMRS)] and measures of brain functioning in individuals with various types of neurologic dysfunction (e.g., traumatic brain injury, epilepsy, stroke, dementia; Johnstone & Glass, 2008; Johnstone et al., 2014, 2012). These studies indicated that *increased* reported spiritual transcendence was consistently associated with *decreased* performance on a measure of visual-spatial perception, the Judgment of Line Orientation Test (JOLO). Given that the JOLO has consistently been shown to be associated with right inferior parietal lobe (RIPL) functioning (i.e., it provides "empirical teeth in the localizing value" for RIPL-related functions; Tranel et al., 2009; p. 219), and the RIPL has also consistently been shown to be associated with disorders of the self (which can also be conceptualized in terms of selflessness; for reviews see Johnstone et al., 2021; Northoff et al., 2006); it was inferred that decreased RIPL functioning may be related to increased experiences of selflessness. This was also suggested given that spiritual experiences have consistently been described in terms of selflessness (which has also been referred to as ego dissolution, ego death, decentering, etc.) throughout history and across religious traditions.

To test if decreased RIPL functioning (and hypothesized increased selflessness) serves as a universal foundation of spiritual transcendence across diverse faith traditions, we conducted a study with a diverse sample of individuals from multiple cultures (i.e., India, United States), ethnicities (i.e., Black, South Asian, White), and religions (i.e., Christianity, Hinduism, Islam; Johnstone et al., 2017). The results generally supported the previous studies and suggested that RIPL-based experiences of selflessness serve as a universal neuropsychological foundation for spiritual experiences for diverse groups, although the interpretations of these experiences are based on different religious beliefs (e.g., Atman/Brahman in Hinduism; Annata in Buddhism; kenosis in Christianity).

Despite these consistent findings, the model was lacking in that we only inferred that selflessness was related to diminished RIPL functioning, given that there were no empirical measures to evaluate "selflessness." Although these preliminary findings were intriguing and made conceptual sense, they confirmed the need to identify empirical measures of selflessness in order to confirm a universal neuropsychological model to explain spiritual transcendence.

A Neuropsychological Model of Spiritual Transcendence

Based on these initial interdisciplinary studies, a neuropsychological model of the self has been developed over time to explain spiritual transcendence (Johnstone et al., 2016, 2021, 2025b; Johnstone & Cohen, 2019). However, it requires a need to conceptualize neuropsychological processes in new ways and differently from the typical manner by which neuropsychological processes are currently conceptualized in terms of relatively singular processes (e.g., affect, behavior, cognition, sensation). The proposed model suggests that the brain *integrates* all neuropsychological inputs (i.e., sensations) and outputs (i.e., affect, behavior, cognition) to create a sense of *relationship* between them so that they are experienced as happening to the same entity at the same time, space, and context (i.e., a unified experience) that is interpreted as a "sense of self/self." This neuropsychological model suggests that the self is therefore an impermanent construct that can change depending on what is, or is not, integrated into the unified experience. The model further suggests that, as a neuropsychological process, the experience of the self can therefore be increased, decreased, or distorted and lead to experiences of "selflessness." This model further proposes that these experiences of selflessness form the neuropsychological foundations of both "negative" neurological disorders of the self, as well as "positive" experiences of spiritual transcendence that have been reported throughout history and across religions.

Explaining the Model through Disorders of the Self

This novel neuropsychological model may be best explained through its application to disorders of the self that have been consistently shown to be related to decreased RIPL functioning (Feinberg et al., 2005; Johnstone et al., 2021; Northoff et al., 2006). These unusual conditions have been conceptualized in terms of neurological, psychiatric, and delusional misidentification disorders (DMD) of the self, but a universal neuropsychological process to explain the nature of these diverse conditions has yet to be developed. This may be because they have generally been conceptualized as disorders of affect, behavior, cognition, and/or sensation, although these processes cannot adequately explain the nature of disorders of the self.

Neurologic disorders of the self are conditions in which individuals will deny distinct aspects of the self, such as stating that their arm does not belong to them (i.e., asomatognosia), denying that they are blind (i.e., Anton's syndrome), or stating that one of their hands has a mind of its own (i.e., alien hand syndrome; Feinberg & Keenan, 2005). Psychiatric disorders of the self involve conditions in which individuals do not recognize their thoughts as their own (i.e., hallucinations, as in schizophrenia), feel that none of their experiences are related to the self or are unreal (i.e., depersonalization disorder), or which involve the existence of multiple selves (i.e., dissociative identity disorder; Hecht, 2010). Whereas neurologic disorders of the self are generally conceptualized as having neurologic etiologies (i.e., brain injury or disease), psychiatric disorders of the self are often conceptualized as having neurodevelopmental or psychological etiologies (i.e., psychological trauma).

DMDs are rare and very unusual conditions that are described as involving "delusions" and "misidentifications" (neither of which is adequately explained according to current understandings of neuropsychological processes; Enoch & Ball, 2002; Breen et al., 2000). For example, individuals with Capgras syndrome can recognize relatives but believe they are impostors while, conversely, individuals with Fregoli syndrome claim that strangers are family members. Individuals with Cotard syndrome state that their intestines are rotting and/or that they are dead or dying, and they often stop using the "I" pronoun.

Although all these neurologic, psychiatric, and DMDs of the self are all conceptualized as disorders of the self, a universal neuropsychological model has yet to be developed to explain their unusual nature (i.e., what universal neuropsychological process can explain how individuals can deny the existence of an arm, believe that thoughts are inserted by others into their brains, or that they are dead?). To date these disorders have generally been conceptualized as disorders of awareness (i.e., a cognitive process), but such a model is limited, as individuals with asomatognosia are typically aware of their arms (i.e., they can acknowledge the arm), individuals with schizophrenia are aware of their thoughts, and individuals with Capgras syndrome are aware of their family members, but they just do not experience a sense of relationship to them. Although these conditions vary in their presentations and have been shown to be related to multiple brain regions/networks, they have all been shown to be primarily related to the right hemisphere in general, and the right inferior parietal lobule (RIPL) more specifically (Northoff et al., 2006).

Although these unique disorders of the self have lacked a universal neuropsychological model to explain their unusual presentations to date, the proposed model provides a framework to do so by suggesting that such disorders are associated with the disintegration of neuropsychological processes that creates a lack of a sense of relationship of the individual neuropsychological processes to the unified experience/self. When this occurs, the disintegrated individual neuropsychological processes are not perceived as being part of the unified experience/sense of self.

For example (see Table 3.1), according to the proposed model, specific disorders of the self should exist for each individual neurological input (i.e., sensations) and neurologic output (i.e., affect, behavior, cognition). The model specifically suggests that asomatognosia involves the disintegration of the tactile sensation of a body part (usually the left arm), which leads to a lack of a sense of relationship between the arm and the unified experience and the resulting experience that it is not part of the self (i.e., "not mine"). This model can also explain the experiential nature of other

TABLE 3.1 Disorders of the Self

Process	*Disorder*	*Distorted Relationship*
Neurologic Inputs (Sensations)		
Tactile	Asomatognosia	No "relationship" to arm
	Cotard syndrome	No "relationship" to internal organs
Visual perceptions	Anton's syndrome	No "relationship" to blindness
	Mirror misidentification	No "relationship" to reflection
Auditory	Phonoagnosia	No "relationship" to own voice
Spatial	Environ. Reduplication	Distorted "relationship" to space
Taste	Ageusia	No "relationship" to associated pleasure
Smell	Anosmia	No "relationship" to associated pleasure
Neurologic Outputs (Mental Experiences)		
Thought	Schizophrenia	No "relationship" to thoughts
	Delusions	Over "relationship" to thoughts
Cognitive Schema	Capgras syndrome	No "relationship" to family
	Fregoli syndrome	Existing "relationship" to strangers
Behavior	Alien hand syndrome	No "relationship" to behavior of the hand
Affect	Alexithymia	No "relationship" to emotions
General Disintegration		
All senses/ experiences	Depersonalization DO	Unreal/unrelated experiences
All senses/ experiences	Anosognosia	No "relationship" to impairments/ attributes
Distorted Integration		
All senses/ experiences	Dissociative Identity	Multiple relationships

disintegrated sensations, including Anton's syndrome (i.e., disintegrated visual processes leading to the denial of blindness) and phonognosia (i.e., disintegrated auditory processes leading to the inability to recognize one's own voice).

The model can also explain the disintegration of neurologic outputs (i.e., affect, behavior, cognition). Specifically, alexithymia can be explained as the disintegration of, and lack of a sense of relationship to, emotions. Alien hand syndrome can be conceptualized as a disorder of disintegrated instinctual behavioral processes that lack a sense of relationship to the unified experience and the subsequent interpretation that the hand is acting of its own volition. Similarly, the model suggests that schizophrenia involves the disintegration of thoughts and the absence of a sense of relationship to them that leads to the experience that they did not originate internally (i.e., hallucinations).

The proposed neuropsychological model can also explain DMDs. For example, individuals with Capgras syndrome are apparently unable to integrate the cognitive schema (i.e., a form of thought) associated with known acquaintances (i.e., spouse/child/sibling), do not experience a sense of relationship to them, and therefore interpret their lack of a sense of relationship as an indication that their acquaintances are impostors. Fregoli syndrome, the opposite of Capgras syndrome, involves an exaggerated experience of relationship to unknown individuals, which leads to the interpretation that strangers are relatives (e.g., an unrelated hospital roommate is a family member). Capgras and Fregoli syndromes are analogous to jamais vu (i.e., a sense of relationship is absent when it should exist) and déjà vu experiences (i.e., a sense of relationship exists when it should not), respectively, which can be considered as normal experiences of mild disintegration of neuropsychological experiences (i.e., a distorted sense of "relationship"). The neuropsychological model further proposes that Cotard syndrome involves the disintegration of the sensations of internal organs which are processed in the insula, which leads to a lack of a sense of relationship to them. This condition can be conceptualized similarly to asomatognosia, but rather than a disintegration of tactile sensations that are processed in the contralateral parietal cortex, Cotard syndrome involves the disintegration of tactile sensations that are processed in the insula.

Whereas all these disorders of the self involve the disintegration of relatively singular neuropsychological processes (i.e., a sensation, thought, emotion, behavior, etc.), other disorders of the self-involve a general disintegration of all neuropsychological processes and an overall diminished experience of the self. For example, depersonalization is a psychiatric disorder in which individuals experience a general disintegration of experiences and therefore report that all experiences feel unreal or unrelated to the self. Similarly, anosognosia is a condition that is associated with severe brain injury and involves the diminished ability to integrate any neuropsychological process, which leads to lack of a sense of relationship between all neuropsychological processes (i.e., there is no self to possess the impairment/trait). The proposed neuropsychological model suggests that these experiences of a generalized "selflessness" also serve as the neuropsychological foundation of spiritual transcendent experiences.

It is noted that the proposed model suggests the need to reconceptualize neuropsychological processes in terms of relatively singular processes (i.e., affect, behavior, cognition, sensation), as well as the experience of *relationship* that is created when they are *integrated* in the RIPL. As such, asomatognosia can be conceptualized as a disorder of *relationship* to tactile sensations rather than a disorder of tactile sensations, schizophrenia can be conceptualized as a disorder of *relationship* to thoughts rather than a thought disorder, and alexithymia can be conceptualized as a disorder of *relationship* to emotions, rather than an emotional disorder.

Our Shirley Ryan/JTF Study

Based on our previous research, our JTF-sponsored study was conducted to validate the proposed neuropsychological model and demonstrate that RIPL-related networks serve as the neurological foundations of selflessness, which in turn serve as the neuropsychological foundation of spiritual transcendence.

It is noted that this study focused on identifying the neuropsychological processes associated with trait experiences of spiritual transcendence (i.e., a general disposition toward transcendence), rather than state experiences of transcendence (i.e., brief, intense experiences of transcendence experienced during religious and meditative practices). Given that the model suggests that spiritual transcendence is associated with brain functioning, it was proposed that the neuropsychological foundations of spiritual transcendence could be best demonstrated through the longitudinal study of individuals with various neurological conditions, some of whom are expected to decline over time (i.e., multiple sclerosis) and some who are expected to improve over time (i.e., traumatic brain injury, stroke). Based on the proposed neuropsychological model, the following hypotheses were offered:

1 Empirically distinct measures of selflessness (i.e., disintegrated inputs, disintegrated outputs) could be empirically distinguished from one another;
2 These empirical measures of selflessness would be significantly associated with empirical measures of spiritual transcendence;
3 To demonstrate a causal link between RIPL functions, selflessness, and transcendence, it was further hypothesized that longitudinal changes (between Time 2 and Time 1) in measures of RIPL functioning, selflessness, and transcendence would be significantly associated with each other. It was specifically hypothesized that as the RIPL functioning of individuals with ABI improved over time, experiences of both selflessness and transcendence would decrease. Conversely, it was hypothesized that as the RIPL functioning of individuals with MS declined over time, experiences of both selflessness and transcendence would increase; and
4 fMRI and neuropsychological measures of RIPL-related networks would be associated with empirical measures of both selflessness and transcendence.

Shirley Ryan/JTF Study Design

The sample included 73 individuals with diverse neurological disorders, including 33 with acquired brain injury (ABI; traumatic brain injury, stroke) and 40 with multiple sclerosis (MS). Individuals completed fMRI analysis and measures of selflessness and spiritual transcendence at Time 1 (baseline) and Time 2 (one year post-baseline). The following constructs of interest were assessed using the following measures:

Spiritual transcendence was assessed using the BMMRS (Fetzer Institute & National Institute on Aging Working Group, 1999). Lower scores on the BMMRS indicate a higher level of spirituality. The original BMMRS includes theoretically derived subscales of spirituality (i.e., Daily Spiritual Experiences, Meaning, Values/Beliefs, Forgiveness, Religious/Spiritual Coping), although our study used the following empirically distinct measures of spirituality that were identified in several factor analytic studies of the BMMRS (Johnstone et al., 2009, 2017, 2021):

- *Positive Spirituality* measures a positive sense of relationship with a higher power (e.g., "I feel the presence of a higher power;" "I feel the love of a higher power for me, directly or through others").
- *Negative Spirituality* measures a negative sense of relationship with a higher power (i.e., "I feel I am being punished by a higher power for my sins or lack of spirituality;" "I wonder whether I have been abandoned by a higher power").
- *Forgiveness* measures the degree to which one forgives others, or feels forgiven by a higher power (e.g., "I have forgiven those who hurt me;" "I know that I am forgiven by a higher power").

Selflessness was assessed using the Cambridge Depersonalization Scale (CDS; Sierra & Berrios, 2000). It is a 29-item measure of depersonalization disorder, a psychiatric disorder of the self that involves experiences of depersonalization and derealization. Higher CDS scores indicate a higher degree of selflessness. The CDS was deemed to be appropriate to use as a measure of selflessness, given that it assesses experiences associated with depersonalization, including experiences of disintegration for all perceived sensations and created mental experiences. Table 3.2 provides examples of CDS items that assess specific disintegrated neuropsychological processes (i.e., sensations, affect, behavior, cognition), as well as the subjective manner by which these experiences are expressed (i.e., disintegrated time, disintegrated space, and disintegrated context/unreality).

Neuropsychological functioning of the RIPL was assessed using the JOLO, which was used to infer the functional integrity of the RIPL as it has been shown to be consistently related to cerebral lesions in the RIPL (Tranel et al., 2009), as well as increased spiritual transcendence (Johnstone et al., 2012; 2014; Johnstone & Glass, 2008).

Neuroanatomical networks associated with selflessness and spiritual transcendence were evaluated with fMRI, including 24 neural networks associated with the RIPL. The data measured the strength of connectivity between the RIPL and 24 regions of interest within both cerebral hemispheres (based on the Harvard-Oxford Cortical and subcortical atlas). To simplify the neuroimaging results, they are described in terms of commonly accepted networks that exist between the RIPL and neuroanatomical regions within the general cerebral lobes (i.e., frontal, temporal, parietal, occipital) and the insular cortices.

TABLE 3.2 CDS Item Examples

Dis-Integrated Neurologic Inputs (i.e., Sensations)

- Dis-integrated tactile sensations (e.g., "Parts of my body feel as if they didn't belong to me")
- Dis-integrated taste/smell (e.g., "The smell/taste of things no longer gives me a feeling of pleasure or dislike")
- Dis-integrated vision (e.g., "What I see looks 'flat' or 'lifeless', as if I were looking at a picture")
- Dis-integrated audition (e.g., "Familiar voices (including my own) sound remote and unreal")

Dis-Integrated Neurologic Outputs (i.e., Affect, Behavior, Cognition)

- Dis-integrated thoughts (e.g., "I feel so detached from my thoughts that they seem to have a 'life' of their own")
- Dis-integrated behaviors (e.g., When I move it doesn't feel as if I were in charge of the movements, so that I feel "automatic" and mechanical as if I were a "robot")
- Dis-integrated emotions (e.g., "When I weep or laugh, I do not seem to feel any emotions at all")

Subjective Expressions of Disintegration

- Dis-integrated space (e.g., "I have the feeling of being outside my body")
- Dis-integrated time (e.g., It seems as if things that I have recently done had taken place a long time ago. For example, anything which I have done this morning feels as if it were done weeks ago")
- Dis-integrated context (e.g., "Whilst doing something I have the feeling of being a 'detached observer' of myself")

Identifying Selflessness as an Empirically Distinct Construct

Our first study focused on identifying selflessness as an empirically distinct construct. According to the proposed model, if the integration of all sensations and mental experiences leads to a unified experience/sense of self, then impairment in this process of integration should lead to decreased experiences of the self (i.e., increased selflessness) for all neurologic inputs (i.e., sensations) and outputs (i.e., affect, behavior, cognition). To confirm this hypothesis, a factor analysis of the CDS based on the 73 participants was conducted (Johnstone et al., 2025a). Overall, the study confirmed the proposed model by identifying the following empirically distinct factors:

Disintegrated Sensations

- *Disintegrated bodily sensations* assess selflessness in terms of experiences of detachment from one's bodily sensations (e.g., asomatognosia), including tactile sensations, body size, and pain (e.g., "Parts of my body feel as if they didn't belong to me").
- *Disintegrated smell/taste* assesses selflessness in terms of the disintegration of one's relationship to qualities of smell and taste (e.g., "The flavour of meals no longer gives me a feeling of pleasure or distaste").

Disintegrated Mental Experiences

- *Disintegrated emotions* assesses abnormal experiences of relationship to emotions (e.g., alexithymia), including detachment from one's experiences of pleasure, affection, fear, and distress (e.g., "When I weep or laugh, I do not seem to feel any emotions at all").
- *Disintegrated cognition* assesses abnormal experiences of relationship to cognition (e.g., schizophrenia), including a sense of detachment from one's thoughts and memories (e.g., "I feel so detached from my thoughts that they seem to have a 'life' of their own").

Experiences of Distorted Space and Reality

Given that the proposed neuropsychological model hypothesizes that the integration of all neuropsychological processes leads to the experience that they are happening at the same time, space, and context (i.e., a unified experience), it is appropriate to assume that impairment in this integrative process will lead to distortions in the experience of time, space, and context. In fact, the CDS includes such items which were identified as distinct factors in the factor analysis, including:

- *Disintegrated spatial perception.* This factor assesses abnormal experiences of spatial perception, including out-of-body experiences (e.g., "I have the feeling of being outside my body").
- *Unreality.* This factor assesses abnormal experiences of context/reality (e.g., detached, strange, and unreal experiences; "Out of the blue, I feel strange, as if I were not real or as if I were cut off from the world").

The neuropsychological model also proposes the existence of individual factors for dis-integrated vision (e.g., Anton's syndrome), hearing (i.e., phonognosia), and behavior (i.e., alien hand syndrome), as well as experiences of dis-integrated time, although these constructs/processes could not be identified in the study, given factor analyses require at least two items to confirm a distinct factor, and the CDS has only one item for each of these areas.

A subsequent literature review indicated that previous factor analytic studies of the CDS based on psychiatric populations identified similar empirically distinct factors of selflessness, although they were labeled differently (e.g., disintegrated bodily sensations as "anomalous bodily experiences," disintegrated emotions as "emotional numbing," disintegrated cognition as "anomalous subjective recall," and disintegrated space as "alienation from surroundings"; Blevins et al., 2013; Fagioli et al., 2015; Sierra et al., 2005). Overall, our study, based on a neurologic sample, and these similar studies based on psychiatric samples generally confirm that individual neuropsychological processes are integrated into a unified experience, and that disintegration of these individual processes can be conceptualized as examples of selflessness.

Demonstrating Relationships between Empirical Measures of Selflessness and Transcendence

With the identification of empirically distinct measures of selflessness, the next focus of our JTF project was to demonstrate relationships between empirical measures of selflessness (i.e., CDS factors) and empirical measures of spiritual transcendence (i.e., BMMRS positive spirituality, negative spirituality; Johnstone et al., 2025b). In this study, Pearson correlations generally indicated that *increased* selflessness was associated with *increased* spiritual transcendence (see Table 3.3). Overall, as hypothesized, the results suggest that increased selflessness serves as a neuropsychological foundation of increased transcendence.

In further support of the model, the results indicated that decreased functioning of the RIPL (i.e., JOLO) was generally associated with both increased selflessness and increased spiritual transcendence. Specifically, decreased RIPL functioning was associated with higher scores on all measures of selflessness, with five of the seven correlations being/approaching statistical significance. Similarly, the results also indicated that decreased RIPL functioning (i.e., JOLO) was correlated with both increased positive spirituality (non-significantly) and increased negative spirituality (significantly). To our knowledge, this was the first study to correlate empirical measures of selflessness, empirical measures of transcendence, and empirical measures of RIPL functioning, suggesting that selflessness and transcendence are empirically measurable constructs that are appropriate to use in scientific research.

Longitudinal Relationships Among RIPL Functioning, Selflessness, and Spiritual Transcendence

Although the previous study identified concurrent relationships between selflessness and spiritual transcendence, a longitudinal study to demonstrate possible causal

TABLE 3.3 Correlations between JOLO, CDS Factors, and BMMRS Factors

	BMMRS Factors		*JOLO (Adjusted Raw Score)*
CDS Factors	*Positive Spiritual Experience*	*Negative Spiritual Experience*	
Bodily Sensations	−0.11	−0.29*	−0.07
Space	−0.12	−0.22†	−0.03
Taste and Smell	0.17	−0.35**	0.02
Cognitive	−0.12	−0.15	−0.18
Affect	0.05	−0.30**	−0.13
Unreality	−0.27*	−0.25*	−0.30*
CDS Total Score	−0.14	−0.19	−0.10
JOLO (adjusted raw score)	0.13	0.24*	-

Note. †$p < 0.1$, *$p < 0.05$, **$p < 0.01$.

relationships between selflessness and transcendence was conducted (unpublished to date). Theoretically, according to the proposed model, if RIPL functioning (i.e., JOLO) improves over time, then experiences of selflessness (i.e., CDS) and spirituality should decrease (i.e., BMMRS). Conversely, if RIPL functioning declines over time, then experiences of selflessness and spirituality should increase. To test this hypothesis, a sample of individuals with neurological conditions but different expectations for recovery was recruited, including individuals expected to improve over time (i.e., ABI) and individuals expecting to decline over time (i.e., MS). Change scores between Time 2 (one year post-baseline) and Time 1 (baseline) were compared in terms of selflessness (i.e., CDS total score, 6 CDS factors), spirituality (i.e., BMMRS positive and negative spirituality), and RIPL-related functioning (i.e., JOLO) for the entire sample.

As hypothesized, Pearson correlations indicated that all measures of selflessness and spirituality were negatively correlated, with 6 of 14 being statistically significant (see Table 3.4). Overall, as selflessness increased, so did spiritual transcendence. Of note, those CDS selflessness factors indicative of broader disintegration (i.e., total score, disintegrated bodily sensations, disintegrated cognition, disintegrated context) were more frequently significantly associated with spiritual transcendence, compared to CDS selflessness factors suggestive of disintegration of more specific processes (e.g., disintegrated taste/smell, disintegrated space). These results suggest that more generalized experiences of selflessness serve as a neuropsychological foundation for spiritual transcendence, consistent with the description of spiritually transcendent experiences throughout history.

Pearson correlations were also calculated for change scores between measures of RIPL functioning and selflessness, and RIPL functioning and spiritual transcendence. Results indicated that the RIPL change scores were negatively correlated with

TABLE 3.4 Longitudinal Correlations

	BMMRS Factors		*JOLO (Adjusted Raw Score)*
CDS Factors	*Positive Spiritual Experience*	*Negative Spiritual Experience*	
Bodily Sensations	−0.33*	−0.42**	−0.31*
Space	−0.06	−0.14	−0.09
Taste and Smell	−0.20	−0.12	0.02
Cognitive	−0.26*	−0.25*	−0.26*
Affect	−0.02	−0.16	−0.01
Unreality	−0.18	−0.42**	−0.30*
CDS Total Score	−0.25†	−0.40*	−0.12
JOLO (adjusted raw score)	0.16	0.07	

Note. †$p < 0.1$, *$p < 0.05$, **$p < 0.01$.

six of seven indices of selflessness, with three being statistically significant (i.e., disintegrated bodily sensations, disintegrated cognition, disintegrated context). Overall, as hypothesized, these results indicate that decreased RIPL functioning over time is associated with increased experiences of selflessness.

In addition, decreasing RIPL functioning over time was associated with higher spiritual transcendence (as hypothesized), although the results were non-significant. These results generally suggest that changes in RIPL functioning are primarily related to changes in indices of selflessness, and less so spirituality, which may relate to the fact that "selflessness" can be considered to be a more pure neuropsychological process, whereas spirituality is related to both neurologic (i.e., RIPL networks) and environmental factors (e.g., religious beliefs and practices).

We believe that this is the first study in which empirical measures of selflessness have been shown to be correlated with empirical measures of spiritual transcendence in a longitudinal study, i.e., that RIPL-based experiences of selflessness form the neuropsychological foundation for spiritually transcendent experiences. These results also suggest that selflessness and spiritual transcendence are empirically distinct constructs from which the neurosciences and humanities can collaborate in the future to better understand, and hopefully influence, humans' relationship to the divine.

The Neuroanatomy of Selflessness

A secondary focus of our JTF project was to use fMRI to identify the neuroanatomical regions/networks associated with selflessness and spiritual transcendence. It was hypothesized that all indices of selflessness would be significantly associated with RIPL-related networks (i.e., where integration hypothetically occurs for all individual neuropsychological processes), but that distinct networks throughout the brain would be associated with distinct disintegrated neuropsychological processes (e.g., sensations, emotions, thoughts, behaviors).

For this (unpublished) study, participants included 53 individuals with diverse neurological conditions who had usable fMRI data. Pearson correlations were conducted between the identified RIPL-related networks of interest and subjective experiences of selflessness (i.e., CDS total score; six CDS factors; see Table 3.5). As hypothesized, all CDS selflessness factors were significantly correlated with at least one RIPL-related network, suggesting that the RIPL (or more generally the right hemisphere association area; conjunction of the frontal, parietal, and temporal lobes) is the general neuroanatomical region in which neuropsychological processes are integrated.

Furthermore, as hypothesized, measures of general selflessness (i.e., CDS total score, disintegrated space, disintegrated context) and disintegrated neurological outputs (i.e., disintegrated emotions, disintegrated cognition) were significantly correlated with the most RIPL-related networks, consistent with the diverse distribution of cognitive processes (i.e., attention, memory, language, visual-spatial,

TABLE 3.5 Correlations between fMRI Data and CDS Factors

	CDS Total	*Bodily Sensation*	*Disintegrated Context*	*Emotional*	*Cognitive*	*Taste and Smell*	*Space*
IPL_R_1	0.17	0.08	0.06	0.24 *	0.08	-0.066	−0.04
IPL_R_3	−0.14	−0.16	0.18	−0.08	−0.24*	0.05	−0.22±
IPL_R_4	0.26*	0.05	0.14	0.26*	0.15	0.03	0.001
IPL_R_5	0.18	0.18	0.19	0.14	0.21	0.07	0.24*
IPL_R_6	0.16	0.20	0.33*	0.24*	0.30*	0.06	0.29*
IPL_R_7	0.14	0.07	0.24*	0.18	0.10	0.18	0.10
IPL_R_8	0.19	0.26*	0.29*	0.32*	0.23	0.07	0.20
IPL_R_9	0.28*	0.10	0.21	0.33**	0.35**	0.10	0.17
IPL_R_10	−0.07	−0.17	−0.24*	−0.02	−0.09	−0.13	−0.28*
IPL_R_13	−0.11	−0.12	−0.15	−0.11	−0.17	0.28*	−0.14
IPL_R_15	0.26*	−0.08	0.05	0.11	0.17	0.02	−0.10
IPL_R_17	−0.27*	−0.06	0.12	0.09	0.25*	−0.02	−0.01
IPL_R_19	0.14	0.11	0.23	0.29*	0.22	0.15	0.10
IPL_R_21	0.07	0.17	0.02	0.02	−0.03	0.25*	0.13
IPL_R_24	0.10	0.14	0.22	0.25*	0.14	0.09	0.14

± $p < 0.01$, * $p < 0.05$, ** $p < 0.001$.
IPL_R= Right inferior parietal lobe.

executive) and emotional experiences (e.g., anger, sadness, happiness, fear, shame, disgust, surprise) across the brain. The results specifically indicated that disintegrated emotion is associated with RIPL-based networks within both right and left hemispheres, as well as frontal, temporal, parietal, and occipital lobes. Similarly, disintegrated cognition is also associated with RIPL-based networks within both the right and left hemispheres, including frontal, temporal, and insular cortices.

In contrast to these measures of general selflessness, indices of relatively distinct disintegrated processes (i.e., disintegrated bodily sensations, disintegrated taste/smell) were significantly related to fewer RIPL-related networks, reflecting the relatively specific neurologic pathways associated with individual sensations.

The Neuroanatomy of Transcendence

A second (unpublished) study was conducted to identify the neuroanatomical correlates of spiritual transcendence (Table 3.6). Again, the results confirmed that all measures of transcendence were significantly associated with at least one RIPL-related network. As hypothesized, all BMMRS spirituality factors were significantly correlated with RIPL-related networks (eight within the right hemisphere, three within the left hemisphere), suggesting the RIPL is the general region in which neuropsychological processes are integrated. In this study, several RIPL-related networks were consistently related to the different indices of spirituality, including the RIPL-right medial temporal gyrus network (with positive spirituality, negative spirituality, and forgiveness), the RIPL-right inferior frontal gyrus network (with both positive and negative spirituality), and the RIPL-right superior parietal lobe network (with negative spirituality and forgiveness). It was concluded that these results generally support the neuropsychological model that suggests that RIPL-networks, and particularly RIPL-networks associated with the right medial temporal gyrus, the right superior parietal lobe, and the right inferior frontal gyrus, serve as the neuroanatomical foundations for spiritually transcendent experiences.

Moving Forward

Overall, these studies generally confirm the hypotheses and suggest that empirically distinct measures of selflessness (that are generally integrated in the RIPL) serve as a neuropsychological foundation of spiritual transcendence. These findings suggest that religion may be best conceptualized in terms of cognitive, behavioral, and emotional processes, but that spirituality may be best conceptualized in terms of the neuropsychological process that integrates individual processes to create experiences of relationship, and specifically the experience of selflessness that results from the disintegration of neuropsychological processes.

Selflessness and an Undivided Unity

Although these studies identify selflessness as a neuropsychological foundation of spiritually transcendent experiences, the need exists to identify the neuropsychological foundations of the experience of an "undivided unity." The sciences have been unable to adequately define and measure such experiences, although the humanities may be able to best guide future research in this area. For example, religious mystics and humanities scholars throughout history have made distinctions between the experiences of a finite consciousness (i.e., a self) and the experiences of an infinite/universal/ unitary consciousness (Stace, 1960; Taves, 2020). Similarly, the nature of the self has been addressed philosophically in terms of "centers

TABLE 3.6 Correlations between fMRI Data and BMMRS Factors

	Positive Spirituality	*Negative Spirituality*	*Forgiveness*
IPL_R_4	*−0.24**	0.15	*0.29**
IPL_R_5	−0.01	−0.09	*0.24**
IPL_R_7	0.08	0.11	*0.27**
IPL_R_8	−0.07	*−0.32**	0.05
IPL_R_9	0.05	0.08	*0.28**
IPL_R_12	*0.27**	*−0.27**	*0.28**
IPL_R_18	0.21	*0.34**	*0.26**

± $p < 0.10$, * $p < 0.05$, ** $p < 0.01$.
IPL_R = Right inferior parietal lobe.

of narrative gravity" (Dennett, 1993) or an "ego tunnel" (Metzinger, 2009), as well as according to the unified field theory in the sciences (McTaggart, 2008). Regardless of whether spiritual transcendence is studied from the perspectives of the sciences or humanities, the current studies suggest that they should focus on selflessness as a scientific and theological foundation of such experiences.

Assessing Spiritual Transcendence

The findings of our JTF study also suggest a need for different ways to both conceptualize and assess this integrative neuropsychological process that creates experiences of selflessness. Whereas individual neuropsychological processes (e.g., attention, memory, language, visual-spatial, executive skills) are generally assessed quantitatively (i.e., more/less), it has been suggested that the integrative process that creates experiences of relationship needs to be conceptualized and measured according to three distinct components including qualitatively, quantitatively, and the center of experience/point of reference from which these integrated processes are experienced (Johnstone et al., 2025c).

Qualitative Relationship. The model suggests that it is first necessary to identify the specific neuropsychological processes that are, or are not, integrated into the unified experience/sense of self. This involves identifying individual processes that may be disintegrated (e.g., tactile sensations in asomatognosia, thoughts in schizophrenia, emotions in alexithymia) or the general disintegration of all processes (e.g., depersonalization, anosognosia).

Quantitative Relationship. The model further suggests that the experience of relationship needs to be measured quantitatively in terms of the degree of experienced relationship (e.g., high/low, more/less). For example, jamais vu experiences can be conceptualized as examples of mild disintegration (i.e., a mild degree of relationship is experienced), whereas asomatognosia can be conceptualized as an example of more severe disintegration (e.g., no degree of relationship to the arm exists).

Center of Experience. Different from how other singular neuropsychological processes are conceptualized and assessed, it is suggested that the center of experience from which these integrated processes are experienced needs to be identified. For example, neuropsychological processes are typically integrated so that they are experienced as occurring within the brain/body (typically behind the eyes), which is the default experience of this integrative process. However, this center of experience/point of reference can also exist outside of the body, as evidenced by out-of-body experiences (OBEs) and near-death experiences (NDEs). Individuals have reported both OBEs and NDEs, including experiences in which individuals report observing themselves from above in an operating room, flying through space during a psychedelic trip, or traveling through a tunnel during NDEs (Blackmore, 2019). During these experiences, a center of experience exists (i.e., a unified experience/sense of self), but one that is centered outside of the brain/body. In fact, experimental studies have also shown that neurostimulation to the brain (and particularly inhibition of RIPL functioning) can create the sensation that one's center of experience can exist several feet behind one's actual body (Blanke, 2012; Blanke et al., 2004; Lenggenhager et al., 2007).

Whereas the previous examples involve the experience of a self, whether within or outside of the body, other experiences have been reported throughout history in which the "normal" experience of the self can be dissolved (i.e., experiences of selflessness) and self/other boundaries obliterated so that no individual sense of self exists. In contrast to experiences of an integrated self that is centered in the body/brain, these experiences of selflessness apparently involve the experience of becoming part of (i.e., being integrated into) a broader experience. Although there are no commonly accepted neuropsychological models to explain such varied experiences of centeredness, they may be best conceptualized in terms of a finite consciousness (i.e., centered within the body/brain) versus an infinite consciousness (i.e., as part of a universal experience; Taves, 2020). Novel research is needed to assess these experiences of "decentering" (McNamara, 2022), which can benefit from collaboration between the neurosciences and the humanities, given their long-standing interest in such experiences.

Practical Implications

Lastly, consistent with the goals of the JTF, these findings can be used to provide a bridge between the neurosciences and humanities to better understand the nature of humanity. Whereas scientists may be able to explain the neuropsychological mechanisms associated with religious and spiritual experiences, clinicians, clergy, and scholars from the humanities need to direct practices and research in this area to provide meaning to the findings and to enhance existing practices (i.e., religious, spiritual, psychological) and develop novel interventions (e.g., entheogens, technologies) to improve our health, thriving, and relationships to the cosmos and divine.

References

Aftanas, L. I., & Golocheikine, S. A. (2001). Human anterior and frontal midline theta and lower alpha reflect emotionally positive state and internalized attention: High-resolution EEG investigation of meditation. *Neuroscience Letters, 310*, 57–60.

APA Dictionary of Psychology. (n.d.). *Transcendence*. https://dictionary.apa.org/transcendence

Azari, N., Nickel, J., Wunderlich, G., Niedeggen, M., Hefter, H., Tellmann, L., Herzog, H., Stoerig, P., Birnbacher, D., & Seitz, R. J. (2001). Neural correlates of religious experience. *European Journal of Neuroscience, 13*, 1649–1652.

Blackmore, S. (2019). *Seeing myself: The new science of out-of-body experiences*. Robinson.

Blanke, O. (2012). Multisensory brain mechanisms of bodily self-consciousness. *Nature Reviews Neuroscience, 13*(8), 556–571. https://doi.org/10.1038/nrn3292

Blanke, O., Landis, T., Spinelli, L., & Seeck, M. (2004). Out-of-body experience and autoscopy of neurologic origin. *Brain, 27*, 243–258. https://doi.org/10.1093/brain/awh040

Blevins, C. A., Witte, T. K., & Weathers, F. W. (2013). Factor structure of the Cambridge depersonalization scale in trauma-exposed college students. *Journal of Trauma Dissociation, 14*, 288–301.

Breen, N., Caine, D., Coltheart, M. Hendy, J., & Roberts, C. (2000). Towards an understanding of delusions of misidentification: Four case studies. *Mind & Language, 15*(1), 74–110. https://doi.org/10.1111/1468-0017.00124

Canby, N. K., Lindahl, J., Britton, W. B., & Córdova, J. V. (2024). Clarifying and measuring the characteristics of experiences that involve a loss of self or a dissolution of its boundaries. *Consciousness and Cognition, 119*, 103655. https://doi.org/10.1016/j.concog.2024.103655

Cristofori, I., Cohen-Zimerman, S., Bulbulia, J., Gordon, B., Krueger, F., & Grafman, J. (2022). The neural underpinning of religious beliefs: Evidence from brain lesions. *Frontiers in Behavioral Neuroscience*, *16*, 977600.

Dennett, D. C. (1993). *Consciousness explained.* Penguin.

Enoch, D., & Ball, H. (2002). *Uncommon psychiatric syndromes* (4th ed). Alder.

Fagioli, F., Telesforo, L., Dell'Erba, A., Consolazione, M., Migliorini, V., Patanè, M., … & Fiori-Nastro, P. (2015). Depersonalization: An exploratory factor analysis of the Italian version of the Cambridge Depersonalization Scale. *Comprehensive Psychiatry, 60*, 161–167.

Feinberg, T. E., DeLuca, J., Giacino, J. T., Roane, D. M., & Solms, M. (2005). Right hemisphere pathology and the self: Delusional misidentification and reduplication. In T. E. Feinberg & J. P. Keenan (Eds.), *The lost self: Pathologies of the brain and identity* (pp. 100–130). Oxford University Press.

Feinberg, T. E., & Keenan, J. P. (Eds.). (2005). *The lost self: Pathologies of the brain and identity*. Oxford University Press.

Grafman, J., Cristofori, I., Zhong, W., & Bulbulia, J. (2020). The neural basis of religious cognition. *Current Directions in Psychological Science*, *29*(2), 126–133.

Hecht, D. (2010). Schizophrenia, the sense of "self" and the right cerebral hemisphere. *Medical Hypotheses, 74*, 186–188. https://doi.org/10.1016/j.mehy.2009.07.032

Herzog, H., Lele, V. R., Kuwert, T., Langen, K. J, Kops, E. R., & Feinendegen, L. E. (1990–91). Changed pattern of regional glucose metabolism during Yoga meditative relaxation. *Neuropsychobiology, 23,* 182–187.

James, W. (1902). *The varieties of religious experience* (Vol. 13). Harvard University Press.

Johnstone, B., Bayan, S., Gutierrez, L., Lardizabal, D., Lanigar, S., Yoon, D. P., & Judd, K. (2014). Neuropsychological correlates of forgiveness. *Religion, Brain, and Behavior, 5*, 24–35.

Johnstone, B., Bhushan, B., Hanks, R., Yoon, D. P., & Cohen, D. (2016). Factor structure of the Brief Multidimensional Measure of Religiousness/Spirituality in US and Indian Samples with traumatic brain injury. *Journal of Religion and Health, 55*(2), 572–586. https://doi.org/10.1007/s10943-015-0170-y

Johnstone, B., Bodling, A., Cohen, D., Christ, S. E., & Wegrzyn, A. (2012). Right parietal lobe-related "selflessness" as the neuropsychological basis of spiritual transcendence. *International Journal for the Psychology of Religion, 22*(4), 267–284. https://doi.org/10.1080/10508619.2012.657524

Johnstone, B., Bruininks, P., Smith, E. I., Yoon, D. P., Cohen, D., Edman, L., Bankard, J., & Witvliet, C. (2021). Conceptualising spirituality and religion as psychological processes:

Validation of the factor structure of the BMMRS. *Mental Health, Religion & Culture, 24*(3), 316–332. https://doi.org/10.1080/13674676.2020.1793311

Johnstone, B., & Cohen, D. (2019). *Neuroscience, selflessness, and spiritual experience: Explaining the science of transcendence* (1st ed.). Academic Press, an imprint of Elsevier.

Johnstone, B., Cohen, D., Anderson, R., Dennison, A. C., & Bosque, L. (2025a). Reconceptualizing disorders of the self as disorders of relationship. *Archives of Physical Medicine and Rehabilitation*, S0003999324014230. https://doi.org/10.1016/j.apmr.2024.12.019

Johnstone, B., Cohen, D., & Dennison, A. (2021). The integration of sensations and mental experiences into a unified experience: A neuropsychological model for the "sense of self." *Neuropsychologia, 159*, 107939. https://doi.org/10.1016/j.neuropsychologia.2021.107939

Johnstone, B., Cohen, D., Konopacki, K., & Ghan, C. (2016). Selflessness as a foundation of spiritual transcendence: Perspectives from the neurosciences and religious studies. *The International Journal for the Psychology of Religion, 26*(4), 287–303. https://doi.org/10.1080/10508619.2015.1118328

Johnstone, B., Cohen, D., Thompson, N., Dennison, A., & Bosque, L. (2025b). Empirical validation of "selflessness" as a neuropsychological foundation of spiritual transcendence. *Psychology of Religion and Spirituality*. Advance online publication https://psycnet.apa.org/doi/10.1037/rel0000593

Johnstone, B., & Glass, B. A. (2008). Support for a neuropsychological model of spirituality in persons with traumatic brain injury. *Zygon, 43*(4), 861–874. https://doi.org/10.1111/j.1467-9744.2008.00964.x

Johnstone, B., Hanks, R., Bhushan, B., Cohen, D., Roseberry, J., & Yoon, D. P. (2017). Selflessness as a universal neuropsychological foundation of spiritual transcendence: Validation with Christian, Hindu, and Muslim traditions. *Mental Health, Religion & Culture, 20*(2), 175–187. https://doi.org/10.1080/13674676.2017.1333090

Johnstone, B., Smith, E., & Cohen, D. (2025c). Neuropsychological integration, a sense of relationship, and the self as unified experience. *Archives of Clinical Neuropsychology, 40(8)*, 1581–1591. https://doi.org/10.1093/arclin/acaf056

Johnstone, B., Yoon, D. P., Franklin, K. L., Schopp, L., & Hinkebein, J. (2009). Re-conceptualizing the factor structure of the Brief Multidimensional Measure of Religiousness/Spirituality. *Journal of Religion and Health, 48*(2), 146–163. https://doi.org/10.1007/s10943-008-9179-9

Lenggenhager, B., Tadi, T., Metzinger, T., & Blanke, O. (2007). Video ergo sum: Manipulating bodily self-consciousness. *Science, 317(*5841*)*, 1096–1099. https://doi.org/10.1126/science.1143439

Lifshitz, M., van Elk, M., & Luhrmann, T. M. (2019). Absorption and spiritual experience: A review of evidence and potential mechanisms. *Consciousness and Cognition, 73*, 102760. https://doi.org/10.1016/j.concog.2019.05.008

McNamara, P. (2009). *The neuroscience of religious experience*. Cambridge University Press.

McNamara, P. (2022). *The cognitive neuroscience of religious experience: Decentering and the self.* Cambridge University Press.

McNamara, P., Durso, R. Brown, A., & Harris, E. (2006). The chemistry of religiosity: Evidence from patients with Parkinson's disease. In P. McNamara (Ed.), *Where God and science meet: The neurology of religious experience* (Vol. 2, pp. 1–14). Praeger.

McNamara, P., & Grafman, J. (2024). Advances in brain and religion studies: A review and synthesis of recent representative studies. *Frontiers in Human Neuroscience, 18*, 1495565.

McNamara, P., Newsome, W., Linkenhoker, B., & Grafman, J. (2024). Neuroscientists must not be afraid to study religion. *Nature, 631*(8019), 25–27.

McTaggart, L. (2008). *The field: Our quest for the secret force of the universe*. Harper.

Metzinger, T. (2009). *The ego tunnel: The science of the mind and the myth of the self.* Basic Books.

Newberg, A. B., Alavi, A., Baime, M., Mozley, P. D., & d'Aquili, E. G. (1997). The measurement of cerebral blood flow during the complex cognitive task of meditation using HMPAO-SPECT imaging. *Journal of Nuclear Medicine, 38*, 95.

Newberg, A. B., Alavi, A., Baime, M., Pourdehnad, M., Santanna, J., & d'Aquili, E. G. (2001). The measurement of regional cerebral blood flow during the complex cognitive task of meditation: A preliminary SPECT study. *Psychiatry Research: Neuroimaging, 106*, 113–122.

Newberg, A. B., Pourdehnad, M., Alavi, A., & d'Aquili, E. G. (2003). Cerebral blood flow during meditative prayer: Preliminary findings and methodological issues. *Perceptual and Motor Skills, 97,* 625–630.

Northoff, G., Heinzel, A., de Greek, M., Bermpohl, F., Dobrowolny, H., & Panksepp, J. (2006). Self-referential processing in the brain: A meta-analysis of imaging studies on the self. *Neuroimage, 31*(1), 440–457. https://doi.org/10.1016/j.neuroimage.2005.12.002

Saver, J. L., & Rabin. J. (1997). The neural substrates of religious experience. *The Journal of Neuropsychiatry and Clinical Neurosciences, 9,* 498–510.

Sierra, M., Baker, D., Medford, N., & David, A. S. (2005). Unpacking the depersonalization syndrome: An exploratory factor analysis on the Cambridge Depersonalization Scale. *Psychological Medicine. 35,* 1523–1532.

Sierra, M., & Berrios, G. E. (2000). The Cambridge Depersonalisation Scale: A new instrument for the measurement of depersonalisation. *Psychiatry research, 93*(2), 153–164.

Stace, W. (1960). *Mysticism and philosophy*. St. Martin's Press.

Taves, A. (2020). Mystical and other alterations in sense of self: An expanded framework for studying nonordinary experiences. *Perspectives on Psychological Science, 15*(3), 669–690.

Tranel, D., Vianna, E., Manzel, K., Damasio, H., & Grabowski, T. (2009). Neuroanatomical correlates of the Benton facial recognition test and judgment of line orientation test. *Journal of Clinical and Experimental Neuropsychology, 31(2),* 219–233. https://doi.org/10.1080/13803390802317542. PMID: 19051129; PMCID: PMC2853018.

Uddin, L. Q., Molnar-Szakacs, I., Zaidel, E., & Iacoboni, M. (2006). rTMS to the right inferior parietal lobule disrupts self–other discrimination. *Social Cognitive and Affective Neuroscience, 1*(1), 65–71. https://doi.org/10.1093/scan/nsl003

Urgesi, C., Aglioti, S. M., Skrap, M, & Fabbro, F. (2010). The spiritual brain: Selective cortical lesions modulate human self-transcendence. *Neuron, 65,* 309–319.

4

THE BODILY INSTANTIATION OF SPIRITUAL FEELINGS

Self-Transcendence and the Predictive Processing of Body Signals

Cosimo Urgesi

Recent advances in cognitive neuroscience have made it possible to address the issue of the cerebral localization of highly complex functions that underpin human self- and body-awareness, and the representation of the social world. Related to these advances is the dramatic increase in research interest in the neural underpinnings of the mental processes called into play during spiritual experiences. Spirituality is the complex pattern of feelings, thoughts, and behaviors (Paloutzian & Park, 2005) that reflects a view of the human condition in self-transcendent contexts and in relation to unseen realities/supernatural agents. Here, a general definition of spirituality is adopted (Paloutzian & Park, 2005) where the human being is seen in a transcendent context, that is, in relation to a world that is not assumed to be entirely transparent to his sense modalities, thus allowing for the existence of a "Beyond" or whatever one may define the "Sacred." This definition of spirituality conceives it as a pattern of feelings, thoughts, and behaviors that may be expressed individually or in a community, as a subjective form of activity independent of a specific faith tradition (Emmons & Paloutzian, 2003).

Neural Bases of Spiritual States and Traits

Spirituality is correlated to biological processes of the highest level of complexity that are instantiated in the human brain and become manifest in specific circumstances (states) or as stable aspects of the personality of an individual (traits). State changes involve at least altered sensory, cognitive, and self-referential awareness, which can arise, for example, during meditation or prayer. Although spiritual experiences are not limited to meditative states, reaching higher forms of self-awareness linked to spirituality is searched for by practitioners of different forms of meditation. Modifications of self-awareness during spiritual experiences include assuming

DOI: 10.4324/9781003158189-4

an allocentric perspective, a feeling of transcendence from one's own thoughts and from contingent sensorimotor body schema representation, and a feeling of an extended self (Cahn & Polich, 2006). Insofar as modifications of self-awareness constitute one of the fundamental components of mystic experiences, the study of spirituality provides us a window into the study of self-representation. Indeed, the feeling of being out of the physical constraints of the human body and the sense of belonging to a unitary whole is what is experienced and searched for by practitioners of meditation across different cultural and religious traditions. Importantly, modifications of self-awareness seem to outlast the actual practice of meditation or prayer, and to induce lasting changes in these dimensions that persist in meditators also when they are not actively engaged in meditation or prayer (i.e., a trait change). Indeed, meditators evaluate themselves and are evaluated by others as being more peaceful and as having an increased feeling of well-being, perceptual awareness, and persistent transcendental self-representations (Cahn & Polich, 2006).

Neuroscientific studies have so far explored the modification of neural activity associated with both spiritual states and traits. State changes related to spiritual experiences have been addressed using electroencephalography (EEG) and event-related potentials (ERPs), or neuroimaging techniques like functional magnetic resonance imaging (fMRI) or positron emission tomography (PET) to measure changes of brain activity during meditation and prayer in both naïve and expert meditators (Beauregard & Paquette, 2006, 2008; Cahn & Polich, 2006; Grafman et al., 2020; Lutz et al., 2009; Newberg et al., 2001; Newberg, 2014; Taylor et al., 2011).

Despite the fact that different brain imaging techniques have been used, and that various types of spiritual experiences and features of participants have been examined, all studies converge in suggesting that spiritual experiences consistently engage key regions such as the prefrontal and cingulate cortices, temporal and parietal areas, thalamus, amygdala, and hypothalamus (review in Newberg & Iversen, 2003). Prefrontal and cingulate cortices, which are involved in the focusing of attention, show an increase of neural activation during meditation and prayer, while the posterior parietal cortex seems to be deactivated, particularly in the right hemisphere. Since this area is involved in the representation of the multiple sensations converging into the construction of the body schema (Berlucchi & Aglioti, 1997, 2010), it has been suggested that such a parietal deafferentation would reflect a reduced or altered sense of one's own body in space (Newberg & Iversen, 2003). Indeed, an important component of spirituality may be associated with transcendental representations of the self. In particular, the reduced awareness of self-other boundaries that often accompanies spiritual experiences may lead to experiences of detachment from the spatiotemporal constraints of the physical body, together with increased feelings of connectedness with a larger reality and with religious or spiritual power (Emmons & Paloutzian, 2003; Fuller, 2008; Paloutzian & Park, 2005).

Such neurocognitive markers accompany expert meditators beyond meditative states and sustain long-lasting changes of individual self-awareness triggered by meditation practice (Cahn & Polich, 2006; Lutz et al., 2004). Studies have indeed compared the structural and functional brain anatomy of people of faith, such as Catholic nuns, Buddhist monks, or experts in different forms of meditation, with that of individuals with no experience in meditation. Differences in cortical thickness have been reported between expert meditators and non-meditators in temporoparietal and prefrontal areas (Hölzel et al., 2008, 2011; Lazar et al., 2005), suggesting that the differences in cognitive and emotional styles of expert meditators may correlate with differences in brain anatomy. Meditation experiences also induce changes in the neural (insula and limbic structures) and psychophysiological responses to the pain of others (Lutz et al., 2008), and in the neurocognitive structures involved in sustained and focused attention (Lutz et al., 2007, 2009). These effects are particularly evident in expert meditators, showing that the ability to experience extended self-representations may induce long-lasting facilitation of affective empathy and attention.

Neural Bases of Self-transcendence

The ability to experience a detachment from current body perceptions and actions and to project self-images into past or future scenarios is inherently linked to human beings (Morin, 2006). However, people differ in their predispositions to spiritual feeling, thinking, and behavior, independently of their meditation expertise and state. Thus, spirituality is an important dimension of personality, as it involves enduring dispositions which are associated with consistent patterns of behavior, thoughts, and feelings that make each individual unique.

According to a widely known psychobiological model of personality, interindividual differences in spiritual feeling and thinking are detected by the Temperament and Character Inventory (TCI; Cloninger et al., 1993), a personality inventory which allows measuring seven temperament and character dimensions, including a supposedly stable personality dimension called Self-transcendence (ST). ST reflects the enduring tendency to transcend contingent sensorimotor representations and to identify the self as an integral part of the universe as a whole. The ST scale from the TCI captures important aspects of spirituality, such as connectedness, a belief in being part of a broader human reality that cuts across places, generations, and groups. Indeed, ST allows detecting interindividual differences in the transcendental representations of the self in relation to the world (Self-forgetfulness), to other people (Transpersonal identification), and to supernatural entities/dimensions (Spiritual acceptance). It is worth noting that ST seems to be only minimally culture-bound, and thus it is thought to be measurable independently of the specific backgrounds of participants.

ST has been widely used in neuroscience studies as a measure of interindividual differences in spiritual attitude. In particular, studies using functional and structural MRI have found specific correlations between ST and metabolic activity (Turner et al., 2003) and gray matter density (Kaasinen et al., 2005) in prefrontal and temporoparietal areas. In keeping with studies on meditation states and traits, individuals with higher ST scores tend to have higher activity at rest and higher gray matter density in the prefrontal cortex and lower activity at rest and gray matter density in the temporoparietal cortices. The correlational approach adopted by these studies, however, cannot establish whether functional and structural brain markers associated with spiritual attitudes indexed by ST actively determine inter-individual differences in cognitive and emotional styles or are epiphenomenal to them.

To investigate the causative involvement of brain activity on ST, a previous neuropsychological study (Urgesi et al., 2010) tested 24 patients with high-grade gliomas and 24 patients with low-grade gliomas involving the anterior or posterior brain areas in the left or right hemispheres. The comparison of ST scores obtained by patients before and after surgery revealed that the removal of high- and low-grade gliomas affecting the posterior brain areas induced a selective increase of ST, independently of which hemisphere was affected. Whereas posterior high-grade glioma patients had higher ST scores than anterior high-grade glioma patients both before and after surgery, posterior low-grade glioma patients presented higher ST scores than anterior low-grade glioma patients only after surgical removal of brain tissue. Thus, the specificity of the anatomo-clinical correlation between the neurofunctional state of the posterior parietal cortex and ST was supported by the definite modulation of the ST increase according to the localization in the brain (posterior vs. anterior areas) and the histological malignancy and growth rate (high vs. low grade) of the tumors. To determine the duration of the effect, a different group of 20 patients who had been operated for the first time 2–48 months before testing was also enrolled in the same study (Urgesi et al., 2010). Their evaluation showed that posterior patients still had higher ST scores than anterior patients several months after surgery, thus pointing to the persistence over time of the ST increase induced by damage to posterior areas. To rule out any non-specific effects of craniotomy on the ST increase observed in patients with gliomas, a group of 20 patients with brain meningiomas was also tested before and after surgery. As meningiomas do not involve the brain tissue, no effect of surgery was expected. Accordingly, comparing ST scores obtained by patients with meningiomas involving anterior or posterior areas revealed no consistent effect.

In sum, this neuropsychological study (Urgesi et al., 2010) found a specific increase of ST after removal of high- and low-grade gliomas affecting the posterior areas of the brain. The site specificity of the effect rules out that the ST increase may be ascribed to non-specific changes of self-conceptions and life perspectives that may have occurred as psychological complications of the awareness of suffering from tumors. Furthermore, no specific change of other personality dimensions depending on the lesion site was observed. In keeping with the evidence that visuo-spatial deficits induced by parietal traumatic brain damage correlate with measures of spirituality (Johnstone & Glass, 2008), the results showed the crucial role of parietal areas in determining ST. Furthermore, they suggested that changes in neural activity in temporoparietal areas may induce modulations of stable personality traits related to transcendental self-referential awareness.

Given that ST attempts to capture the individual differences in a large part of the sorts of states and traits that are normally associated with spirituality, as defined above, this suggests the possible association between the identified brain areas and spiritual inclinations. However, the ST scale of TCI requires subjective, explicit evaluations of the responders on their own thinking, feeling, and behaviors, which may be influenced by cultural understanding of terms, emotional states, and social pressure. Not only that, several studies have documented that a large part of our mental activity is not made explicit to consciousness, and several measures have been developed to test the implicit attitude of the responders toward specific objects (Nosek et al., 2011).

Neural Bases of Implicit Spiritual Attitudes

To address the concerns related to the use of explicit measures to measure religiosity and spirituality, further studies (Crescentini et al., 2014a, 2014b, 2015) have adapted the implicit association test (IAT; Greenwald et al., 1998) to indirectly infer people's implicit associations between the self and spiritual/religious concepts. The IAT uses a word categorization task to measure the strength of automatic concept-attribute associations, assuming that strongly associated concept-attribute pairs are easier to classify together, by pressing the same response key, compared to weakly associated pairs. The spiritual/religious IAT evaluates the association between words referring to the concept of self (e.g., me, mine, etc.) or other (e.g., them, you, etc.) and words associated with religious/spiritual (e.g., spirit, divine, etc.) or of non-religious/non-spiritual (e.g., physical, atheist, etc.) attributes, ultimately providing a measure of the varying levels with which people automatically perceive the self as more religious/spiritual than non-religious/non-spiritual. A self-esteem IAT procedure can be used to control for general associations of positive versus negative attributes to the self. Using these measures, Crescentini and colleagues (2014, 2015) showed that altering with non-invasive brain stimulation the excitability of the temporoparietal cortex, in particular of an area (temporoparietal junction, TPJ) that is critical for the representation of the body and the self (Blanke & Mohr, 2005), may induce fast plastic changes of implicit spirituality/religiosity in healthy individuals. In a first study (Crescentini et al., 2014a), the left or right TPJ was targeted with paired-pulse transcranial magnetic stimulation (TMS), a type of stimulation known to transiently disrupt the activity of the stimulated regions. This led participants to more strongly associate the self with spiritual/religious attributes compared to when the TMS targeted the left or right dorsolateral prefrontal cortex. In the second study (Crescentini et al., 2015), the authors targeted the same area with inhibitory, excitatory or sham theta burst stimulation, in separate sessions, to, respectively, reduce, enhance, or leave unaltered the excitability of the temporoparietal cortex. Participants' implicit spirituality/religiosity attitudes were reduced after excitatory stimulation of TPJ compared to inhibitory or sham stimulation. These results align well with the neuropsychological studies of patients (Johnstone & Glass, 2008; Urgesi et al., 2010), suggesting that hampering or boosting the processing of bodily signals in the temporoparietal cortex may increase or decrease individuals' implicit spirituality/religiosity. Overall, the temporoparietal cortex seems to serve as a central neurocognitive substrate of implicit spirituality and religiosity, since its down-regulation alteration may lead individuals to experience an extended self-awareness in which the self is projected into dimensions that transcend sensorimotor contingencies of the body and are connected with things beyond the self. These findings can be interpreted in the light of the body deafferentation account of mystical experience (Newberg, 2014; Newberg & Iversen, 2003), according to which spirituality and religiosity are linked to a partial and flexible weakening of the spatial unity between the body and the self.

Dissociating the Neural Bases of Spirituality and Religiosity

The measures used in the previous studies largely confounded spirituality, the more experiential and subjective dimension of understanding and searching for the meaning of life, and religiosity, intended as the institutional aspect of believing in a supernatural being (Paloutzian & Park, 2005). There is ample consensus about the fact that spirituality and religiosity are different concepts, and they may have quite distinct empirical and philosophical treatments (Emmons & Paloutzian, 2003; Paloutzian & Park, 2005). Accordingly, people may report to be spiritual but not religious (Fuller, 2008).

New versions of the IAT procedure have been developed to separately measure spirituality and religiosity (Finisguerra et al., 2019) based on Glock's multidimensional model of religious commitment (Glock, 1962). According to this model, religious commitment can be expressed by five main dimensions: (1) the ideological dimension, reflecting belief in religious doctrines and teachings; (2) the ritualistic dimension, which involves participation in religious practices, such as prayer or attending services; (3) the experiential dimension, referring to personal religious experiences or feelings of connection with the divine; (4) the intellectual dimension, for knowledge about the religion's teachings, scriptures, and history; and (5) the consequential dimension, which entangles the influence of religious beliefs on a person's daily behavior and moral decisions. The spiritual IAT was implemented by selecting words that mapped the experiential dimension, defined as the spiritual, emotional component, and understanding of the meaning of life. Conversely, the religious IAT conflated the ritualistic dimension, defined as the whole body of religious/spiritual rites and practices, and the three cognitive dimensions (i.e., ideological, intellectual, and consequential), defined as the set of descriptions, characteristics, beliefs, and rules associated with a faith. Importantly, a validation of the manipulation of the constructs confirmed that participants evaluated the words used in the spiritual IAT as tapping more the spirituality than the religiosity dimension, while the opposite was reported for the words used in the religious IAT (Finisguerra et al., 2019).

These IATs were used to go deeper into the brain bases of spirituality and religiosity. A reanalysis of the brain tumor data first reported in (Urgesi et al., 2010) revealed that a brain network centered on the periaqueductal gray was associated with changes at the spiritual acceptance, but not at other ST subscales (Ferguson et al., 2022). Importantly, this network intersected a network associated with neuropsychological correlates of self-reported religiosity, pointing to different neural mechanisms mediating the spirituality and religious dimensions, which involve cortical and subcortical structures. According to the bodily deafferentation model of spirituality and religiosity (Newberg, 2014; Newberg & Iversen, 2003), indeed, bodily deafferentation also involves cortical medial and subcortical structures that convey information about the internal state of the body (i.e., interoception). In particular, the parasympathetic-mediated suppression of the activity of the noradrenergic neurons of the locus coeruleus, which are involved in arousal and alerting and project to the posterior parietal cortex, would be crucial in attenuating the influence of sensory input from the body to the parietal cortex in spiritual experiences.

To investigate this mechanism, Finisguerra and colleagues (2019) capitalized on a non-invasive brain stimulation technique, the transcutaneous vagus nerve stimulation (tVNS), that allows a bottom-up approach to brain stimulation. As a key component of the parasympathetic branch of the autonomic nervous system, the vagus nerve carries ascending interoceptive sensory information about internal organs and the enteric nervous system and is, thus, crucial for interoception (Barrett & Simmons, 2015). By delivering electrical pulses to the sensory afferent fibers of the auricular, thick-myelinated branch of the vagus nerve in the outer ear, tVNS activates the nuclei of the nerve located in the brainstem, and, in particular, the nucleus tractus solitarius and locus coeruleus (Yakunina et al., 2017). Accordingly, it has been shown that tVNS improves interoception accuracy in a heartbeat discrimination task, in which participants had to judge whether sequences of auditory tones were synchronous or asynchronous with their heartbeats (Villani et al., 2019).

To test whether the improved interoception abilities during tVNS may impact spirituality and religiosity, Finisguerra and colleagues applied tVNS to the cymba conchae, which has high density of vagus nerve afferents, or to the ear lobe, which is free of cutaneous vagal innervation, while participants performed the spiritual and religious IATs as well as a self-esteem IAT as a control. The results showed that tVNS applied to the cymba conchae reduced the strength to which participants associated the self with spiritual attributes, analogously to the effects observed after inhibition of the temporoparietal cortex with TMS (Crescentini et al., 2014a). This effect, however, was specific to the spiritual IAT and did not extend to the religious or self-esteem IATs, pointing to a neurofunctional dissociation between the spirituality and religiosity constructs. In particular, the results suggest that boosting the processing of sensory internal information may weaken spirituality, but not religiosity.

Spirituality and the Predictive Coding of Internal Bodily Signals

The fact that altering interoceptive processing via tVNS alters spirituality but not religiosity aligns well with a recently proposed framework of spirituality and religiosity (van Elk & Aleman, 2017) as mediated by different predictive processing mechanisms, respectively related to different weighting of perception of internal bodily states and external events. Adopting a predictive processing account of brain functioning (Friston, 2010), this model views the brain as a predictive machine that uses prior knowledge to explain away the sensory evidence coming from the internal (interoceptive) and external (exteroceptive) world. This way, the brain tries to minimize the mismatch between its forecasts and incoming signals (prediction error), updating its internal generative models. In this context, spiritual and religious experiences arise from altered precision-weighting of prediction errors, meaning the brain rebalances how much it relies on priors versus external sensory information. Across different neural systems, how the brain's hierarchical inference mechanisms weight and integrate prediction errors may shape spiritual experiences, agency attribution, and religious belief. In other words, spirituality and religiosity may be associated with greater reliance on priors and/or reduced error monitoring, at the expense of the processing of sensorial evidence. This proposal may explain the positive and negative associations of spirituality and religiosity with schizotypal and autistic traits, respectively (Crespi et al., 2019). Indeed, high schizotypic individuals are prone to rely on priors, whereas high autistic traits individuals favor incoming sensory evidence (Tarasi et al., 2022).

Importantly, van Elk and Aleman (2017) also proposed a neurocognitive distinction between spirituality and religiosity, grounded in differences in phenomenological content (keeping with Glock's multidimensional model of religious commitment), cognitive processing, and underlying brain mechanisms. From a neurocognitive standpoint, spiritual experiences are hypothesized to result from changes in the weighting of interoceptive signals and disruptions in multisensory integration, particularly involving regions of the default mode network (e.g., the posterior cingulate cortex, precuneus) and TPJ. These alterations lead to atypical hierarchical inference and increased susceptibility to internally generated percepts, consistent with mystical or anomalous experiences. In contrast, religiosity relies on theory of mind processes and agency detection, facilitated by regions such as the medial prefrontal cortex, temporoparietal junction, and superior temporal sulcus (Grafman et al., 2020). Furthermore, the anterior cingulate cortex and dorsolateral prefrontal cortex are implicated in sustaining religious beliefs by modulating prediction-error sensitivity, thereby contributing to the stability and persistence of belief despite contradictory evidence. In summary, while both spirituality and religiosity involve hierarchical predictive processes, they may differ in the relative contribution of bottom-up sensory and interoceptive signals (dominant in spirituality) versus top-down social-cognitive and cultural priors about the external world (dominant in religiosity). This distinction supports a nuanced neurocognitive taxonomy of religious and spiritual phenomena within a unified computational framework and allows generation of specific testable predictions, as the effects of sensory or interoceptive manipulation on spiritual experiences.

A recent study (Pyasik et al., *preprint*) aimed to evaluate the changes in the levels of implicit spirituality and religiosity following an experimental manipulation of either prior beliefs or prediction error related to interoception. Seeking causal evidence, the study investigated whether and to what extent inducing a change in the weighting of prior or prediction error related to interoception affects spirituality compared to religiosity. A variant of the heartbeat discrimination task was used in which participants reported whether their heartbeat was faster or slower than a rhythmic sound. Using this task, two preregistered behavioral experiments were conducted. In the first experiment, prior beliefs about heart rate perception were manipulated via sham TMS to the right frontotemporal region (simulating a stimulation of the insula), paired with verbal suggestions that the stimulation would induce participants to perceive their heartbeat as either slower or faster. This manipulation aimed to increase the weight of top-down prior beliefs. In the second experiment, prediction error reliability was manipulated by delivering either true or false error feedback after each trial, thereby modifying the reliability of bottom-up error signals. Both experiments employed the spiritual and religious IATs to assess changes in implicit self-concepts related to spirituality and religiosity after performing the heartbeat discrimination task at baseline or with the experimental manipulation. The results of the first experiment showed that priming the participants with the belief that the sham TMS would lead them to perceive their heartbeat as slower successfully shifted their heartbeat perception in the direction of the induced prior, particularly in individuals who had high autistic traits (and thus likely had low interoceptive prior at baseline). Importantly, boosting prior beliefs led to a significant increase in implicit spirituality, but not religiosity. Indeed, after performing the task with the sham-TMS induced prior, participants showed a stronger association between the self and spiritual attributes; no comparable effects were observed for the association between the self and religious attributes. The results of the second experiment showed that modulating prediction error reliability successfully influenced interoceptive accuracy, since participants were more precise in discriminating their heartbeat when they received true compared to false feedback. This improvement in interoceptive accuracy, however, was not accompanied by a modification of implicit spirituality or religiosity as measured with the spiritual or religious IAT.

These findings provide empirical support for a relation between spirituality and predictive interoceptive processing. A likely explanation for the effects is that increasing the weighting of the beliefs about one's body states decreased the weighting of the actual processing of bodily signals, enhancing the blurring of the boundaries of the self, which is one of the core components of spirituality. Compared to implicit religiosity, implicit spirituality appears more susceptible to top-down modulation of bodily self-representations, consistent with its experiential and embodied nature. These findings support the idea that spirituality is rooted in the perception of bodily signals and experiences (Newberg & Iversen, 2003; van Elk & Aleman, 2017), to the extent that altering the processing of bodily signals is able to change spiritual self-representations.

However, these preliminary results should be corroborated in order to provide further support to the interoceptive predictive processing view of spirituality and religiosity. In particular, supporting the dissociation between spirituality and religiosity would require evidence that altering the predictive processing of the external world would influence implicit religiosity, but not spirituality. In a similar vein, future studies should provide data suggesting that reducing the weight people give to interoceptive priors reduces implicit spirituality, to rule out that the prior induction in Pyasik et al. (preprint) exerted its effects on spirituality merely by enhancing attention to internal bodily signals. While the study looked for such a dissociation with the manipulation of the validity of performance feedback, this enhanced the precision of heartbeat discrimination, but no effects were detected on measures of response bias, suggesting that it did not affect the weighting of prediction error. Finally, future studies should compare the role of the predictive processing of visceral (e.g., cardiac interoception) and somatic (e.g., limb proprioception) signals of the body in shaping self-awareness and spiritual self-representations.

Conclusions

This chapter has provided an integrative overview of the neurocognitive foundations of spirituality, advancing the notion that spiritual experiences emerge from embodied processes rooted in the predictive processing of bodily signals. Drawing on converging evidence from neuropsychological, neuroimaging, behavioral, and brain stimulation studies, it has been shown that alterations in the processing and precision-weighting of bodily signals can modulate implicit spiritual self-representations, while leaving religiosity relatively unaffected. These findings support the view that spirituality, as a form of intrinsic religiosity, is closely tied to dynamic, bottom-up bodily inference mechanisms involving temporoparietal and midline cortical structures, as well as subcortical pathways associated with interoception and parasympathetic regulation. This view aligns with recent predictive coding accounts, which posit that the brain's hierarchical generative models differentially weight prior beliefs and sensory inputs depending on the phenomenological content and cognitive architecture of each domain. The reviewed evidence thus contributes to a growing theoretical framework situating spiritual and religious cognition within the domain of embodied predictive processing. It offers a promising platform for future research aiming to disentangle the phenomenological, neural, and computational dimensions of transcendental experience. Moreover, by demonstrating the malleability of spiritual self-representations through manipulation of the processing of bodily signals, these findings open new avenues for clinical and contemplative interventions aimed at modulating self-awareness, affective meaning-making, and existential well-being. In sum, this chapter underscores the need for a neurocognitive taxonomy of spiritual and religious phenomena that recognizes their overlapping yet distinct neural architectures, and that takes the role of the body seriously in shaping the spiritual dimensions of human experience.

Acknowledgments

This work was funded by the JTF and was performed by the University of Udine (Italy) under subcontract with the Shirley Ryan AbilityLab (Chicago, IL). Cosimo Urgesi is supported by grants from the Italian Ministry of Health (Ricerca Corrente, 2025, Scientific Institute, IRCCS E. Medea).

References

Barrett, L. F., & Simmons, W. K. (2015). Interoceptive predictions in the brain. *Nature Reviews Neuroscience*, *16*(7), 419–429. https://doi.org/10.1038/nrn3950

Beauregard, M., & Paquette, V. (2006). Neural correlates of a mystical experience in Carmelite nuns. *Neuroscience Letters*, *405*(3), 186–190. https://doi.org/10.1016/j.neulet.2006.06.060

Beauregard, M., & Paquette, V. (2008). EEG activity in Carmelite nuns during a mystical experience. *Neuroscience Letters*, *444*(1), 1–4. https://doi.org/10.1016/j.neulet.2008.08.028

Berlucchi, G., & Aglioti, S. (1997). The body in the brain: neural bases of corporeal awareness. *Trends in Neurosciences*, *20*(12), 560–564.

Berlucchi, G., & Aglioti, S. M. (2010). The body in the brain revisited. *Experimental Brain Research*, *200*(1), 25–35. https://doi.org/10.1007/s00221-009-1970-7

Blanke, O., & Mohr, C. (2005). Out-of-body experience, heautoscopy, and autoscopic hallucination of neurological origin. Implications for neurocognitive mechanisms of corporeal awareness and self-consciousness. *Brain research. Brain research reviews*, *50*(1), 184–199. https://doi.org/10.1016/j.brainresrev.2005.05.008

Cahn, B. R., & Polich, J. (2006). Meditation states and traits: EEG, ERP, and neuroimaging studies. *Psychological Bulletin*, *132*(2), 180–211. https://doi.org/10.1037/0033-2909.132.2.180

Cloninger, C. R., Svrakic, D. M., & Przybeck, T. R. (1993). A psychobiological model of temperament and character. *Archives of General Psychiatry*, *50*(12), 975–990. https://doi.org/10.1001/archpsyc.1993.01820240059008

Crescentini, C., Aglioti, S. M., Fabbro, F., & Urgesi, C. (2014a). Virtual lesions of the inferior parietal cortex induce fast changes of implicit religiousness/spirituality. *Cortex*, *54*, 1–15. https://doi.org/10.1016/j.cortex.2014.01.023

Crescentini, C., Di Bucchianico, M., Fabbro, F., & Urgesi, C. (2015). Excitatory stimulation of the right inferior parietal cortex lessens implicit religiousness/spirituality. *Neuropsychologia*, *70*, 71–79. https://doi.org/10.1016/j.neuropsychologia.2015.02.016

Crescentini, C., Urgesi, C., Campanella, F., Eleopra, R., & Fabbro, F. (2014b). Effects of an 8-week meditation program on the implicit and explicit attitudes toward religious/spiritual self-representations. *Consciousness and Cognition*, *30*, 266–280. https://doi.org/10.1016/j.concog.2014.09.013

Crespi, B., Dinsdale, N., Read, S., & Hurd, P. (2019). Spirituality, dimensional autism, and schizotypal traits: The search for meaning. *PLoS One*, *14*(3). https://doi.org/10.1371/journal.pone.0213456

Emmons, R. A. R. A., & Paloutzian, R. F. (2003). The psychology of religion. *Annual Review of Psychology*, *54*(1), 377–402. https://doi.org/10.1146/annurev.psych.54.101601.145024

Ferguson, M. A., Schaper, F. L. W. V. J., Cohen, A., Siddiqi, S., Merrill, S. M., Nielsen, J. A., Grafman, J., Urgesi, C., Fabbro, F., & Fox, M. D. (2022). A neural circuit for spirituality and religiosity derived from patients with brain lesions. *Biological Psychiatry*, *91*(4), 380–388. https://doi.org/10.1016/j.biopsych.2021.06.016

Finisguerra, A., Crescentini, C., & Urgesi, C. (2019). Transcutaneous vagus nerve stimulation affects implicit spiritual self-representations. *Neuroscience*, *412*, 144–159. https://doi.org/10.1016/j.neuroscience.2019.05.059

Friston, K. (2010). The free-energy principle: a unified brain theory? *Nature Reviews Neuroscience*, *11*(2), 127–138. https://doi.org/10.1038/nrn2787

Fuller, R. C. (2008). *Spirituality in the Flesh: Bodily Sources of Religious Experiences* (Vol. 8). Oxford University Press.

Glock, C. Y. (1962). On the study of religious commitment. *Religious Education*, *57*(sup4), 98–110. https://doi.org/10.1080/003440862057S407

Grafman, J., Cristofori, I., Zhong, W., & Bulbulia, J. (2020). The neural basis of religious cognition. *Current Directions in Psychological Science*, *29*(2), 126–133. https://doi.org/10.1177/0963721419898183

Greenwald, A. G., McGhee, D. E., & Schwartz, J. L. (1998). Measuring individual differences in implicit cognition: the implicit association test. *Journal of personality and social psychology*, *74*(6), 1464–1480. https://doi.org/10.1037//0022-3514.74.6.1464

Hölzel, B. K., Carmody, J., Vangel, M., Congleton, C., Yerramsetti, S. M., Gard, T., & Lazar, S. W. (2011). Mindfulness practice leads to increases in regional brain gray matter density. *Psychiatry Research*, *191*(1), 36–43. https://doi.org/10.1016/j.pscychresns.2010.08.006

Hölzel, B. K., Ott, U., Gard, T., Hempel, H., Weygandt, M., Morgen, K., & Vaitl, D. (2008). Investigation of mindfulness meditation practitioners with voxel-based morphometry. *Social Cognitive and Affective Neuroscience*, *3*(1), 55–61. https://doi.org/10.1093/scan/nsm038

Johnstone, B., & Glass, B. A. (2008). Support for a neuropsychological model of spirituality in persons with traumatic brain injury. *Zygon: Journal of Religion and Science*, *43*(4), 861–874. https://doi.org/10.1111/j.1467-9744.2008.00964.x

Kaasinen, V., Maguire, R. P., Kurki, T., Brück, A., & Rinne, J. O. (2005). Mapping brain structure and personality in late adulthood. *NeuroImage*, *24*(2), 315–322. https://doi.org/10.1016/j.neuroimage.2004.09.017

Lazar, S. W., Kerr, C. E., Wasserman, R. H., Gray, J. R., Greve, D. N., Treadway, M. T., McGarvey, M., Quinn, B. T., Dusek, J. A., Benson, H., Rauch, S. L., Moore, C. I., & Fischl, B. (2005). Meditation experience is associated with increased cortical thickness. *Neuroreport*, *16*(17), 1893–1897. https://doi.org/10.1097/01.wnr.0000186598.66243.19

Lutz, A., Brefczynski-Lewis, J., Johnstone, T., & Davidson, R. (2008). Regulation of the neural circuitry of emotion by compassion meditation: effects of meditative expertise. *PLoS One*, *3*(3), 1–10. https://doi.org/10.1371/journal.pone.0001897

Lutz, A., Greischar, L. L., Rawlings, N. B., Ricard, M., & Davidson, R. J. (2004). Long-term meditators self-induce high-amplitude gamma synchrony during mental practice. *Proceedings of the National Academy of Sciences of the United States of America*, *101*(46), 16369–16373. https://doi.org/10.1073/pnas.0407401101

Lutz, A., Schaefer, H. S., Levinson, D. B., Davidson, R. J., & Brefczynski-Lewis, J. a. (2007). Neural correlates of attentional expertise in long-term meditation practitioners.

Proceedings of the National Academy of Sciences of the United States of America, 104(27), 11483–11488. https://doi.org/10.1073/pnas.0606552104

Lutz, A., Slagter, H. A., Rawlings, N. B., Francis, A. D., Greischar, L. L., & Davidson, R. J. (2009). Mental training enhances attentional stability: neural and behavioral evidence. *The Journal of Neuroscience, 29*(42), 13418–13427. https://doi.org/10.1523/JNEUROSCI.1614-09.2009

Morin, A. (2006). Levels of consciousness and self-awareness: a comparison and integration of various neurocognitive views. *Consciousness and Cognition, 15*(2), 358–371. https://doi.org/10.1016/j.concog.2005.09.006

Newberg, A. B. (2014). The neuroscientific study of spiritual practices. *Frontiers in Psychology, 5*(March), 215. https://doi.org/10.3389/fpsyg.2014.00215

Newberg, A., Alavi, A., Baime, M., Pourdehnad, M., Santanna, J., & d'Aquili, E. (2001). The measurement of regional cerebral blood flow during the complex cognitive task of meditation: a preliminary SPECT study. *Psychiatry Research, 106*(2), 113–122. https://doi.org/10.1016/s0925-4927(01)00074-9

Newberg, A. B., & Iversen, J. (2003). The neural basis of the complex mental task of meditation: neurotransmitter and neurochemical considerations. *Medical Hypotheses, 61*(2), 282–291. https://doi.org/10.1016/S0306-9877(03)00175-0

Nosek, B. A., Hawkins, C. B., & Frazier, R. S. (2011). Implicit social cognition: from measures to mechanisms. *Trends in Cognitive Sciences, 15*(4), 152–159. https://doi.org/10.1016/j.tics.2011.01.005

Paloutzian, R. F., & Park, C. L. (2005). *Handbook of the Psychology of Religion and Spirituality* (1st ed.). Guilford Press.

Pyasik, M., Marini, E., Ippolito, G., Fusco, G., Tarasi, L., Finisguerra, A., Romei, V., & Urgesi, C. (preprint). *Biasing Predictive Processing of Interoceptive Information Affects Implicit Spirituality But Not Religiosity*. PsyArXiv [Preprint], https://doi.org/10.31234/osf.io/kwtq5_v2

Tarasi, L., Trajkovic, J., Diciotti, S., di Pellegrino, G., Ferri, F., Ursino, M., & Romei, V. (2022). Predictive waves in the autism-schizophrenia continuum: a novel biobehavioral model. *Neuroscience & Biobehavioral Reviews, 132*, 1–22. https://doi.org/10.1016/j.neubiorev.2021.11.006

Taylor, V. A., Grant, J., Daneault, V., Scavone, G., Breton, E., Roffe-Vidal, S., Courtemanche, J., Lavarenne, A. S., & Beauregard, M. (2011). Impact of mindfulness on the neural responses to emotional pictures in experienced and beginner meditators. *NeuroImage, 57*(4), 1524–1533. https://doi.org/10.1016/j.neuroimage.2011.06.001

Turner, R. M., Hudson, I. L., Butler, P. H. D., & Joyce, P. R. (2003). Brain function and personality in normal males: a SPECT study using statistical parametric mapping. *NeuroImage, 19*(3), 1145–1162. https://doi.org/10.1016/S1053-8119(03)00171-X

Urgesi, C., Aglioti, S. M., Skrap, M., & Fabbro, F. (2010). The spiritual brain: selective cortical lesions modulate human self-transcendence. *Neuron, 65*(3), 309–319. https://doi.org/10.1016/j.neuron.2010.01.026

van Elk, M., & Aleman, A. (2017). Brain mechanisms in religion and spirituality: an integrative predictive processing framework. *Neuroscience and Biobehavioral Reviews, 73*, 359–378. https://doi.org/10.1016/j.neubiorev.2016.12.031

Villani, V., Tsakiris, M., & Azevedo, R. T. (2019). Transcutaneous vagus nerve stimulation improves interoceptive accuracy. *Neuropsychologia, 134*. https://doi.org/10.1016/j.neuropsychologia.2019.107201

Yakunina, N., Kim, S. S., & Nam, E. C. (2017). Optimization of transcutaneous vagus nerve stimulation using functional MRI. *Neuromodulation: Technology at the Neural Interface, 20*(3), 290–300. https://doi.org/10.1111/NER.12541

5

REDEMPTIVE TURNING POINTS, SPIRITUAL EXPERIENCE, AND DECENTERING

Spiritual Experiences and Narrative Identity Construction in Spiritual Life History Interviews

Patrick McNamara

Introduction

Narrative identity theory argues that human beings make sense of their lives by constructing internalized life stories that integrate past, present, and anticipated future events into a coherent whole (McAdams, 2001). Central to these life stories are turning points, moments perceived as having significantly altered the trajectory of one's life. Among the most studied narrative forms is the redemption sequence, in which adversity is ultimately transformed into growth, moral insight, or spiritual deepening. Prior research has linked redemptive life stories to higher well-being, generativity, and resilience (McAdams, 2013).

However, there are significant gaps in our understanding of these redemptive turning points. For example, the role of spiritual experiences in defining these experiences or deriving meaning from them is understudied. Many turning points involve religious or spiritual experiences—prayer, divine guidance, mystical encounters—but the study of these elements has been sparse. Second, little is known about the underlying psychological operations that support redemption turning points. Recent work on the cognitive process of decentering (Bernstein et al., 2015; McNamara, 2022) suggests that transformational experiences often involve (a) down-regulation of agency or perspective shift on experiential states from first person to third person, (b) entering a liminal space, (c) model updating via cultural or spiritual narratives, and (d) final integration. Whether this four-step process co-occurs with redemption-related spiritual experiences has not been empirically established.

McNamara (2009; 2022) presented evidence and arguments for the idea that a brain-based, cognitive process which decentered or down-regulated the subjective sense of agency or self was central to transformative spiritual and religious

DOI: 10.4324/9781003158189-5

experience. This decentering process promoted a subjective and dynamical shift from first-person perspective to third-person perspective and then back again to an enriched first-person perspective. Decentering also functioned to facilitate the growth of new and culturally shaped perceptual capacities as well as ongoing personal transformation. The brain dedicates significant neural machinery to the decentering process as it appears to be fundamentally important for reducing uncertainty via the updating of predictive models (embodied in the self-world relational model) of the world the individual has to navigate each day. Decentering involves: (1) taking offline the self-model, or disengaging executive control systems such that the sense of self or agency is transiently diminished, predictive modeling is temporarily suspended, and the individual is more open to sensory input and to cultural influences, (2) then the individual finds him/her diminished sense of self in a liminal suppositional space or possible-worlds meta-stable brain state where the self-world relational model can be edited or worked upon using available cultural materials, (3) then a search in memory and semantic stores ensues, looking for cultural master narratives and cognitive materials to update the self-world model guided by existing cultural scripts, symbols, or narratives, until a more computationally efficient and better predictive self-world model (given current environmental challenges) is found, thus ultimately enriching the individual's sense of self. The final dynamical step involved (4) instantiating or binding the new self-world model into a position of executive control in the neural system that is matched to some extent to a culturally appropriate or ideal cultural scripts/symbols resulting hopefully in a wider, better-adapted sense of self. Steps 2 and 3 are typically experienced phenomenologically as a kind of liminal or in-between space with high cognitive uncertainty and anxious affect. Phenomenological analyses of narratives of everyday religious experiences and encounters with SAs have been found to be entirely consistent with the decentering account of religious experiences (Wildman and McNamara, 2010; McNamara et al., 2015).

To explore the potential role of decentering in spiritual experiences associated with turning-point redemptive narratives, we adopted an approach modeled on McAdam's work on narrative life histories (McAdams, 2006; McAdams & McLean, 2013). McAdams et al. define a *redemptive sequence* as a narrative arc in which a protagonist encounters suffering, adversity, or failure but ultimately interprets the event as leading to positive outcomes, personal growth, or moral insight (McAdams et al., 2001; McAdams, 2013). These sequences move from negative affect at the beginning of the story toward a positive resolution, imbuing the event with meaning and contributing to a coherent and hopeful life story. The opposite arc is the *contamination sequence*, in which an initially good or hopeful event is "spoiled" by subsequent negative outcomes, leaving the narrator with a sense of loss, disillusionment, or bitterness. Redemptive stories are associated with higher levels of well-being, generativity, and purpose, whereas contaminated stories predict depressive symptoms and lower life satisfaction (McAdams, 2013).

In McAdams's life story model, *turning points* are key autobiographical events that the narrator perceives as marking a decisive change in the direction of life (McAdams, 2001; McAdams & Bowman, 2001). They are the "hinges" of the life narrative, moments when the plot shifts, leading to a new trajectory of goals, relationships, or self-understanding. Turning points are often emotionally intense, personally meaningful, and recalled with rich detail even years later. They may involve losses, gains, moral choices, spiritual awakenings, or sudden opportunities, and they play a disproportionate role in shaping identity because they are used by narrators to explain "how I became who I am."

Turning points are not merely objective events but *interpretive constructions*—the meaning the person makes of the event is as important as the event itself. Redemptive turning points—where adversity is reframed as leading to positive transformation—are especially associated with life satisfaction and a sense of purpose, whereas contaminated turning points—where positive events are narrated as spoiled—are linked to distress and rumination. Given that decentering is postulated to be the underlying cognitive process that drives these narrative reconstructions, it seems reasonable to assume that the intensity of decentering would be associated with whether or not the redemptive arc was "contaminated." Thus, redemptive arcs provide a natural "laboratory" for studying the potential role of decentering in processes of meaning-making, emotional regulation, and identity development.

The present study addresses the potential role of decentering in the spiritual experiences associated with redemptive arcs or narratives within turning-point narratives. I hypothesized that markers of the four-step decentering process would reliably occur in redemptive narratives but that decentering markers would differ as a function of "contamination."

Methods

Participants

We used a set of transcripts of in-depth McAdams styled "life-chapter" interviews that were done as part of another study on sleep dreams and spiritual experiences. The methods for those studies are described elsewhere (Balch et al., 2025). Briefly, for that study we recruited volunteers who answered online adverts for a remote study on sleep, dreams, and religion. To be eligible, participants were required to: be at least 18 years old, reside in the United States, speak and read English, have reliable Wi-Fi, and not have a current psychiatric or neurological diagnosis. Eligibility criteria regarding psychiatric and neurological diagnosis was self-reported by participants and was not screened using questionnaires at the time of invitation, however those who scored severe or higher on any of the three categories of the Depression, Anxiety, Stress (DASS; Lovibond & Lovibond, 1995) scale in a baseline survey were not invited to participate further in the study due to concerns about participant burden. Interviews were drawn from a corpus of 107 participants, each of whom completed our spiritual life history version of McAdams's Life Story Interview. Each transcript was labeled with a unique numeric participant ID corresponding to its original filename, allowing us to analyze narratives both at the segment level and aggregated by participant.

IRB/Ethics: The study was overseen by the National University Institutional Review Board, study number 2022–184-OTH, dated May 17, 2022, and informed consent was received prior to participation. Due to the remote nature of the study, participants were provided with a PDF of the consent form via email and met on Zoom with a researcher who read the consent letter aloud and answered any participant questions.

We administered the following questionnaires to get an idea of the religious background and personalities of the participants.

Mood: Depression, Anxiety, and Stress Scales: (DASS-42; Lovibond & Lovibond, 1995). The DASS consists of 42 items with 14 each in the domains of depression, anxiety, and stress, as well as a total score. Participants are instructed to indicate on a scale of 0 (did not apply to me at all) to 3 (applied most of the time) the extent to which each statement applied to them over the last week. Crawford and Henry (2003) have previously reported high (>.82) reliability and validity for the DASS subscales. The DASS Manual (Order DASS manual) (Lovibond & Lovibond, 1995) reports the cutoff scores for depression (normal = 0–9, mild = 10–13, moderate = 14–20, severe = 21–27, and extremely severe = 28+); anxiety (normal = 0–7, mild = 8–9, moderate = 10–14, severe = 15–19, and extremely severe = 20+), and stress (normal = 0–14, mild = 15–18, moderate = 19–25, severe = 26–33, and extremely severe = 34+).

Personality: We utilized the well-validated Big Five Inventory (BFI; Rammstedt & John, 2007) to measure the personality traits of our participants. Specifically, we used the 60-item BFI-2, which has been shown to have strong factor structure in the main five dimensions as well as robust sub-facets for each factor.

Religiosity/Spirituality: Brief Multidimensional Measure of Religiosity/Spirituality

Participants also completed the BMMRS (Fetzer Institute, 1999). The BMMRS was developed in the late 1990s by a panel of experts in the scientific study of religion who were asked by the Fetzer Institute and the National Institute on Aging to develop an assessment tool that would capture the multidimensional nature of the construct of religiosity. Their primary aim was to develop items for assessing health-relevant domains of religiousness and spirituality. The BMMRS captures 12 domains of spirituality/religion: Daily Spiritual Experiences, Meaning, Values/Beliefs, Forgiveness, Private Religious Practices, Religious/Spiritual Coping, Religious Support, Religious/Spiritual History, Commitment, Organizational Religiousness, Religious Preference, and Overall Self-Ranking as a religious/spiritual person. We were interested only in the following subscales: private religious practices, organizational religiousness, daily spiritual experiences, and religious coping as these subscales seem most relevant to the issue of the role of religious/spiritual experiences in turning-point experiences and redemptive narrative arcs.

Procedure and Materials

Each participant completed our spiritual life history version of the Life Story Interview (McAdams, 2001), which includes sections on major life chapters, high and low points, and turning points. Turning points are defined as "key episodes that mark an important change or transformation in the direction of your life story." Interviews were transcribed and merged into a single corpus, preserving participant IDs as section headers. While closely following McAdams's (2008) procedures, our adapted Spiritual Life History interview focused specifically on how participants narrated the story of their religious or spiritual changes or development. Individuals were first asked to give a broad overview of their religious or spiritual life, beginning as early as they wished and breaking the story into chapters. Having given a brief overview of their religious or spiritual life, participants were then asked to focus in depth on three key scenes: a high point of their religious or spiritual life; a low point; and a turning point.

Coding of Redemptive Motifs

Each turning-point narrative was scored for redemption on a five-point scale (−2 to +2) following McAdams et al.'s redemption coding manual: −2 = full contamination, −1 = partial contamination, 0 = neutral, +1 = partial redemption, +2 = full redemption. Redemption was scored using a hybrid approach: a sentiment-shift heuristic (comparing valence words in the first vs. last third of the segment) combined with coder review for narrative meaning and growth language. Narratives were assigned −2 if they moved from positive to strongly negative (full contamination), −1 for partial contamination, 0 for neutral or flat affect, +1 for partial redemption (negative to mildly positive), and +2 for full redemption (negative to strongly positive, with clear evidence of growth or insight). Scoring combined automated sentiment-shift heuristics with manual coder review to ensure that changes in affect were meaningful within the narrative context rather than driven by isolated words.

Identification and Scoring of Turning Points

Turning-point segments were identified by scanning for interviewer prompts containing a "turning point" query and extracting a context window of approximately eighteen paragraphs after the prompt. This yielded 247 distinct turning-point segments ($M = 2.3$ per participant). Segments were reviewed for coherence, and those with fewer than 20 words were excluded. There also had to be inclusion of a clear event or episode that was framed by the participant as life-changing. Each segment was then coded for whether it qualified as a turning point according to McAdams's criteria (i.e., it marked a meaningful change in life direction, was elaborated with some detail, and included emotional and interpretive content). Segments failing to meet these criteria (e.g., vague, purely factual statements) were excluded from further analysis. The resulting set of validated turning-point narratives formed the basis for subsequent scoring of redemption, spiritual content, and decentering.

Decentering Coding

Decentering was conceptualized as a four-step process encompassing (a) agency down-regulation/self-distancing, (b) liminality or disorientation, (c) model updating and cultural script search, and (d) integrative binding to a moral or spiritual framework. Our goal was to systematically identify markers of each step within turning-point narratives, with particular attention to spiritual or religious themes. Building on prior decentering frameworks (McNamara, 2022), we developed an enriched coding scheme that combined lexical, phrasal, and narrative-level indicators to capture subtle and diverse manifestations of decentering.

Lexical and Phrasal Expansion

For Step a (agency down-regulation), our marker list included not only explicit phrases of diminished agency (e.g., "I couldn't do anything," "I had no control") but also stuckness and immobilization language ("I felt stuck," "I couldn't move forward," "I was lost"), emotional collapse markers ("I felt hopeless," "I was in despair," "I felt dead inside"), physiological surrender terms ("I collapsed," "I wept," "I froze"), and fatalistic expressions ("it was meant to be," "I had no choice").

For Step b (liminality), we identified markers of temporal dislocation ("time stopped," "everything slowed"), dream-like or altered-state descriptors ("everything felt unreal," "I was in a fog"), and threshold metaphors ("I was between worlds," "in limbo"), enabling us to detect moments where narrators described a suspension of ordinary identity structures.

Step c (model updating) emphasized cognitive verbs ("I realized," "I reframed," "I asked why"), explicit references to meaning-making efforts (therapy, prayer, consulting scripture), and mentions of narrative restructuring ("I made sense of it," "I saw the pattern").

Step d (binding/integration) focused on language indicating resolution and reorientation ("I found peace," "I was born again," "I saw the bigger picture"), invocation of supernatural agency (God, Spirit, angels, providence), and ethical or vocational reframing ("I forgave," "I discovered my purpose").

Each marker list was developed iteratively by reviewing transcripts, adding new phrasal variants, and refining pattern-matching rules. Beyond single keywords, we considered contextual and syntactic cues that signaled decentering. For example, Step a could be inferred from a cluster of passive constructions even without an explicit "I surrendered" phrase (e.g., "things just happened to me"). Step b could be inferred from narrative disorientation or imagery of liminality even when the word "liminal" was absent. This enriched approach allowed detection of less obvious residues of decentering even when markers were metaphoric or distributed across multiple sentences.

Scoring Intensity/Confidence for decentering

Each decentering step was scored on a 0–2 scale: 0 = absent, 1 = single marker, 2 = multiple markers or sustained thematic presence. This allowed us to capture gradations of decentering rather than binary presence/absence. The greater the score (up to 8), the greater the number of markers of decentering. Confidence that we are indeed seeing a decentering process therefore increased with intensity score. Total decentering intensity (0–8) was computed by summing across steps and markers. For analytic purposes, these totals were categorized into 0–1 (minimal), 2–3 (low-moderate), 4–5 (moderate-high), and 6–8 (near-complete) categories. Narratives with three or more overt steps present (intensity > 0) were classified as multistep decentering sequences.

Results

Sample Characteristics

There were 85 females and 22 males. Mean age for the entire sample was 46.1 (14.7), mean education was 16 years (1.8) ().

To summarize our sample characteristics, our participants reported relatively low levels of psychological distress. On the Depression Anxiety Stress Scales (DASS), mean scores were within the normal severity range and below population norms for depression ($M = 4.14$, $SD = 5.19$; norm $M \approx 6.34$), anxiety ($M = 2.29$, $SD = 3.15$; norm $M \approx 4.70$), and stress ($M = 5.37$, $SD = 4.91$; norm $M \approx 10.11$), suggesting a psychologically healthy sample. Religiousness and spirituality, measured by the BMMRS, were typical to slightly elevated relative to U.S. national norms (Idler et al., 2003). Measuring multiple dimensions of religion and spirituality for health research: Conceptual background and findings from the 1998 General Social Survey. Research on Aging, 25(4), 327–365), with somewhat higher scores for organizational religiousness ($M = 4.56$, $SD = 1.47$; norm $M \approx 4.2$) and private religious practices ($M = 26.03$, $SD = 10.39$; norm $M \approx 24.6$). Personality traits assessed with the BFI were broadly typical, though participants scored slightly higher than norms (John et al., 2008) on agreeableness ($M = 38.98$, $SD = 3.45$; norm $M \approx 36.9$) and conscientiousness ($M = 38.78$, $SD = 3.02$; norm $M \approx 36.1$), indicating a sample that may be somewhat more prosocial and achievement-oriented than average. Together, these findings characterize the sample as psychologically healthy, moderately religious/spiritual, and slightly more agreeable and conscientious than the general population.

Across 107 participants, we identified 247 turning-point narratives ($M = 2.3$ per participant). Mean length was 216 words.

With regard to the presence of decentering mechanisms within the 247 turning-point narratives, Step a was present in 31.6% of turning-point segments ($n = 78$). Step b (liminality) appeared in 23.1% ($n = 57$), Step c (model updating) in 56.7% ($n = 140$), and Step d (binding/integration) in 87.9% ($n = 217$). Full four-step sequences occurred in 18 segments, permitting sequential analysis.

Of the 18 turning-point narratives that evidenced clear markers of all four steps, a clear sequential process was noted with Step 1 occurring before all other steps in all 18 narratives and Step 4 occurring last in all narratives, but Steps 2 and 3 occurring roughly equally in positions 2 and 3.

We turned next to examining decentering markers in the redemption arcs embedded in the 247 turning-point narratives. Within the 247 turning-point narratives, there were 124 contaminated sequences, 41 neutral sequences, and 82 non-contaminated redemptive sequences. There were five contaminated sequences that evidenced 6–8 decentering steps and 0 redemptive sequences that evidenced high (6–8) decentering markers. There were 34 contaminated sequences that evidenced 4–5 decentering markers and only 10 redemptive sequences that evidenced 4–5 markers. There were roughly equal numbers of contaminated and redemptive sequences that exhibited 2 or 3 markers and there were 29 contaminated sequences and 19 redemptive sequences with 0–1 markers. Thus, contaminated sequences were more likely to embody a high number of markers of a decentering experience.

We next examined decentering markers across the 247 turning-point narratives by redemption level. Contaminated arcs (−2 and −1 combined; $n = 124$) contained 29 narratives (23.4%) with 0–1 markers, 56 (45.2%) with 2–3 markers, 34 (27.4%) with 4–5 markers, and 5 (4.0%) with 6–8 markers. In contrast, redemptive arcs (+1 and +2 combined; $n = 82$) showed 19 narratives (23.2%) with 0–1 markers, 53 (64.6%) with 2–3 markers, 10 (12.2%) with 4–5 markers, and 0 (0%) with 6–8 markers.

A chi-square test of association confirmed that high-intensity decentering (≥ 4 markers) was significantly more likely to occur in contaminated arcs (31.4%) than in redemptive arcs (12.2%), $\chi^2(1) = 9.06$, $p = 0.003$. These results suggest that contaminated narratives often involve intense but unresolved decentering experiences, whereas redemptive arcs cluster in the moderate decentering range, consistent with an adaptive level of perspective shifting sufficient to support narrative integration.

Discussion

Turning-point narratives are central to transformative growth, yet the role of spiritual experiences and associated cognitive mechanisms that transform adversity into growth remains unclear. We analyzed 247 turning-point narratives from 107 participants using McAdams's redemption framework and McNamara's decentering scheme. Decentering steps were identified through lexical, phrasal, and narrative markers of agency down-regulation (Step a), liminality (Step b), model updating (Step c), and integrative meaning-making or binding to a supernatural agent (Step d). Markers of each of the four steps of decentering occurred between 25% and 90% of turning-point narratives with 18 narratives containing all four steps. In these 18 narratives, Step 1 always occurred before the other three steps and Step 4 always occurred after the other three steps implying some sequential process. With regard to redemptive narratives embedded within the 247 turning-point narratives, a chi-square test of association confirmed that high-intensity decentering ($\geq$ 4 markers) was significantly more likely to occur in contaminated arcs (31.4%) than in redemptive arcs (12.2%). These results suggest that decentering processes reliably characterize spiritual experiences involved in turning point/redemptive narratives, and that contaminated narratives often involve intense but unresolved decentering experiences, whereas redemptive arcs cluster in the moderate decentering range, consistent with an adaptive level of perspective shifting sufficient to support narrative integration.

This study provides evidence that redemptive turning points are deeply intertwined with spiritual experience and supported by a multistep decentering process. Participants who constructed highly redemptive narratives engaged in self-distancing, experienced liminality, sought cultural or spiritual frameworks for meaning, and achieved narrative integration, often invoking God or other transcendent forces.

The finding that decentering was most intense (highest number of markers) in contaminated arcs suggests that individuals who perceive key turning points in their life stories as non-redemptive recall the experience as intensely decentering with down-regulation of agency and prolonged times spent in liminal spaces without resolution (Step d). Note that you can have high numbers of decentering phrasal markers while still evidencing lack of a full decentering process. These narratives suggest that participants had begun the process of agency down-regulation and meaning search but had not yet fully achieved integrative resolution. This pattern may reflect a transitional state where negative experience is being actively reworked but remains emotionally charged, consistent with McAdams's view of the life story as a dynamic process rather than a static product. These cases may correspond to liminal or pilgrim phases of spiritual development, where the self is suspended between disintegration and reintegration. Clinically, such narratives may represent points of leverage for intervention, as they show openness to growth but may benefit from additional support to complete the integrative arc. Taking into account the decentering cognitive mechanisms apparently at work in these redemption versus contamination narratives may assist in creating targets for therapeutic integration where we can help a person move from contamination to redemption.

These findings contribute to narrative identity theory by showing that redemption is not simply a positive reappraisal but a process of narrative transformation, frequently spiritual in nature. They also highlight decentering as a potential mechanism by which difficult events are metabolized into personal growth. Future research should examine whether interventions that facilitate decentering (e.g., mindfulness, guided autobiography, psychedelics) increase the likelihood of constructing redemptive life stories, and whether spiritual framing enhances the durability of these transformations.

Acknowledgments

The author thanks John Balch, Ph.D., Chanel Reed, and Rachel Raider for conducting the interviews and transcribing the interviews into anonymized transcripts.

References

Balch, J., Hodulik, G., Raider, R., David, A., Reed, C., Wildman, W. J., … & McNamara, P. (2025). Dream content influences daily spirituality. Available at SSRN 5066183.

Bernstein, A., Hadash, Y., Lichtash, Y., Tanay, G., Shepherd, K., & Fresco, D. M. (2015). Decentering and related constructs: A critical review and metacognitive processes model. *Perspectives on Psychological Science*, *10*(5), 599–617.

Crawford, J. R., & Henry, J. D. (2003). The Depression Anxiety Stress Scales (DASS): Normative data and latent structure in a large non-clinical sample. *British Journal of Clinical Psychology*, *42*(2), 111–131.

John, O. P., Naumann, L., & Soto, C. J. (2008). Paradigm shift to the integrative Big Five taxonomy: History, measurement, and conceptual issues. In O. P. John, R. W. Robins, & L. A. Pervin (Eds.), *Handbook of personality: Theory and research* (3rd ed., pp. 114–158). Guilford.

Lovibond, P. F., & Lovibond, S. H. (1995). The structure of negative emotional states: Comparison of the Depression Anxiety Stress Scales (DASS) with the Beck Depression and Anxiety Inventories. *Behaviour Research and Therapy*, *33*(3), 335–343.

McAdams, D. P. (2001). The psychology of life stories. *Review of General Psychology*, *5*(2), 100–122. https://doi.org/10.1037/1089-2680.5.2.100

McAdams, D. P. (2008). Personal narratives and the life story. In *Handbook of personality: Theory and Research, 3rd ed* (pp. 242–262). The Guilford Press.

McAdams, D. P. (2013). *The redemptive self: Stories Americans live by* (Rev. & expanded ed.). New York: Oxford University Press.

McAdams, D. P., & McLean, K. C. (2013). Narrative identity. *Current Directions in Psychological Science, 22*(3), 233–238. https://doi.org/10.1177/0963721413475622

McAdams, D. P., Reynolds, J., Lewis, M., Patten, A. H., & Bowman, P. J. (2001). When bad things turn good and good things turn bad: Sequences of redemption and contamination in life narrative and their relation to psychosocial adaptation in midlife adults and in students. *Personality and Social Psychology Bulletin*, *27*(4), 474–485.

McNamara, P., Minsky, A., Pae, V., & Gusev, A. (2015) Cognitive phenomenology of religious experience in religious narratives, dreams, and nightmares. *Archive for the Psychology of Religion, 37*, 343–357.
McNamara, P., & Giordano, M. (2017). Cognitive Neuroscience and Religious Language. *Religion, Language, and the Human Mind*, 115.
McNamara, P. (2009). *The neuroscience of religious experience*. Cambridge University Press.
McNamara, P. (2022). *The cognitive neuroscience of religious experience: Decentering and the self*. Cambridge University Press.
Rammstedt, B., & John, O. P. (2007). Measuring personality in one minute or less: A 10-item short version of the Big Five Inventory in English and German. *Journal of Research in Personality, 41*(1), 203–212.
Wildman, W. J., & McNamara, P. (2010). Evaluating reliance on narratives in the psychological study of religious experiences. *The International Journal for the Psychology of Religion, 20*, 223–254.

6

THE GOD RECEPTOR

Naturalistic, Psychotic and Entheogenic Neurocognition in the Origins and Phenomenology of Spiritual and Religious Thought

Bernard Crespi, Nancy Yang, and Sam Doesburg

Suddenly, my whole being was filled with light and loveliness and with an upsurge of deeply moving feeling from within myself to meet and reciprocate the influence that flowed into me. I was in a state of the most vivid awareness and illumination. What can I say of it? A cloudless, cerulean blue sky of the mind, shot through with shafts of exquisite, warm, dazzling sunlight. In its first and most intense stage it lasted perhaps half an hour. It seemed that some force or impulse from without was acting on me, looking into me; that I was in touch with a reality beyond my own; that I had made direct contact with the secret, ultimate source of life. What I had read of the accounts of others acquired a new meaning suddenly. It flashed across my mind, "This is what the mystics mean by the direct experience of God."

M. Coate, describing psychotic experience.
Beyond All Reason. New York: J.B. Lippincott, 1965, page 21.

Introduction

Spirituality and religion represent central features of human experience and culture. Their existence and forms remain enigmatic, however, on two main fronts. First, under what selective pressures, and through what other genetic and environmental processes, did these uniquely human and culturally ubiquitous traits originate and evolve? Is the conception of God, gods, or higher powers an adaptation, a by-product, a delusion, an accident, or some combination of these options? Second, how are spirituality and religion instantiated in the human brain? Brains are comprised of functional modules and networks—are there regions or networks that evolved to represent gods and spirits, like the fusiform face area evolved to encode human faces? These questions remain especially puzzling because spiritual and

DOI: 10.4324/9781003158189-6

religious experiences differ qualitatively from ordinary life, because the causal connections of spirituality and religion to components of reproductive fitness in humans remain largely obscure, and because the existence of gods and spirits is manifestly impossible to verify in any logical or scientific way.

The past ten years have seen substantial progress in addressing these questions, especially through neuroimaging studies of humans engaging in spiritual or religious thought or activities (e.g., Ferguson et al., 2022; McNamara & Grafman, 2024). These studies have demonstrated that activations of specific regions and networks in the brain are positively or negatively associated with such forms of cognition and affect. However, essentially all of the relevant brain architecture implicated in spirituality or religiosity has been functionally spoken for by previous, secular, neuroimaging studies; spiritual and religious forms of cognition recruit regions of the brain that subserve sociality, agency, salience, logic, pleasure, pain, and other basic or advanced human adaptations, among others (e.g., Rim et al., 2019; McNamara & Grafman, 2024). On one hand, such findings should not be surprising, because the human brain has evolved predominantly via expansion, grafting, and co-option of pre-existing areas and circuits for new or expanded roles, such as language. On the other hand, the ubiquity, uniqueness, and central importance of religiosity to humans suggest that this cognitive phenotype should have a specific and detectable neural substrate—a god-region, god-network, or god-signature of some form that is beyond a cobbling together of otherwise, elsewhere dedicated parts.

In this article, we evaluate the hypothesis that the core neural bases of spiritual and religious cognition are mediated not by brain regions or networks, but microscopically, by activation of specific receptors, in particular ways, in the context of the aforementioned macroscopic regions and their circuits. By this hypothesis, the novelty of god-cognition in humans derives predominantly from the novelty of supraphysiological activation of HT2A receptors, that subserves the mechanisms of predictive coding centrally regulating human perception, consciousness, and learning. Such supraphysiological activation is driven by three human-elaborated or unique mechanisms, two internal (stress-challenge responses and psychosis, that are overlapping with one another) and one external (psychedelic biochemicals), that converge in their effects on cognition via the downstream effects of high HT2A activation—all in the context of the already highly social, and thus primed-for-god, human brain. Diverse aspects of this hypothesis have been addressed before, especially in the literature on psychedelic drugs in relation to spirituality and religion, but the relevant threads have yet to be woven fully together.

We first sketch the God-receptor hypothesis, and its components, in broad strokes.

Second, we provide essential background regarding the HT2A receptor, especially with regard to its roles in predictive coding in the contexts of perception and self-perception.

Third, we describe how most psychedelic biochemicals hyper-activate HT2A receptors, and how their effects appear to lead to a suite of novel experiences that overlap broadly with those derived from non-psychedelic causes. We also provide a brief overview of the uses of psychedelic biochemicals in diverse human cultures, especially with regard to how psychedelic experiences often form the bases, or have promoted the origins, of spiritual and religious thought and its cultural instantiations.

Fourth, we discuss the connections of the HT2A receptor hyper-activation with psychosis and schizophrenia, in the framework of cognitive models and predictive coding frameworks for this condition. We also describe relevant overlaps of psychotic and psychedelic experience with one another, as well as with spiritual and religious experience.

Finally, we synthesize these diverse lines of evidence in the context of human evolution, and discuss the predictions and limitations of the God-receptor model with special emphasis on what data are needed for robust tests.

We recognize that each of the academic domains represented by a section of this article is deeper and broader than we can hope to comprehensively address. In this context, our main goal is to outline the God-receptor hypothesis and provide a synopsis and synthesis of the relevant evidence. Most generally, we believe that the hypothesis is consilient with virtually all previous theory regarding the evolution and neural basis of spirituality and religion, and is best conceived in this light.

The God-Receptor Hypothesis

The God-receptor hypothesis, in the form described here, was motivated by the observations that spiritual and religious cognition are apparently unique to humans, represent an evolutionary novelty, exhibit no apparent adaptive significance in their earliest and simplest forms, and are evidently not instantiated within specific macroscopic brain areas or networks (Ferguson et al., 2022; McNamara & Grafman, 2024). Given these conditions, novel phenotypes must arise by novel or unselected evolutionary mechanisms, not driven by the typical processes of selection for adaptive variants. By the hypothesis proposed and evaluated here, religiosity and spirituality derive from three inter-related mechanisms.

The first such mechanism is adaptive, to a point. Humans are periodically subject to forms of stress or challenge that have selected for means of coping with them. One such means involves challenge-induced activation of the HT2A receptor, that results in a cascade of cognitive effects leading to enhanced associative learning and insight, among a suite of additional adaptive shifts in neural functions (Brouwer & Carhart-Harris, 2021; Brouwer et al., 2024). Extreme ecological and social stresses can also lead, however, to *hyper*-activation of the HT2A receptor (defined here in terms of emergent sequelae that are not adaptive in terms of stress coping), that results in novel, extreme-of-adaptation cognitive-affective states that serendipitously engender spiritual and religious mental phenotypes. The cause here is selection for adaptive responses to stressors, where responses sometimes overshoot their neurocognitive goals.

A second such mechanism is internal and pathological, deriving from large mental perturbations that generate maladaptive neuropsychological states. Such internal effects are postulated here to derive mainly from psychosis—reality distortion involving altered perception, hallucinations, and delusions—as well as some cases of temporal lobe epilepsy (e.g., Elliott et al., 2009). Psychosis apparently represents a qualitative extreme of human personality-related, psychological states related to the salience (meaning) (Kapur, 2003; Corlett & Fraser, 2025) and imagination (Nettle, 2001; Crespi et al., 2016) that have been instrumental in making humans what they are in terms of creative cognition (Looijestjin et al., 2015; Acar et al., 2018). It also centrally involves hyper-activation of HT2A receptors, especially in conjunction with alterations to dopaminergic and glutamatergic systems. The cause here is variation in personality and psychology, due proximately to variation in genes and environments.

A third mechanism is the effects on the human brain from external, qualitatively novel environmental inputs. In the context of religiosity and spiritual cognition, such effects derive from fungus and plant-derived biochemicals (so-called psychedelics) that happen to hyper-activate human HT2A receptors because they resemble serotonin in their chemical structure (Cameron et al., 2023). The cognitive-affective effects are thus evolutionarily new. The cause here is serendipity.

These mechanisms of spiritual and religious experience recall the "three visions" theory of Saint Augustine, who considered a trio of sources for visionary events: the natural and physical world, the human imagination, and God. Our present-day, science-based trinity of causes is clearly inter-related in being underlain by a single core neurophysiological structure. Thus, supraphysiological activation of HT2A can result from (1) overshoot of natural, adaptive processes of external, stress-induced learning, (2) psychotic-affective extremes of internal, psychological-personality variation that are similarly exacerbated by stressors, or (3) the external, artificial mechanism of psychedelics. In this context, and as described in more detail below, religious and spiritual perception, cognition, and affect thus emerge as extreme manifestations of the brain-wide suite of changes that drive responses to actual or induced challenges, all in the contexts of the evolution of human sociality, psychological variation, imagination, and culture.

Neither the serendipitous external mechanisms of psychedelics, the maladaptive internal mechanisms of psychosis, nor the overlapping but typically adaptive mechanisms of socioecological or physiological stress, work, of course, on a mental *tabula rasa*. In all three situations, the effects of the novelty channel through neural circuitry that evolved in other selective contexts, and that serves especially in the interpretation of perceptual-cognitive-affective experiences driven by HT2A hyper-activation. A primary such framework, fundamental among animals but developed especially highly in humans, is using the mind to draw inferences and meaning from the world via the neural machinery of Bayesian predictive coding. By this central mechanism of cognitive function, internal, *a priori* hypotheses (as models or predictions) about the world are continually compared to perceptual inputs, with discrepancies between the two ("prediction errors") being resolved through adjustments to beliefs, yielding improved *a posteriori* models of perceived "reality" (reviews in Smith et al., 2021; Pezzulo et al., 2022). Predictive coding models are of key importance here because mental models about the world instantiate human beliefs, feelings, values, goals, and meaning, all of which are massively modified in spiritual and religious thought. They do so in the specific human context of highly developed social cognition, which involves theory of mind, inference of mental states and intentions of others, social imagination and scenario-building, human social relationships involving important ancestors and leaders, and neurally based conceptualizations of the self and its existence. Spirituality and religion thus presumably must be built using the scaffold of predictive coding, and the blocks of mental modules and circuits subserving human sociality, imagination, and learning.

The key to the God-receptor hypothesis is that psychedelic biochemicals, psychosis, and overactivated stress responses all show clear evidence of involving high activation of the serotonin receptor HT2A, thus generating novel cognitive-affective states that result in thoughts and feelings that overlap broadly with those typical of spiritual and religious cognition (Barrett & Griffiths, 2018; McNamara, 2022). Most importantly, HT2A also shows evidence of mediating neural mechanisms of predictive coding in such a way that its hyper-activation generates spiritual/religious experiences cenetred around surprise, awe, consciousness, self, and meaning, thus connecting foundational neural processes with the intersecting phenomenologies of psychedelic experience, psychosis, stress, and spirituality and religion (van Elk & Aleman, 2017; Brouwer & Carhart-Harris, 2021).

In full, the God-receptor hypothesis posits several broad stages in the origins of spirituality and religiosity:

1 Evolutionarily novel mental experiences, involving visions and profound perceived insights, caused by some combination of entheogenic, psychotic-affective spectrum, and stress-related effects;
2 Imaginative interpretation of such visions and insights as indicative of supernatural gods and spirits, that are culturally instantiated into stories, narrative arcs, and institutions that serve to explain the otherwise-inexplicable vagaries of past, current, and expected future life and events, and that motivate forms of within-group unity deriving from shared, powerful beliefs and entities, including actual or perceived ancestors;
3 Fitness-related benefits from belief in such stories, entities, and participation in such institutions, due primarily to enhanced cooperation among individuals within families and groups, as well as loss of benefits or punishment for non-cooperators.

Health and fitness benefits of spirituality and religiosity have been described in detail elsewhere (e.g., Borges et al., 2021; Lynch et al., 2022). We focus predominantly on the first and second stages, especially as regards the neural bases of spiritual and religious experiences and their interpretations. The God-receptor hypothesis makes extraordinary claims; what is the evidence?

The God Receptor

HT2A is a G-protein-coupled receptor that is widely expressed in the central nervous system (Guiard & Giovanni, 2018). Its activation mediates the effects of psychedelic drugs, which serve as agonists of the receptor due to the structural similarities of serotonin to LSD, psilocin, and their chemical relatives (Cameron et al., 2023). By contrast, antagonism of HT2A underlies many of the effects of most atypical antipsychotic drugs, in addition to the effects of these drugs in down-regulating hyper-dopaminergic states via effects on DRD2 (Kantrowitz, 2020).

How might HT2A agonism trigger the profound cognitive-affective effects of psychedelics? A suite of convergent evidence supports the hypothesis that HT2A activation mediates the neural instantiation of prediction errors, the mismatches of predicted with actual sensory inputs used by the brain to continually update internal, top-down models for extracting meaning from interactions with the world (Smith et al., 2021; De Filippo & Schmitz, 2024). Such mismatches can be conceptualized, in typical cognition, as *surprise*, that specifically compels updating of information in the brain, especially for beliefs. By acting as HT2A agonists, psychedelics may thus generate "synthetic" and enhanced surprise, with increased prediction errors that mediate increased top-down updating of beliefs (De Filippo & Schmitz, 2024). In turn, hyper-updating of top-down predictions guides and shapes the processing of bottom-up inputs, leading to the novel landscape of sensations and feelings that characterize psychedelic experience. This model represents an extension and update of the Relaxed Beliefs Under Psychedelics (REBUS) model for predictive coding in psychedelic experience (Carhart-Harris & Friston, 2019), and it was developed to alleviate some of its shortcomings and better account for the subjective experiences involved.

The synthetic surprise model for understanding the neural and psychological effects of HT2A agonism, in relation to spiritual, religious, and mystical experiences, and models based on relaxed belief effects from psychedelics more generally, are underpinned by several lines of information:

1 Psychedelics show evidence of activating HTR2A receptors on SST interneurons, providing an apparent neural mechanism for enhanced prediction error effects (De Fillipo et al., 2021);
2 Serotoninergic neurotransmission encodes novelty in the brain, and activation of HT2A receptors underlies reversal learning, which is driven by prediction error signaling (Kanen et al., 2021);
3 The physiological effects of surprise include enlarged pupil diameter, which is driven by serotonergic neurotransmission (Cazettes et al., 2021), and which

characterizes effects from psychedelics (Aday et al., 2021) as well as problem-solving via sudden insight (Salvi et al., 2020);

4 Psychedelics, and surprise, exert similar effects on cortical alpha-wave oscillations (De Filippo & Schmitz, 2024), which have also been implicated in mechanisms of predictive coding (Alamia & Van Rullen, 2019);
5 N170 event-related potentials have been shown to reflect perceptual surprise (Robinson et al., 2020), and activation of HT2A receptors underpins the effects of psilocybin on alpha-wave oscillations and N170 potentials, in the context of hallucinations (Kometer et al., 2013);
6 Psychedelic experience is uniquely characterized by high levels of "imaginative suggestibility," the ability to become immersed in novel, externally generated scenarios, which implicates enhanced openness to new top-down models, and which may help to explain its therapeutic effects (Carhart-Harris et al., 2015);
7 Greatly increased levels of surprise can accurately and usefully be described as *awe*, an emotion that is fundamental to the effects of psychedelics (Hendricks, 2018; De Filippo & Schmitz, 2024). Awe, in turn, can be designated as a feeling derived from vastness, power, and mystery, that challenges existing systems of belief, and requires foundational adjustments to mental ideas and structures in order to assimilate the meaning of the new experience (Keltner & Haidt, 2003; Ihm et al., 2019).

The contexts of awe in non-psychedelic experience centrally include spirituality and religion; indeed, Ihm et al. (2019) suggest that "precursors to modern religions were conceived and developed during awe-like states in our hominid ancestors." These considerations provide notable links of the synthetic surprise model with the trappings of spirituality, mysticism, and religion, from the magnificence of beauty in the natural world, to the vastness of cathedrals and the grandeur of religious art and music, and to emotional subjugation to fearsome highly powerful individuals and beings—all in the context of novel systems of generation of meaning from the otherwise-inscrutable vagaries and apparent meaninglessness of existence (Keltner & Haidt 2003; Haidt, 2012; Vaillant, 2013; Ihm et al., 2019). Increases in the accessibility of different models of the world, that derive from synthetic surprise, may also help to explain the overlaps of psychedelic with spiritual experiences in terms of enhanced openness, discovery of novel connections and perspectives, feelings of insight and revelation, ego-dissolution via cognition less bounded by prior entrenched models of the self, and beliefs that "everything is connected," with additional links to "insight experiences" among individuals experiencing the schizophrenia prodrome or psychosis itself (Stoliker et al., 2022; Harding et al., 2024).

These considerations suggest central roles of the HT2A receptor in the surprise component of predictive coding of brain function, with mechanistic linkages to spirituality, religion, and psychosis that derive from receptor agonism, and from the role of serotonin in encoding the value of surprising rewards (Harkin et al., 2025).

The primary empirical and theoretical shortcomings of this hypothesis derive from an inadequate understanding of how prediction-error signaling and belief instantiation actually work in relevant areas of the brain, especially with regard to the roles of prediction-error precision (as opposed to magnitude) in cognitive states related to HT2A hyper-activation, since precision is believed to influence the levels of confidence ascribed to bottom-up and top-down information. Moreover, religious beliefs, and delusions in psychosis, commonly involve unusually inflexible top-down belief systems—the antithesis of relaxed beliefs and cognitive flexibility. Apparently, then, there are neural mechanisms that hyper-stabilize newfound, especially strong beliefs with synthetic, entheogenic, or delusional and psychopathological origins (Zeifman et al., 2025), perhaps via temporary down-regulation of HT2A (Brouwer & Carhart-Harris, 2021) or through dopaminergic effects on delusion formation and stability (Huber et al., 2022). Belief and meaning systems thus follow an arc from uncertain, to especially flexible, to remarkably fixed, for reasons that still require explanation in terms of neurophysiological mechanisms and cause.

HT2A Activation Effects in the Religious Bayesian Brain

In 1748, the philosopher David Hume made an argument, based on probabilities, for the unlikelihood of miracles such as personal observation of the resurrection of Jesus. The Reverend Thomas Bayes proved that Hume's logic was incorrect, and in doing so laid the foundation for conception of the brain as a Bayesian engine for predictive inference (Friston, 2003). Bayes believed that religious miracles, visions, and epiphanies were objectively true, but we explore here the argument that they can instead arise from supraphysiological activation of the HT2A receptor in areas of the brain with functions accidentally relevant to religious belief and experience.

How, then, do the HT2A receptor and predictive coding work in different religion-related neural regions and networks, in typical, adaptive cognition and, also in hyper-activation? Many brain regions are involved, but four appear to be especially important.

First, as described above, HT2A receptor activation mediates surprise, considered as the difference between expected and experienced "actual" events; this function is mediated in large part by the anterior cingulate cortex, part of the salience (meaning) network, although a suite of other regions is involved (e.g., Mousavi et al., 2022). The hyper-activated extreme of surprise, awe, represents a central feature of religious experience, that connects directly with hyper-salient meaning. The ACC also appears to be involved in the acquisition and maintenance of religious beliefs (van Elk & Aleman, 2017), as expected if the hyper-salience of awe inspired these effects.

Second, abundant HT2A receptors in the visual system subserve the balanced top-down, bottom-up dynamics of visual stimuli, whereby the brain generates and maintains predictive models regarding this form of sensory input through mental imagery (Dijkstra et al., 2019). Given the close anatomical and activational overlaps of the visual-perception system with the mental-imagination system (e.g., Dentico et al. 2014; Ganis et al. 2004), hyper-activation of HT2A in these brain regions appears to increase the influence of top-down influences in such a way that imagination can prevail, resulting in visual hallucinations (Kometer et al., 2013), sometimes in the context of religious visions depending upon cultural context, setting, and expectations.

Third, different dimensions of the self are instantiated in several brain regions with high densities of HT2A receptors and links to religiosity, the default mode network (the narrative self), the insula (the interoceptive self), and the claustrum (apparently, the integrative, conscious self) (Craig 2019; Yeshurun et al., 2021; Mantas et al., 2024; Tisserand et al., 2023; Anderson et al., 2024). These brain areas mediate the self in the context of self-other boundaries, which subserve emotional empathy and mentalistic perspective-taking, with boundaries being broader and more permeable among individuals with more psychotic-affective patterns of cognition (Minas et al. 1994; Bakhshaie et al. 2011; Crespi & Dinsdale, 2019; Lee et al., 2021). Hyper-activation of HT2A receptors in these brain areas appears responsible for the forms of ego-dissolution that characterizes psychedelic use, psychosis, and religious and mystical experiences, such that it apparently involves hyper-extension of self-other and self-nonself boundaries to the point of fusion and unity, via some combination of top-down and bottom-up effects on neural self-system and embodiment functions (e.g., Vollenweider et al. 1998; Kometer et al., 2012; Quednow et al., 2012; Stoliker et al., 2022). Mechanistically, such ego-dissolution and loss of self-nonself boundaries are associated with desynchronization of neural oscillations with relevant brain regions (Muthukumaraswamy et al., 2013; Carhart-Harris et al., 2016), and decreases in connectivity involving the default and salience networks (Lebedev et al., 2015). Showing some convergence with HT2A-mediated psychedelic effects, yogic practice has also been shown to be associated with such broadband desynchronization of EEG rhythms (Niazi et al., 2022), and the perceived efficacy of religious ritual is likewise associated with reductions in alpha and beta band power (Cho et al., 2018).

Finally, spirituality has recently been associated with the periaqueductal gray (PAG) (Ferguson et al., 2024), a brain region rich in HT2A receptors that subserves periconsciousness (non-reflexive, automatic neural processes that underlie complex conscious experience), involving aspects of basic emotion and experience such as pain modulation, anxiety, and attachment (the psychological basis of social bonding and love)(Nelson & Panksepp, 1998); indeed, increased HT2A activation shows evidence of reducing pain and anxiety through its downstream effects on release of enkephalins, endorphins, serotonin, dopamine, and oxytocin (Nelson & Panksepp, 1998; Silva & McNaughton, 2019; McPherson & Ingram, 2022). Given that production of such endogenous agents not only reduces pain, but can also, at higher levels, induce pleasure, hyper-activation of HT2A receptors in the PAG may, in part, be responsible for the hedonic, ecstatic, and love-imbued (as well as antidepressant more generally) nature of many mystical and religious experiences (Sierra et al., 2022; Salinsky et al., 2023). This hypothesis is consistent with the antinociceptive effects, for example, of LSD, and with the antidepressive and antinociception therapeutic effects of some psychedelics (Castellanos et al., 2020; Ramaekers et al., 2021; Ko et al., 2023; Kooijman et al., 2023). The PAG is also known to play key roles in the encoding of prediction errors regarding aversive stimuli (Grahl et al., 2018), and descending modulation of pain especially through stimulating the release of endorphins and enkephalins.

The four brain regions evaluated here in the context of the God-receptor hypothesis provide only preliminary evidence regarding the roles of HT2A receptor activation, and hyper-activation, in religious, spiritual, and mystical experiences (Figure 6.1), but they suggest an empirical way forward to better understand their neural bases, with clear predictions. These predictions are motivated by the observation that HT2A agonist psychedelic drugs can reliably produce such experiences, but, given that high activation of HT2A can and does also result from natural, endogenous, and socioecological causes (as discussed in more detail below), psychedelics are by no means implicated as necessary or sufficient in the origins of spiritual and religious thought and experience.

What is important for empirical work, under this hypothesis, is the prediction that the brain areas and systems linked with spirituality and religion should harbor notable densities of HT2A receptors that have region-specific normal and adaptive functions that, when hyper-activated, regularly produce elements of spirituality and religion experiences, that are explicable in terms of amplification (or other hyper-activational effects) of predictive coding mechanisms. This prediction

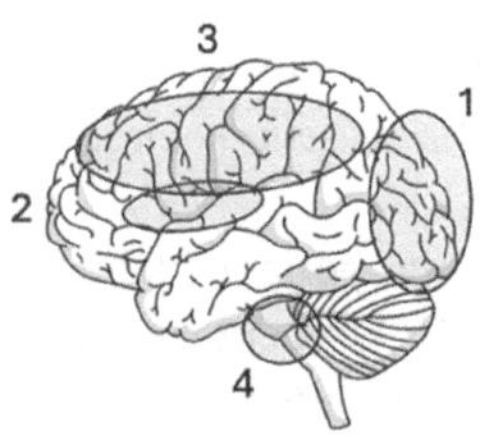

Brain region	Typical function	HT2A hyperactivation
1 Visual cortex	Perception of visual visual stimuli	Visual hallucination, mediated by imagination filtering into perception due to increased top-down predictive coding effects
2 Anterior cingulate cortex	Surprise, registered as prediction errors	Awe, vastness, peak experience, challenge to meaning system
3 Default mode, insula and claustrum	Instantiation of self (narrative, bodily, and multisensory)	Ego-dissolution, due to loss of neural oscillation synchronicity in default mode, and loss of internal bodily and mental state integration; one with others and universe; loss of space, time, self-other boundaries
4 Periaqueductal gray	Pain modulation, basic attachment, basic emotions, periconsciousness	Emotional well-being, bonding, love, connectedness, pleasure

FIGURE 6.1 Four Brain Regions Show Evidence of Being Centrally Involved in the Instantiation of Neural Functions That, Under HT2A Hyper-Activation, Generate Manifestations of Spiritual and Religious Experiences.

provides for specific tests of the idea that HT2A activation represents a "master key" to the doors of religious and spiritual perception and thought. What is not explicable by this framework is why this should all be so, in terms of the adaptive significance of HT2A receptor functions. What, then, could it be about these functions that, when hyper-activated, result in such a remarkable set of religious and spiritual cognitive-affective phenotypes?

The Evolved, Adaptive Significance of HT2A Activation

The life of any organism can be represented as a series of opportunities and threats. To the extent that these potentially affect fitness, they can be considered as stressors or challenges. In turn, organisms have evolved means of dealing with such stresses, many of which are cognitive, affective, and behavioral. The HT2A receptor in particular has been shown to be activated and upregulated in response to stressors, be they social, ecological, or physiological (Leonard, 2005; Murnane, 2019). Brouwer and Carhart-Harris (2021) provide a comprehensive review of evidence linking HT2A to acute or chronic stresses, and suggest an adaptive reason for these responses: that HT2A activation causes a suite of neural changes that facilitate increased neural plasticity and enhanced associative learning (e.g., Kanen et al., 2023; Vargas et al., 2023), thereby generating "pivotal" mental states that are better-suited for alleviating or overcoming the challenge, especially via active coping (Brouwer & Carhart-Harris, 2021). The clearest and simplest evidence for this hypothesis comes from experimental studies whereby administration of HT2A agonists notably facilitate associative learning, for example, in rabbits (Harvey et al. 1983) and humans (Hensman et al., 1991) given LSD. More generally, activation of HT2A receptors in response to stresses can be seen as an adaptive system for learning through associative-imaginative insight (Brouwer & Carhart-Harris, 2021; Tulver et al., 2023; McGovern et al., 2024) in situations where it is especially important, for fitness, to do so.

Under typical conditions, enhanced learning in response to HT2A activation is expected to involve surprise, insight, recognition of salience (meaning) in some association, process, or pattern, and the emergence of novel beliefs about the world that help in dealing with the relevant task. Successfully overcoming stress through these mechanisms should also result in pleasure, the body's reward for a job done well. Learning should be facilitated by increased mental exploration of possible responses to challenges (e.g., divergent thinking, strong imagination, and mental imagery), and by thinking that reaches outside of the self to better encompass the dimensions of the external social or ecological threats. Stresses also commonly engender conditional suppression of pain, such as hungry mice feeling less pain (Alhadeff et al., 2018), or humans suppressing pain during fight-flight events (Melzack, 2014), as enabled via descending antinociceptive pathways. The full arc from initial stress or challenge to resolution involves a well-orchestrated suite of changes, with learning insight and HT2A activation, at the core (Figure 6.2).

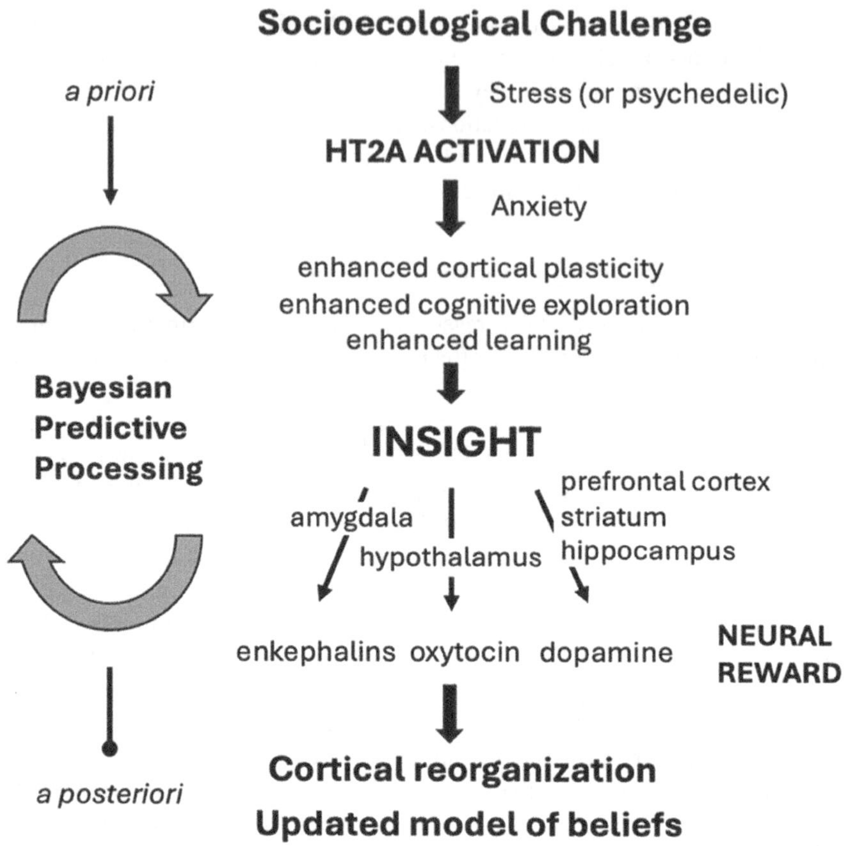

FIGURE 6.2 A Key Evolved Function of HT2A Activation Is the Generation of Neural Plasticity in Response to Stressors or Challenges, Leading, If Successful, to Insight Problem-Solving, Reward, and Updated Beliefs. Hyper-Activation of This System Due to High Levels of Stress, Psychotic-Affective Mental States, or Psychedelic Drugs Can Lead to Spiritual and Religious Experiences That Involve Profound Insights and Novel Supernatural and Delusional Beliefs.

Relatively extreme stresses are expected to commonly involve increased, hyper-activation of HT2A receptors, that can lead to cognitive-affective extremes that should include awe, novel insights and beliefs, hyper-salience (meaning), hallucinations or visions, ego-dissolution, and euphoria. To the extent that hallucinations or visions require logical "explanation" by the brain, to maintain a coherent reality, they should also engender delusions: imagined, self-generated narratives that can make sense, in cultural perspectives, of the extraordinary and otherwise-inexplicable experience (Graseman et al., 2009; Mishara & Corlett, 2009). Delusions of the supernatural, and all-powerful "gods," would be most effective at explaining to one's self, and to others, otherwise ineffable and awe-inspiring experiences, and these can then be enmeshed in culture-specific narratives.

Of course, all of these hypothesized manifestation of HT2A hyper-activation are hallmarks of religious, spiritual, and mystical experience, whether they derive from psychedelics, forms of psychosis, "spirit quests" that involve fasting, social isolation, and other self-induced stress (e.g., 40 days in wilderness), or related causes (Friesen, 2013; Taves, 2020; Demmrich et al., 2023). In principle, this hypothesis can link HT2A activation, and its hyper-activation due to many causes, to diverse religious, spiritual, and mystical experiences. Such experiences thus become emergent properties of an adaptive evolved system that centrally involves perhaps the most human of cognitive-affective traits: imagination, narrative, mentalistic explanation, and social bonding. Hyper-development of these properties, in turn, motivates the genesis of the major features of gods: awesomeness, omnipresence, omnipotence, provision of meaning in the world, and love.

HT2A, Psychedelics, and the Origins of Human Spirituality and Religion

The God-receptor hypothesis posits that the de novo origins of spiritualistic bodies of thought, and religions, should involve some combination of entheogenic, adaptive stress-related, and psychological psychotic-affective influences. The idea of entheogenic (psychoactive drug mediated) origins for human spirituality and religions has been evidenced by a large body of anthropological and historical studies that draw links between (1) use of various naturally occurring psychedelic substances, (2) spiritual and religious experiences that involve visions, ego-dissolution, and interactions with godlike entities, and (3) scriptures and histories of large-scale religions, and current practices in small-scale groups (e.g., Rush, 2013; Brown & Lupu, 2014; Hoffman, 2019; Nemu, 2019; Samorini, 2019; Winkelman, 2019; Spiers et al., 2024). As regards neurological and psychological considerations, perhaps the most telling evidence for entheogenic origins of religions is the remarkable similarities of spiritual and religious insight or revelation experiences with the more general cognitive and affective experiences caused by psychedelic drugs (Buckley, 1981; Carhart-Harris et al., 2013; Lebedev et al., 2015; Griffiths et al., 2019; Friesen, 2022; Brouwer et al., 2024).

Despite such compelling cross-cultural and historical evidence, and the apparent lack of comprehensive alternative scientific explanations for convergent visionary and hallucinatory religious inspiration experiences across thousands of years and diverse cultures, the entheogenic-origins hypothesis for human spirituality and religions remains challenging to evaluate in a robust scientific manner. Such limitations involve several factors:

1 In even the most otherwise-persuasive cases, the specific psychoactive compounds and their sources usually remain unclear, apparently due in part to the highly secretive treatment of "sacred" agents on one hand, and the usual later

suppression of such agents by self-interested parties in established religious institutions that are sustained through their administrations.

2 Many cases are known of dramatic spiritual and religious experiences, even among founders of particular religious groups or subgroups, that clearly do not involve the use of entheogens (though they may involve stress-induced visions). Examples include the visions of Francis of Assisi and Ignatius Loyola, each of which led to successful religious movements.
3 Entheogenic theories for the origins of human religions beg the question of the actual origins of the concept of gods or God in human societies, which would appear to represent more an explanation for psychedelic experiences than a necessary or likely sequel to visions, perceived insights, and hallucinations. Indeed, at the actual origin of psychoactive drugs use in humans, there would presumably be no established cultural context (or a god-being or equivalent) within which to interpret the experiences, other than long-dead, memorable, powerful human ancestors, who may indeed have represented the first gods (Crespi, 2021). As such, the question of the psychological and neural context for the initial psychological creation of gods and spirits remains unresolved.
4 In any given human group, only a small number or proportion of individuals would likely ingest, or have ingested, entheogenic substances in the context of spirituality and religion. Some such individuals would have had large influences in their society and beyond, as prophets, saints, shamans, or seers with personal experience of the supernatural, but the growth and maintenance of religions would still depend upon the psychocultural assimilation of others (O'Grady, 2012).

Taken together, these considerations suggest that, while entheogens may have been instrumental in the origins and early evolution of human spirituality and religion, in generating a direct route to supernatural experiences through HR2A hyperactivation, they are clearly only one of multiple contributory neural and psychological factors. What other causes are involved?

HT2A and Psychosis

Psychedelic drugs represent external and evolutionarily novel causes of spiritual and religious experiences. Such experiences can also be mediated by the two forms of internal causes that are not evolutionarily new: high levels of stress and psychosis. As described above, stress can apparently induce such experiences through hyper-expression of neurophysiological mechanisms that underlie insight through associative learning. By contrast, psychosis represents reality distortion, usually hallucinations and delusions, as seen most prominently in people with schizophrenia or bipolar disorder with mania. Whereas the diagnoses of schizophrenia and bipolar disorder are dichotomous, their psychological features and personality-related underpinnings grade into typical cognition (e.g., Kwapil & Barrantes-Vidal, 2015;

Yamada et al., 2020). Psychosis-related experiences are thus by no means uncommon, and many are enjoyable, such as hypomania (mild forms of mania that involve elation, high energy levels), positive delusions about one's abilities or self-importance (a mild form of delusions of grandeur), or auditory hallucinations that are positively valanced, such as kind hallucinated words from a beloved, deceased aunt or uncle (e.g., Corentin et al., 2023). Typically, forms of psychosis are brought to the attention of psychiatrists only when they are disturbing to ones-self or to others, as in schizophrenia with delusions of persecution.

A striking proportion, around 20%–60% depending upon the population and study, of hallucinations and delusions are religious or spiritual in nature (Grover et al., 2014). Most of these experiences and beliefs are positive, raising the obvious questions of whether a line can be drawn, and where to draw it, between religiosity or spirituality and psychosis, since both involve ideation that is hallucinatory or delusional in its inability to be verified in any objective way. Here, the current criteria are generally twofold: if the delusion is shared by members of some culturally identified group, and if it is emotionally agreeable, it is deemed mentally "healthy" (Pierre, 2001). These criteria, however, do not apply to non-Westernized and ancestral cultures, for whom "natural" and "supernatural" need not be distinguished from one another, although members of such cultures presumably vary in how much they attribute events in the world to divine versus observable causes.

Are the broad overlaps of psychosis with religiosity and spirituality underlain by shared effects of HT2A receptor activation? Diverse, independent lines of evidence link psychoses, as expressed in schizophrenia or bipolar disorder, with this receptor, all in the broader context of psychosis being mediated by shifts in integrated serotoninergic-glutamatergic-dopaminergic activity (e.g., Stahl, 2018):

First, most antipsychotic drugs exert antagonistic effects on the HT2A receptor (e.g., Casey et al., 2022), and some psychosis-inducing agents, notably ketamine and MK801, act as agonists (e.g., Lin et al., 2018; Nasrallah et al., 2019). By contrast, drugs that block the NMDA receptor, such as ketamine and phencyclidine, induce psychosis as well as activating HT2A (Kapur & Seeman, 2002).

Second, HT2A stimulation increases midbrain dopaminergic activity, which exacerbates psychotic (as well as negative) symptoms of schizophrenia. HT2A also exhibits increased functional activity among individuals with schizophrenia compared to controls (Diez-Alarcia et al., 2021). Increased midbrain dopamine also mediates learning via enhanced prediction errors (Gibbs et al., 2007), such that the hyper-salience of psychosis can also engender forms of delusional "hyper-learning" to make sense and meaning of the experience (Graseman et al., 2009), thus linking conceptually to learning under stress in typical, adaptive conditions (Brouwer & Carhart-Harris, 2021).

Third, the schizophrenia "prodrome," a period of some months or years before frank psychosis, is characterized by a suite of psychological changes that include heightened sensitivity to stressors and enhanced attribution of significance and meaning to "ordinary" or "irrelevant" stimuli (e.g., Kim, 2021; Buckley, 1981;

Roiser et al., 2013). Such exaggerated perception of salience or meaning, which is often imbued with mystery, may be followed by moments of sudden, deep insight as psychosis develops, such that the trajectories of psychotic experience can closely parallel those of psychedelics, in ways that implicate HT2A effects in both. More broadly, schizophrenia itself has been usefully described as "salience dysregulation syndrome" (van Os, 2009), whereby assignment of meaning or importance to stimuli is altered, and frequently exaggerated, in cognitive or affective (mood-related) ways. As such, psychosis involves the same sort of anxiogenic, aversive initial stage as do psychedelics as well as genetic stressors (Figure 6.3).

Fourth, as noted above, individuals with schizophrenia or high in positive schizotypy exhibit reductions in the sharpness of self-other boundaries compared to controls, such that their sense of self tends to merge more readily and broadly into the external worlds of people and non-human features of the environment (Bleuler, 1950; Lee et al., 2021; Green & Jimenez, 2022). Such lessening of self-nonself borders expresses itself in various ways, from embodiment as indexed by the rubber hand illusion (Crespi & Dinsdale, 2019), to increases in empathy as evidenced by genetic correlations (Warrier et al., 2018), and to broader reduction in ego boundaries, and loss of sense of ownership of thoughts and actions, as originally described by Bleuler over 100 years ago. These phenomena on the psychotic spectrum closely resemble losses of ego boundaries, and more general losses of the unitary, perceived, agentic self, under psychedelics, which can be attributed to agonism of HT2A.

A key limitation on comparisons of spiritual and religious experiences under psychedelics with idiopathic psychotic-affective disorders such as schizophrenia

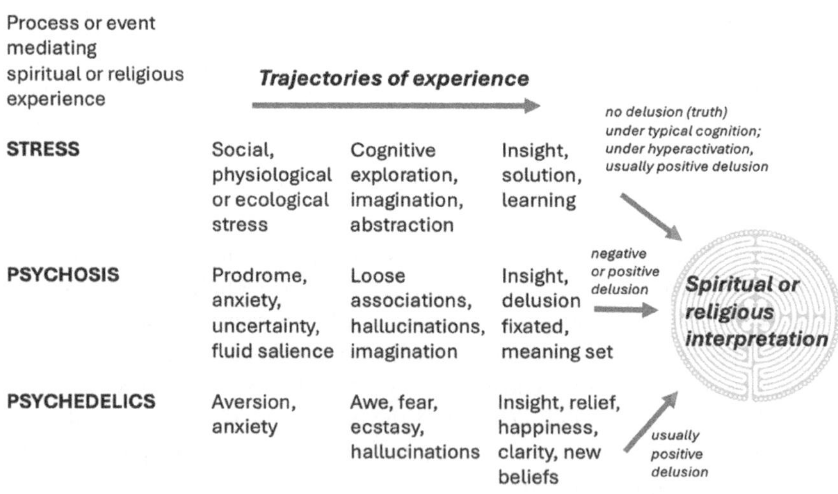

FIGURE 6.3 The Series of Neuropsychological Events That Lead to Insight and Belief Updating Is Notably Similar Under Causation by Stress, Psychosis, and Psychedelic Drugs, Due to Common Underlying Mechanisms Instigated and Orchestrated by HT2A Hyper-Activation.

is that the same data-collection or experimental paradigms have seldom been used for both sets of conditions. However, the broad phenomenological similarities between psychotic, psychedelic, and religious-spiritual experience, and the links of each to HT2A activation, implicate this receptor in the perception of meaning in the world, and gods as their imaginative instantiation (Buckley, 1981; Carhart-Harris et al., 2013; Lebedev et al., 2015; Griffiths et al., 2019; Friesen, 2022; Brouwer et al., 2024). A further commonality appears to be psychosocial and other forms of stress: it represents a crucial environmental trigger for the development of psychosis (van Winkel et al., 2008), and drives HT2A activation itself in the context of adaptation-related challenges more generally as described above; moreover, the early stages of psychedelic experience commonly involve acute stress responses and anxiety (Brouwer & Carhart-Harris, 2021; Brouwer et al., 2024; Figure 6.3). Determining the extent to which these three contexts overlap and recapitulate one another, mediated by trajectories of HT2A activation in different brain regions with downstream effects on cognition and mood, should represent one of the major goals for the cognitive neuroscience of religion and spirituality.

The similarities described above are striking. What, then, of the differences in experience, and its causes, between psychotic-affective disorders, spirituality and religion, and psychedelics? One of the main distinctions, that is crucial as regards mental health and well-being, is valence, with spirituality, religion, psychedelics, mania, and megalomania typically manifesting as positive, but other psychotic symptoms, such as hostile hallucinatory voices, paranoia, other intense aversive delusions, and severe depression, being extremely negative. Positive emotion in mania appears to be mediated by high dopamine that enhances pleasure-seeking and reward, with dopaminergic system activation also leading, in some circumstances, to the release of oxytocin (mediating feelings of bonding and love)(Carter, 2022) and endorphins (mediating feelings of euphoria and overall well-being)(Corder et al., 2018). Aversive psychotic and depressive states, as seen in schizophrenia and schizoaffective disorder, may be related to deleterious exaggerations of social defeat effects (Selten et al., 2013), high social threat sensitivity (Reininghaus et al., 2016), and dysregulated negative feedbacks in mood regulation, but the neurophysiological bases of these specific phenotypes remain unclear. The clear therapeutic benefits of psychedelics in the specific contexts of depression and PTSD may, in this context, stem from their ability to reorganize the structure and valence of meaning-related cognition and affect in relevant brain systems, apparently through HT2A-mediated recapitulation of evolved mechanisms for successful problem-solving through insight.

Discussion

In this chapter, we have proposed and evaluated the "God-receptor" hypothesis for the neural bases of human spirituality and religion. The hypothesis was motivated and evaluated through integration of information from: (1) studies of psychedelic drug effects in the brain; (2) evidence regarding the entheogenic origins and forms of human spirituality and religions; (3) analyses of how psychoactive drugs and HT2A hyper-activation affect predictive coding of cognition and affect; (4) studies of what specific brain regions are most involved in spiritual and religious thought and experience, and the adaptive and hyper-activational effects of HT2A stimulation and predictive coding systems in these areas; and (5) research on how the causes and effects of psychosis and its subclinical forms overlap with spiritual/religious cognition, in the specific context of HT2A typical and hyper-active functions.

By the God-receptor model, the concept of God is most-parsimoniously represented, mechanistically, by the serendipitous cognitive-affective results of supraphysiological activation of the HT2A receptor. Such activation, which can be due to either external, entheogenic or internal, psychophysiological causes, results in a suite of HT2A-mediated alterations to predictive-coding systems that orchestrate central brain functions, most notably: (a) belief in profound, novel insights, driven by lowered thresholds for inferences of meaning, (b) awe, the extreme of prediction-error surprise, that enhances the strength of these beliefs; and (c) ego-dissolution and feelings of oneness with the world as a manifestation of God, apparently due to relaxation of priors regarding self-instantiation and self-other boundaries at different hierarchical levels in the brain including the PAG, default mode network (DMN), and claustrum. These feelings of insight, awe, and oneness are interpreted, via instantiations of culture-specific imagination, in terms of supernatural and preternatural presences, powers, minds, agents, events, and narrative arcs, that take on unique roles in human cognitive-affective and cultural landscapes through the provision of meaning, purpose, and explanation for existence. As such, hyper-stimulation of HT2A can elucidate the origins of god-perception and god-experiences, which come to form the core inspirations and shared delusionary beliefs upon which a supernatural-based religion is initially built.

Ultimately, the God-receptor model is based on the physiological and psychological connections between the evolved, adaptive, usual functions of the HT2A receptor and the effects of receptor hyper-activation, that are supraphysiological and novel but mechanistically and experientially connected to normal function. The adaptive functions of HT2A (and its interacting ligand-receptor systems such as those involving DRD2 and NMDA) in the typically functioning brain depend, in turn, on the specific brain region, network, or operation concerned, but they can, at least in some instances, be linked with supraphysiological effects, including imagination with hallucination, surprise with awe, dissociation with universal oneness, and momentary pleasure with ecstasy and euphoria.

Given that the origins of religiosity and spirituality are indeed mediated by HT2A hyper-activation, the key question becomes just what factors contribute to the hyper-activation process, and how they do so. The first factor is intrinsic susceptibility to high levels of activation, which results from genetic, personality-related, psychiatric, and neurological influences related to psychotic-affective spectrum phenotypes and their subclinical manifestations. Intrinsic susceptibility would thus be enhanced by an associated suite of traits, including positive schizotypal personality, openness to experience, absorption, tendency to dissociation, and strong imagination (Lifshitz et al., 2019). At the extreme, frank psychosis (or salient forms of epilepsy) can occur more or less spontaneously, resulting in hallucinations and delusions that are interpreted in spiritual and religious frameworks often involving sudden insights leading to novel and deeply held beliefs.

Second, among individuals less intrinsically prone to psychosis, hyper-activation effects from HT2A would be driven more by forms of physiological and neurological stress and challenge, that mediates associative, prediction-error-based learning commonly manifesting as imaginative insight moments. Such moments would usually be useful and adaptive, but would sometimes gravitate to novel beliefs that were false and delusional, though they may have adaptive elements in helping to cope with unusual perceptions. This mechanism is part and parcel of the cognitive changes that have made us human, and that underlie the functions of the expanded transmodal association neocortical regions whose development, function, and neurological plasticity are orchestrated in notable part by HT2A effects (Luppi et al., 2024). Most importantly, it is the adaptive trajectory of stress, associative cognitive exploration, insight, learning, and belief that apparently generates potential for the remarkable constellation of supraphysiological effects in different brain regions (especially awe, universal oneness, and love) that make up transformative spiritual and religious experiences. In essence, such experiences represent extremes of adaptive mental states.

The third mechanism for HT2A activation is, of course, psychedelic biochemicals, whose cognitive-affective effects on HT2A in humans are entirely accidental but, once discovered, can be regulated as to time, person, and place, thus laying the groundwork for organization and control of spiritual and religious experience and institutions among nascent groups. As evidenced by a host of anthropological and historical studies, many religions indeed derive in part or whole from such entheogenic events or rituals, that lend them supernatural legitimacy through miracles and compelling narratives directly connecting humans with gods (Brown & Lupu, 2014; Beckstead et al., 2019; Hoffman, 2019; Nemu, 2019; Samorini, 2019; Winkelman, 2019; Spiers et al., 2024).

Because they are all mediated by HT2A, these three mechanisms are essentially one and the same, explaining the deep and broad similarities between psychedelic, spiritual/religious, and positively valenced psychotic experiences (Buckley, 1981; Brouwer et al., 2024; Figure 6.3).

The God-receptor hypothesis has several important implications for the study of the cognitive neuroscience of religion. Perhaps the most noteworthy is that it shifts the focus of the field toward analysis of the neurophysiology and adaptive functions of the HT2A receptor, and the neurotransmitter-receptor systems directly associated with it, in different regions of the brain. Here, we have concentrated on the visual system, brain areas mediating surprise, self-instantiation, and the PAG, as four regions whose connections to the phenomenology of HT2A hyper-activation effects appear most obvious and relevant to spirituality and religion. Many other brain areas and systems must also be intimately involved, together representing a network of God-related activation and receptor effects (e.g., Gobbi, 2024). Predictive coding theory provides the key cognitive-science instrument for understanding how the network components work separately and together, and it will need to be elaborated in concert with studies of HT2A's adaptive and hyper-activated functions.

Finally, studies of the neurocognitive physiological basis of spirituality and religion should generate novel insights into the mechanisms of psychedelic-based therapies, that are beginning to revolutionize treatments for depression and trauma (Velit-Salazar et al., 2024). Do psychedelic therapies work because they amplify the evolved, adaptive, plasticity-inducing process of challenge, exploration, and discovery that is typically imbued with fitness-related pleasure and love? Can this process be optimized, personalized, or recapitulated through psychophysiological rather than just biochemical means? Finding God throughout the human brain may be only the origin of this field, and its many profound applications to human health and well-being.

Acknowledgments

We are grateful to Ari Brouwer for insightful comments and the Templeton Foundation and NSERC for financial support.

References

Acar, S., Chen, X., & Cayirdag, N. (2018). Schizophrenia and creativity: A meta-analytic review. *Schizophrenia Research, 195*, 23–31. https://doi.org/10.1016/j.schres.2017.08.036

Aday, J., Wood, J., Bloesch, E., & Davoli, C. (2021). Psychedelic drugs and perception: A narrative review of the first era of research. *Reviews in the Neurosciences*, *32*(5), 559–571. https://doi.org/10.1515/revneuro-2020-0094

Alamia, A., & VanRullen, R. (2019). Alpha oscillations and traveling waves: Signatures of predictive coding? *PLoS Biology, 17*(10), e3000487. https://doi.org/10.1371/journal.pbio.3000487

Alhadeff, A. L., Su, Z., Hernandez, E., Klima, M. L., Phillips, S. Z., Holland, R. A., Guo, C., Hantman, A. W., De Jonghe, B. C., & Betley, J. N. (2018). A neural circuit for the suppression of pain by a competing need state. *Cell, 173*(1), 140–152. https://doi.org/10.1016/j.cell.2018.02.057

Anderson, T. L., Keady, J. V., Songrady, J., Tavakoli, N. S., Asadipooya, A., Neeley, R. E., Turner, J. R., & Ortinski, P. I. (2024). Distinct 5-HT receptor subtypes regulate claustrum excitability by serotonin and the psychedelic, DOI. *Progress in Neurobiology, 240*, 102660. https://doi.org/10.1016/j.pneurobio.2024.102660

Bakhshaie, J., Sharifi, V., & Amini, J. (2011). Exploratory factor analysis of SCL-90-R symptoms relevant to psychosis. *Iranian Journal of Psychiatry, 6*(4), 128.

Barrett, F. S., & Griffiths, R. R. (2018). Classic hallucinogens and mystical experiences: Phenomenology and neural correlates. In A. C. Halberstadt, F. X. Vollenweider, & D. E. Nichols (Eds.), *Behavioral neurobiology of psychedelic drugs* (pp. 393–430). Springer. https://doi.org/10.1007/7854_2017_474

Beckstead, R., Blankenagel, B., Noconi, C., & Winkelman, M. (2019). The entheogenic origins of Mormonism: A working hypothesis. *Journal of Psychedelic Studies, 3*(2), 212–260. https://doi.org/10.1556/2054.2019.020

Bleuler, E. (1950). *Dementia praecox or the group of schizophrenias*. International Universities Press.

Borges, C. C., Dos Santos, P. R., Alves, P. M., Borges, R. C. M., Lucchetti, G., Barbosa, M. A., Porto, C. C., & Fernandes, M. R. (2021). Association between spirituality/religiousness and quality of life among healthy adults: A systematic review. *Health and Quality of Life Outcomes, 19*, 1–13. https://doi.org/10.1186/s12955-021-01878-7

Brouwer, A., & Carhart-Harris, R. L. (2021). Pivotal mental states. *Journal of Psychopharmacology, 35*(4), 319–352. https://doi.org/10.1177/0269881120959637

Brouwer, A., Raison, C. L., & Shults, F. L. (2024). The trajectory of psychedelic, spiritual, and psychotic experiences: implications for cognitive scientific perspectives on religion. *Religion, Brain & Behavior*, 1–17. https://doi.org/10.1080/2153599X.2024.2349151

Brown, J. & Lupu, M. (2014). Sacred plants and the gnostic church: Speculations on entheogen-use in early Christian ritual. *Journal of Ancient History, 2*(1), 64–77. https://doi.org/10.1515/jah-2014-0010

Buckley, P. (1981). Mystical experience and schizophrenia. *Schizophrenia Bulletin, 7*(3), 516–521. https://doi.org/10.1093/schbul/7.3.516

Cameron, L. P., Benetatos, J., Lewis, V., Bonniwell, E. M., Jaster, A. M., Moliner, R., Castrén, E., McCorvy, J. D., Palner, M., & Aguilar-Valles, A. (2023). Beyond the 5-HT2A receptor: Classic and nonclassic targets in psychedelic drug action. *Journal of Neuroscience, 43*(45), 7472–7482. https://doi.org/10.1523/JNEUROSCI.1384-23.2023

Carhart-Harris, R. L., & Friston, K. J. (2019). REBUS and the anarchic brain: Toward a unified model of the brain action of psychedelics. *Pharmacological Reviews, 71*(3), 316–344. https://doi.org/10.1124/pr.118.017160

Carhart-Harris, R. L., Kaelen, M., Whalley, M. G., Bolstridge, M., Feilding, A., & Nutt, D. J. (2015). LSD enhances suggestibility in healthy volunteers. *Psychopharmacology, 232*, 785–794. https://doi.org/10.1007/s00213-014-3714-z

Carhart-Harris, R. L., Leech, R., Erritzoe, D., Williams, T. M., Stone, J. M., Evans, J., Sharp, D. J., Feilding, A., Wise, R. G., & Nutt, D. J. (2013). Functional connectivity measures after psilocybin inform a novel hypothesis of early psychosis. *Schizophrenia Bulletin, 39*(6), 1343–1351. https://doi.org/10.1093/schbul/sbs117

Carhart-Harris, R. L., Muthukumaraswamy, S., Roseman, L., Kaelen, M., Droog, W., Murphy, K., Tagliazucchi, E., Schenberg, E. E., Nest, T., Orban, C., & Leech, R. (2016). Neural correlates of the LSD experience revealed by multimodal neuroimaging. *Proceedings of the National Academy of Sciences, 113*(17), 4853–4858. https://doi.org/10.1073/pnas.1518377113

Carter, C. S. (2022). Oxytocin and love: Myths, metaphors and mysteries. *Comprehensive Psychoneuroendocrinology, 9*, 100107. https://doi.org/10.1016/j.cpnec.2021.100107

Casey, A. B., Cui, M., Booth, R. G., & Canal, C. E. (2022). "Selective" serotonin 5-HT2A receptor antagonists. *Biochemical Pharmacology, 200*, 115028. https://doi.org/10.1016/j.bcp.2022.115028

Castellanos, J. P., Woolley, C., Bruno, K. A., Zeidan, F., Halberstadt, A., & Furnish, T. (2020). Chronic pain and psychedelics: A review and proposed mechanism of action.

Regional Anesthesia & Pain Medicine, 45(7), 486–494. https://doi.org/10.1136/rapm-2020-101273

Cazettes, F., Reato, D., Morais, J. P., Renart, A., & Mainen, Z. F. (2021). Phasic activation of dorsal raphe serotonergic neurons increases pupil size. *Current Biology, 31*(1), 192–197. https://doi.org/10.1016/j.cub.2020.09.090

Cho, P. S., Escoffier, N., Mao, Y., Ching, A., Green, C., Jong, J., & Whitehouse, H. (2018). Groups and emotional arousal mediate neural synchrony and perceived ritual efficacy. *Frontiers in Psychology, 9*, 2071. https://doi.org/10.3389/fpsyg.2018.02071

Corder, G., Castro, D. C., Bruchas, M. R., & Scherrer, G. (2018). Endogenous and exogenous opioids in pain. *Annual Review of Neuroscience, 41*, 453–473. https://doi.org/10.1146/annurev-neuro-080317-061522

Corentin, C., Fitzgerald, C., & Goodwin, J. (2023). Benefits of hearing voices groups and other self-help groups for voice hearers: A systematic review. *Issues in Mental Health Nursing, 44*(4), 228–244. https://doi.org/10.1080/01612840.2023.2189953

Corlett, P. R., & Fraser, K. M. (2025). 20 years of aberrant salience in psychosis: What have we learned. *American Journal of Psychiatry, 182*(9). https://doi.org/10.1176/appi.ajp.20240556

Craig, A. D. (2009). How do you feel—now? The anterior insula and human awareness. *NatureRreviews Neuroscience, 10*(1), 59–70.

Crespi, B. (2021). The kin selection of religion. In J. R. Liddle & T. K. Shackelford (Eds.), *The Oxford handbook of evolutionary psychology and religion* (pp. 135–152). Oxford University Press.

Crespi, B., & Dinsdale, N. (2019). Autism and psychosis as diametrical disorders of embodiment. *Evolution, Medicine, and Public Health, 2019*(1), 121–138. https://doi.org/10.1093/emph/eoz021

Crespi, B., Leach, E., Dinsdale, N., Mokkonen, M., & Hurd, P. (2016). Imagination in human social cognition, autism, and psychotic-affective conditions. *Cognition, 150*, 181–199. https://doi.org/10.1016/j.cognition.2016.02.001

De Filippo, R., Rost, B. R., Stumpf, A., Cooper, C., Tukker, J. J., Harms, C., Beed, P., & Schmitz, D. (2021). Somatostatin interneurons activated by 5-HT2A receptors suppress slow oscillations in the medial entorhinal cortex. *eLife, 10*, e66960. https://doi.org/10.7554/eLife.66960

De Filippo, R., & Schmitz, D. (2024). Synthetic surprise as the foundation of the psychedelic experience. *Neuroscience & Biobehavioral Reviews, 157*, 105538. https://doi.org/10.1016/j.neubiorev.2024.105538

Demmrich, S., Koppold-Liebscher, D., Klatte, C., Steckhan, N., & Ring, R. M. (2023). Effects of religious intermittent dry fasting on religious experience and mindfulness: A longitudinal study among Baha'is. *Psychology of Religion and Spirituality, 15*(4), 459. https://doi.org/10.1037/rel0000423

Dentico, D., Cheung, B. L., Chang, J. Y., Guokas, J., Boly, M., Tononi, G., & Van Veen, B. (2014). Reversal of cortical information flow during visual imagery as compared to visual perception. *Neuroimage, 100*, 237–243. https://doi.org/10.1016/j.neuroimage.2014.05.081

Diez-Alarcia, R., Muguruza, C., Rivero, G., García-Bea, A., Gómez-Vallejo, V., Callado, L. F., Llop, J., Martín, A., & Meana, J. J. (2021). Opposite alterations of 5-HT2A receptor brain density in subjects with schizophrenia: Relevance of radiotracers' pharmacological profile. *Translational Psychiatry, 11*, 302. https://doi.org/10.1038/s41398-021-01430-7

Dijkstra, N., Hinne, M., Bosch, S. E., & van Gerven, M. A. J. (2019). *Individual differences in the influence of mental imagery on conscious perception* [Preprint]. bioRxiv. https://doi.org/10.1101/607770

Elliott, B., Joyce, E., & Shorvon, S. (2009). Delusions, illusions and hallucinations in epilepsy: 1. Elementary phenomena. *Epilepsy Research, 85*(2–3), 162–171.

Ferguson, M. A., Schaper, F. L., Cohen, A., Siddiqi, S., Merrill, S. M., Nielsen, J. A., ... & Fox, M. D. (2022). A neural circuit for spirituality and religiosity derived from patients with brain lesions. *Biological Psychiatry, 91*(4), 380–388.

Ferguson, M. A., Asp, E. W., Kletenik, I., Tranel, D., Boes, A. D., Nelson, J. M., Schaper, F. L. W. V. J., Siddiqi, S., Turner, J. I., Anderson, J. S., Nielsen, J. A., Bateman, J. R., Grafman, J., & Fox, M. D. (2024). A neural network for religious fundamentalism derived from patients with brain lesions. *PNAS Proceedings of the National Academy of Sciences of the United States of America, 121*(36), Article e2322399121. https://doi.org/10.1073/pnas.2322399121

Friesen, N. (2013). Vision quest structures in the ethnographic and archaeological record, with examples from Saskatchewan. In T. Cyr-Steenkamp, B. Riehl-Fitzsimmons, & N. Friesen (Eds.), *Contributions to Northern Plains Archaeology* (pp. 61–84). Saskatoon, SK: Saskatchewan Archaeological Society and the Department of Archaeology and Anthropology, University of Saskatchewan. https://autumn.ca/wp-content/uploads/2023/04/Vision_Quest_Structures_in_the_Ethnograp-1.pdf

Friesen, P. (2022). Psychosis and psychedelics: Historical entanglements and contemporary contrasts. *Transcultural Psychiatry, 59*(5), 592–609. https://doi.org/10.1177/13634615221129116

Friston, K. (2003). Learning and inference in the brain. *Neural Networks, 16*(9), 1325–1352. https://doi.org/10.1016/j.neunet.2003.06.005

Ganis, G., Thompson, W. L., & Kosslyn, S. M. (2004). Brain areas underlying visual mental imagery and visual perception: An fMRI study. *Cognitive Brain Research, 20*(2), 226–241. https://doi.org/10.1016/j.cogbrainres.2004.02.012

Gibbs, A. A., Naudts, K. H., Spencer, E. P., & David, A. S. (2007). The role of dopamine in attentional and memory biases for emotional information. *American Journal of Psychiatry, 164*(10), 1603–1609. https://doi.org/10.1176/appi.ajp.2007.06081241

Gobbi, G. (2024). The psychopharmacology of psychedelics: Where the brain meets spirituality (CCNP Innovations in Neuropsychopharmacology Award). *Journal of Psychiatry and Neuroscience, 49*(5), E301–E318. https://doi.org/10.1503/jpn.240037

Grahl, A., Onat, S., & Büchel, C. (2018). The periaqueductal gray and Bayesian integration in placebo analgesia. *Elife, 7*, e32930. https://doi.org/10.7554/eLife.32930

Grasemann, U., Hoffman, R., & Miikkulainen, R. (2009). Hyperlearning: A connectionist model of psychosis in schizophrenia. In *Proceedings of the Annual Meeting of the Cognitive Science Society* (Vol. 31, No. 31). https://escholarship.org/uc/item/31d5h9qq

Green, M. F., & Jimenez, A. M. (2022). Clinical observations and neuroscientific evidence tell a similar story: Schizophrenia is a disorder of the self-other boundary. *Schizophrenia Research, 242,* 45–48. https://doi.org/10.1016/j.schres.2021.12.032

Griffiths, R. R., Hurwitz, E. S., Davis, A. K., Johnson, M. W., & Jesse, R. (2019). Survey of subjective "God encounter experiences": Comparisons among naturally occurring experiences and those occasioned by the classic psychedelics psilocybin, LSD, ayahuasca, or DMT. *PLOS ONE, 14*(4), e0214377. https://doi.org/10.1371/journal.pone.0214377

Grover, S., Davuluri, T., & Chakrabarti, S. (2014). Religion, spirituality, and schizophrenia: A review. *Indian Journal of Psychological Medicine, 36*(2), 119–124. https://doi.org/10.4103/0253-7176.130962

Guiard, B. P., & Di Giovanni, G. (Eds.). (2018). *5-HT2A receptors in the central nervous system*. Springer International Publishing.

Haidt, J. (2012). *The righteous mind: Why good people are divided by politics and religion.* Vintage Books.

Harding, J. N., Wolpe, N., Brugger, S. P., Navarro, V., Teufel, C., & Fletcher, P. C. (2024). A new predictive coding model for a more comprehensive account of delusions. *The Lancet Psychiatry, 11*(4), 295–302. https://doi.org/10.1016/S2215-0366(23)00411-X

Harkin, E. F., Grossman, C. D., Cohen, J. Y., Béïque, J. C., & Naud, R. (2025). A prospective code for value in the serotonin system. *Nature, 641*(8064), 952–959.

Harvey, J. A., Gormezano, I., & Cool-Hauser, V. A. (1983). Effects of scopolamine and methylscopolamine on classical conditioning of the rabbit nictitating membrane response. *The Journal of Pharmacology and Experimental Therapeutics, 225*(1), 42–49. https://doi.org/10.1016/S0022-3565(25)33549-4

Hendricks, P. S. (2018). Awe: A putative mechanism underlying the effects of classic psychedelic-assisted psychotherapy. *International Review of Psychiatry, 30*(4), 331–342. https://doi.org/10.1080/09540261.2018.1474185

Hensman, R., Guimarães, F. S., Wang, M., & Deakin, J. F. W. (1991). Effects of ritanserin on aversive classical conditioning in humans. *Psychopharmacology, 104*, 220–224. https://doi.org/10.1007/BF02244182

Hoffman, M. A. (2019). Entheogens (psychedelic drugs) and the ancient mystery religions. In P. Wexler (Ed.), *Toxicology in antiquity* (2nd ed., pp. 353–362). Academic Press. https://doi.org/10.1016/B978-0-12-815339-0.00025-1

Huber, M. K., Schwitzer, J., Kirchler, E., & Lepping, P. (2022). Delusion and dopamine: Neuronal insights in psychotropic drug therapy. In *NeuroPsychopharmacotherapy* (pp. 1–20). Cham: Springer International Publishing.

Ihm, E. D., Paloutzian, R. F., van Elk, M., & Schooler, J. W. (2019). Awe as a meaning-making emotion: On the evolution of awe and the origin of religions. In S. M. McNamara & C. E. R. Webb (Eds.), *The evolution of religion, religiosity, and theology* (pp. 138–153). Routledge.

Kanen, J. W., Apergis-Schoute, A. M., Yellowlees, R., Arntz, F. E., van der Flier, F. E., Price, A., … & Robbins, T. W. (2021). Serotonin depletion impairs both Pavlovian and instrumental reversal learning in healthy humans. *Molecular Psychiatry, 26*(10), 7200–7210. https://doi.org/10.1038/s41380-021-01240-9

Kanen, J. W., Luo, Q., Kandroodi, M. R., Cardinal, R. N., Robbins, T. W., Nutt, D. J., Carhart-Harris, R. L., & den Ouden, H. E. M. (2023). Effect of lysergic acid diethylamide (LSD) on reinforcement learning in humans. *Psychological Medicine, 53*(14), 6434–6445. https://doi.org/10.1017/S0033291722002963

Kantrowitz, J. T. (2020). Targeting serotonin 5-HT2A receptors to better treat schizophrenia: Rationale and current approaches. *CNS Drugs, 34*(9), 947–959. https://doi.org/10.1007/s40263-020-00752-2

Kapur, S. (2003). Psychosis as a state of aberrant salience: A framework linking biology, phenomenology, and pharmacology in schizophrenia. *American Journal of Psychiatry, 160*(1), 13–23. https://doi.org/10.1176/appi.ajp.160.1.13

Kapur, S., & Seeman, P. (2002). NMDA receptor antagonists ketamine and PCP have direct effects on the dopamine D2 and serotonin 5-HT2 receptors—implications for models of schizophrenia. *Molecular Psychiatry, 7*(8), 837–844. https://doi.org/10.1038/sj.mp.4001093

Keltner, D., & Haidt, J. (2003). Approaching awe, a moral, spiritual, and aesthetic emotion. *Cognition and Emotion, 17*(2), 297–314. https://doi.org/10.1080/02699930302297

Kim, S. A. (2021). 5-HT1A and 5-HT2A signaling, desensitization, and downregulation: Serotonergic dysfunction and abnormal receptor density in schizophrenia and the prodrome. *Cureus, 13*(6), e15811. https://doi.org/10.7759/cureus.15811

Ko, K., Kopra, E. I., Cleare, A. J., & Rucker, J. J. (2023). Psychedelic therapy for depressive symptoms: A systematic review and meta-analysis. *Journal of Affective Disorders*, *322*, 194–204. https://doi.org/10.1016/j.jad.2022.09.168

Kometer, M., Schmidt, A., Bachmann, R., Studerus, E., Seifritz, E., & Vollenweider, F. X. (2012). Psilocybin biases facial recognition, goal-directed behavior, and mood state toward positive relative to negative emotions through different serotonergic subreceptors. *Biological Psychiatry, 72*(11), 898–906. https://doi.org/10.1016/j.biopsych.2012.04.005

Kometer, M., Schmidt, A., Jäncke, L., & Vollenweider, F. X. (2013). Activation of serotonin 2A receptors underlies the psilocybin-induced effects on α oscillations, N170 visual-evoked potentials, and visual hallucinations. *Journal of Neuroscience*, *33*(25), 10544–10551. https://doi.org/10.1523/JNEUROSCI.3007-12.2013

Kooijman, N. I., Willegers, T., Reuser, A., Mulleners, W. M., Kramers, C., Vissers, K. C., & van Der Wal, S. E. (2023). Are psychedelics the answer to chronic pain: A review of current literature. *Pain Practice*, *23*(4), 447–458. https://doi.org/10.1111/papr.13203

Kwapil, T. R., & Barrantes-Vidal, N. (2015). Schizotypy: Looking back and moving forward. *Schizophrenia Bulletin, 41*, S366–S373. https://doi.org/10.1093/schbul/sbu186

Lebedev, A. V., Lövdén, M., Rosenthal, G., Feilding, A., Nutt, D. J., & Carhart-Harris, R. L. (2015). Finding the self by losing the self: Neural correlates of ego-dissolution under psilocybin. *Human Brain Mapping, 36*(8), 3137–3153. https://doi.org/10.1002/hbm.22833

Lee, H.-S., Hong, S.-J. J., Baxter, T., Scott, J., Shenoy, S., Buck, L., Bodenheimer, B., & Park, S. (2021). Altered peripersonal space and the bodily self in schizophrenia: A virtual reality study. *Schizophrenia Bulletin, 47*(4), 927–937. https://doi.org/10.1093/schbul/sbab024

Leonard, B. E. (2005). The HPA and immune axes in stress: The involvement of the serotonergic system. *European Psychiatry*, *20*(S3), S302–S306. https://doi.org/10.1016/S0924-9338(05)80180-4

Lifshitz, M., Van Elk, M., & Luhrmann, T. M. (2019). Absorption and spiritual experience: A review of evidence and potential mechanisms. *Consciousness and Cognition, 73*, 102760. https://doi.org/10.1016/j.concog.2019.05.008

Lin, H., Kim, J. G., Park, S. W., Noh, H. J., Kim, J. M., Yoon, C. Y., Woo, N. S., Kim, B., Cho, I. S., Choi, B. H., & Sung, D. J. (2018). Enhancement of 5-HT2A receptor function and blockade of Kv1.5 by MK801 and ketamine: Implications for PCP derivative-induced disease models. *Experimental & Molecular Medicine, 50*(4), 1–8. https://doi.org/10.1038/s12276-018-0073-6

Looijestijn, J., Blom, J. D., Aleman, A., Hoek, H. W., & Goekoop, R. (2015). An integrated network model of psychotic symptoms. *Neuroscience & Biobehavioral Reviews, 59*, 238–250. https://doi.org/10.1016/j.neubiorev.2015.09.016

Luppi, A. I., Girn, M., Rosas, F. E., Timmermann, C., Roseman, L., Erritzoe, D., Nutt, D. J., Stamatakis, E. A., Spreng, R. N., Xing, L., Huttner, W. B., & Carhart-Harris, R. L. (2024). A role for the serotonin 2A receptor in the expansion and functioning of human transmodal cortex. *Brain, 147*(1), 56–80. https://doi.org/10.1093/brain/awad311

Lynch, R., Shenk, M. K., Shaver, J. H., & Spake, L. (2022). Fertility and faith: Insights from human behavioral ecology, evolutionary psychology, and life history theory. *Religion, Brain & Behavior, 12*(4), 406–413. https://doi.org/10.1080/2153599X.2021.2023617

Mantas, I., Flais, I., Masarapu, Y., Ionescu, T., Frapard, S., Jung, F., Le Merre, P., Saarinen, M., Tiklova, K., Salmani, B. Y., & Gillberg, L. (2024). Claustrum and dorsal endopiriform cortex complex cell-identity is determined by Nurr1 and regulates hallucinogenic-like states in mice. *Nature Communications, 15*(1), 8176. https://doi.org/10.1038/s41467-024-52429-9

McGovern, H. T., Grimmer, H. J., Doss, M. K., Hutchinson, B. T., Timmermann, C., Lyon, A., Corlett, P. R., & Laukkonen, R. E. (2024). An integrated theory of false insights and beliefs under psychedelics. *Communications Psychology, 2*(1), 69. https://doi.org/10.1038/s44271-024-00120-6

McNamara, P. (2022). *The cognitive neuroscience of religious experience: Decentering and the self.* Cambridge University Press.

McNamara, P., & Grafman, J. (2024). Advances in brain and religion studies: A review and synthesis of recent representative studies. *Frontiers in Human Neuroscience, 18*, 1495565. https://doi.org/10.3389/fnhum.2024.1495565

McPherson, K. B., & Ingram, S. L. (2022). Cellular and circuit diversity determines the impact of endogenous opioids in the descending pain modulatory pathway. *Frontiers in Systems Neuroscience, 16*, 963812. https://doi.org/10.3389/fnsys.2022.963812

Melzack, R. (2014). Pain and stress: Clues toward understanding chronic pain. In M. E. Lamb & R. M. Lerner (Eds.), *Advances in psychological science: Vol. 2. Social, personal, and cultural aspects* (pp. 63–85). Psychology Press.

Minas, I. H., Klimidis, S., Stuart, G. W., Copolov, D. L., & Singh, B. S. (1994). Positive and negative symptoms in the psychoses: Principal components analysis of items from the Scale for the Assessment of Positive Symptoms and the Scale for the Assessment of Negative Symptoms. *Comprehensive Psychiatry, 35*(2), 135–144. https://doi.org/10.1016/0010-440X(94)90059-Q

Mishara, A. L., & Corlett, P. (2009). Are delusions biologically adaptive? Salvaging the doxastic shear pin. *Behavioral and Brain Sciences, 32*(6), 530–531. https://doi.org/10.1017/S0140525X09991464

Mousavi, Z., Kiani, M. M., & Aghajan, H. (2022). Spatiotemporal signatures of surprise captured by magnetoencephalography. *Frontiers in Systems Neuroscience, 16*, 865453. https://doi.org/10.3389/fnsys.2022.865453

Murnane, K. S. (2019). Serotonin 2A receptors are a stress response system: Implications for post-traumatic stress disorder. *Behavioural Pharmacology, 30*(2–3), 151–162. https://doi.org/10.1097/FBP.0000000000000459

Muthukumaraswamy, S. D., Carhart-Harris, R. L., Moran, R. J., Brookes, M. J., Williams, T. M., Errtizoe, D., Sessa, B., Papadopoulos, A., Bolstridge, M., Singh, K. D., Feilding, A., Friston, K. J., & Nutt, D. J. (2013). Broadband cortical desynchronization underlies the human psychedelic state. *Journal of Neuroscience, 33*(38), 15171–15183. https://doi.org/10.1523/JNEUROSCI.2063-13.2013

Nasrallah, H. A., Fedora, R., & Morton, R. (2019). Successful treatment of clozapine-nonresponsive refractory hallucinations and delusions with pimavanserin, a serotonin 5HT-2A receptor inverse agonist. *Schizophrenia Research, 208*, 217–220. https://doi.org/10.1016/j.schres.2019.02.018

Nelson, E. E., & Panksepp, J. (1998). Brain substrates of infant–mother attachment: Contributions of opioids, oxytocin, and norepinephrine. *Neuroscience & Biobehavioral Reviews, 22*(3), 437–452. https://doi.org/10.1016/S0149-7634(97)00052-3

Nemu, D. (2019). Getting high with the most high: Entheogens in the Old Testament. *Journal of Psychedelic Studies, 3*(2), 117–132. https://doi.org/10.1556/2054.2019.004

Nettle, D. (2001). *Strong imagination: Madness, creativity and human nature* (Online ed., 31 Oct. 2023). Oxford University Press. https://doi.org/10.1093/oso/9780198507062.001.0001

Niazi, I. K., Navid, M. S., Bartley, J., Shepherd, D., Pedersen, M., Burns, G., Taylor, D., & White, D. E. (2022). EEG signatures change during unilateral Yogi nasal breathing. *Scientific Reports, 12*(1), 520. https://doi.org/10.1038/s41598-021-04461-8

O'Grady, S. (2012). *And man created God: Kings, cults, and conquests at the time of Jesus*. Atlantic Books Ltd.

Pezzulo, G., Parr, T., & Friston, K. (2022). The evolution of brain architectures for predictive coding and active inference. *Philosophical Transactions of the Royal Society B, 377*(1844), 20200531. https://doi.org/10.1098/rstb.2020.0531

Pierre, J. M. (2001). Faith or delusion? At the crossroads of religion and psychosis. *Journal of Psychiatric Practice, 7*(3), 163–172. https://doi.org/10.1097/00131746-200105000-00004

Quednow, B. B., Kometer, M., Geyer, M. A., & Vollenweider, F. X. (2012). Psilocybin-induced deficits in automatic and controlled inhibition are attenuated by ketanserin in healthy human volunteers. *Neuropsychopharmacology, 37*(3), 630–640. https://doi.org/10.1038/npp.2011.228

Ramaekers, J. G., Hutten, N., Mason, N. L., Dolder, P., Theunissen, E. L., Holze, F., Liechti, M. E., Feilding, A., & Kuypers, K. P. (2021). A low dose of lysergic acid diethylamide decreases pain perception in healthy volunteers. *Journal of Psychopharmacology, 35*(4), 398–405. https://doi.org/10.1177/0269881120940937

Reininghaus, U., Kempton, M. J., Valmaggia, L., Craig, T. K. J., Garety, P., Onyejiaka, A., Gayer-Anderson, C., So, S. H., Hubbard, K., Beards, S., Dazzan, P., Pariante, C., Mondelli, V., Fisher, H. L., Mills, J. G., Viechtbauer, W., McGuire, P., van Os, J., Murray, R. M., Wykes, T., Myin-Germeys, I., & Morgan, C. (2016). Stress sensitivity, aberrant salience, and threat anticipation in early psychosis: An experience sampling study. *Schizophrenia Bulletin, 42*(3), 712–722. https://doi.org/10.1093/schbul/sbv190

Rim, J. I., Ojeda, J. C., Svob, C., Kayser, J., Drews, E., Kim, Y., Tenke, C. E., Skipper, J., & Weissman, M. M. (2019). Current understanding of religion, spirituality, and their neurobiological correlates. *Harvard Review of Psychiatry, 27*(5), 303–316. https://doi.org/10.1097/HRP.0000000000000232

Robinson, J. E., Breakspear, M., Young, A. W., & Johnston, P. J. (2020). Dose-dependent modulation of the visually evoked N1/N170 by perceptual surprise: A clear demonstration of prediction-error signalling. *European Journal of Neuroscience, 52*(11), 4442–4452. https://doi.org/10.1111/ejn.13920

Roiser, J. P., Howes, O. D., Chaddock, C. A., Joyce, E. M., & McGuire, P. (2013). Neural and behavioral correlates of aberrant salience in individuals at risk for psychosis. *Schizophrenia Bulletin, 39*(6), 1328–1336. https://doi.org/10.1093/schbul/sbw025

Rush, J. A. (Ed.). (2013). *Entheogens and the development of culture: The anthropology and neurobiology of ecstatic experience*. North Atlantic Books.

Salinsky, L. M., Merritt, C. R., Zamora, J. C., Giacomini, J. L., Anastasio, N. C., & Cunningham, K. A. (2023). μ-opioid receptor agonists and psychedelics: Pharmacological opportunities and challenges. *Frontiers in Pharmacology*, *14*, 1239159. https://doi.org/10.3389/fphar.2023.1239159

Salvi, C., Simoncini, C., Grafman, J., & Beeman, M. (2020). Oculometric signature of switch into awareness? Pupil size predicts sudden insight whereas microsaccades predict problem-solving via analysis. *NeuroImage*, *217*, 116933. https://doi.org/10.1016/j.neuroimage.2020.116933

Samorini, G. (2019). The oldest archeological data evidencing the relationship of Homo sapiens with psychoactive plants: A worldwide overview. *Journal of Psychedelic Studies, 3*(2), 63–80. https://doi.org/10.1556/2054.2019.008

Selten, J. P., van der Ven, E., Rutten, B. P. F., & Cantor-Graae, E. (2013). The social defeat hypothesis of schizophrenia: An update. *Schizophrenia Bulletin, 39*(6), 1180–1186. https://doi.org/10.1093/schbul/sbt134

Sierra, S., Muchhala, K. H., Jessup, D. K., Contreras, K. M., Shah, U. H., Stevens, D. L., Jimenez, J., Lavilla, X. K., de la Fuente Revenga, M., Lippold, K. M., & Shen, S. (2022). Sex-specific role for serotonin 5-HT2A receptor in modulation of opioid-induced antinociception and reward in mice. *Neuropharmacology, 209*, 108988. https://doi.org/10.1016/j.neuropharm.2022.108988

Silva, C., & McNaughton, N. (2019). Are periaqueductal gray and dorsal raphe the foundation of appetitive and aversive control? A comprehensive review. *Progress in Neurobiology, 177*, 33–72. https://doi.org/10.1016/j.pneurobio.2019.02.001

Smith, R., Badcock, P., & Friston, K. J. (2021). Recent advances in the application of predictive coding and active inference models within clinical neuroscience. *Psychiatry and Clinical Neurosciences, 75*(1), 3–13. https://doi.org/10.1111/pcn.13138

Spiers, N., Labate, B. C., Ermakova, A. O., Farrell, P., Romero, O. S. G., Gabriell, I., & Olvera, N. (2024). Indigenous psilocybin mushroom practices: An annotated bibliography. *Journal of Psychedelic Studies, 8*(1), 3–25. https://doi.org/10.1556/2054.2023.00297

Stahl, S. M. (2018). Beyond the dopamine hypothesis of schizophrenia to three neural networks of psychosis: Dopamine, serotonin, and glutamate. *CNS Spectrums, 23*(3), 187–191. https://doi.org/10.1017/S1092852918001013

Stoliker, D., Egan, G. F., Friston, K. J., & Razi, A. (2022). Neural mechanisms and psychology of psychedelic ego dissolution. *Pharmacological Reviews, 74*(4), 876–917. https://doi.org/10.1124/pharmrev.121.000508

Taves, A. (2020). Mystical and other alterations in sense of self: An expanded framework for studying nonordinary experiences. *Perspectives on Psychological Science, 15*(3), 669–690. https://doi.org/10.1177/1745691619895047

Tisserand, A., Philippi, N., Botzung, A., & Blanc, F. (2023). Me, myself and my insula: An oasis in the forefront of self-consciousness. *Biology, 12*(4), 599. https://doi.org/10.3390/biology12040599

Tulver, K., Kaup, K. K., Laukkonen, R., & Aru, J. (2023). Restructuring insight: An integrative review of insight in problem-solving, meditation, psychotherapy, delusions and psychedelics. *Consciousness and Cognition, 110*, 103494. https://doi.org/10.1016/j.concog.2023.103494

Vaillant, G. E. (2013). Psychiatry, religion, positive emotions and spirituality. *Asian Journal of Psychiatry, 6*(6), 590–594. https://doi.org/10.1016/j.ajp.2013.08.073

van Elk, M., & Aleman, A. (2017). Brain mechanisms in religion and spirituality: An integrative predictive processing framework. *Neuroscience & Biobehavioral Reviews, 73*, 359–378. https://doi.org/10.1016/j.neubiorev.2016.12.031

van Os, J. (2009). A salience dysregulation syndrome. *The British Journal of Psychiatry, 194*(2), 101–103. https://doi.org/10.1192/bjp.bp.108.054254

van Winkel, R., Stefanis, N. C., & Myin-Germeys, I. (2008). Psychosocial stress and psychosis: A review of the neurobiological mechanisms and the evidence for gene-stress interaction. *Schizophrenia Bulletin, 34*(6), 1095–1105. https://doi.org/10.1093/schbul/sbn101

Vargas, M. V., Dunlap, L. E., Dong, C., Carter, S. J., Tombari, R. J., Jami, S. A., Cameron, L. P., Patel, S. D., Hennessey, J. J., Saeger, H. N., & McCorvy, J. D. (2023). Psychedelics promote neuroplasticity through the activation of intracellular 5-HT2A receptors. *Science, 379*(6633), 700–706. https://doi.org/10.1126/science.adf0435

Velit-Salazar, M. R., Shiroma, P. R., & Cherian, E. (2024). A systematic review of the neurocognitive effects of psychedelics in healthy populations: Implications for depressive disorders and post-traumatic stress disorder. *Brain Sciences, 14*(3), 248. https://doi.org/10.3390/brainsci14030248

Vollenweider, F. X., Vollenweider-Scherpenhuyzen, M. F., Bäbler, A., Vogel, H., & Hell, D. (1998). Psilocybin induces schizophrenia-like psychosis in humans via a serotonin-2 agonist action. *Neuroreport, 9*(17), 3897–3902.

Warrier, V., Toro, R., Chakrabarti, B., iPSYCH-Broad Autism Group, Børglum, A. D., Grove, J., 23andMe Research Team, Hinds, D. A., Bourgeron, T., & Baron-Cohen, S. (2018). Genome-wide analyses of self-reported empathy: Correlations with autism, schizophrenia, and anorexia nervosa. *Translational Psychiatry, 8*(1), 35. https://doi.org/10.1038/s41398-017-0082-6

Winkelman, M. (2019). Introduction: Evidence for entheogen use in prehistory and world religions. *Journal of Psychedelic Studies, 3*(2), 43–62. https://doi.org/10.1556/2054.2019.024

Yamada, Y., Matsumoto, M., Iijima, K., & Sumiyoshi, T. (2020). Specificity and continuity of schizophrenia and bipolar disorder: Relation to biomarkers. *Current Pharmaceutical Design, 26*(2), 191–200. https://doi.org/10.2174/1381612825666191216153508

Yeshurun, Y., Nguyen, M., & Hasson, U. (2021). The default mode network: Where the idiosyncratic self meets the shared social world. *Nature Reviews Neuroscience, 22*(3), 181–192. https://doi.org/10.1038/s41583-020-00420-w

Zeifman, R. J., Spriggs, M. J., Kettner, H., Lyons, T., Rosas, F. E., Mediano, P. A., Erritzoe, D., & Carhart-Harris, R. L. (2025). From relaxed beliefs under psychedelics (REBUS) to revised beliefs after psychedelics (REBAS). *Scientific Reports, 15*(1), 3651. https://doi.org/10.1038/s41598-023-28111-3

7

RELIGIOUS COGNITION IN DREAMS

Attributing Agency and Meaning to (Lucid) Dreaming

Michelle Carr and Kennedy Robertson

Introduction: Dreaming as a Religious and Cognitive Experience

Dreams have long served as a bridge between human cognition and the sacred, offering spaces where the boundaries of self, culture, and spirituality are renegotiated. Across history, they have been regarded not only as private experiences but also as vehicles of prophecy, divine affirmation, and symbolic meaning that shape religious worldviews. Whether in theistic traditions, where dreams have conveyed the voice of God, or non-theistic orientations, where they have guided individuals toward meaning or enlightenment, dreaming has functioned as a powerful medium of religious cognition. Contemporary scholarship has extended these insights by exploring how dreams reflect and reinforce pre-existing beliefs. Neurocognitive perspectives have proposed that altered states of consciousness can give rise to experiences of supernatural agency, interactions with other-worldly figures (Peters, 2021). Some suggest lucid dreaming, where a dreamer becomes aware that they are dreaming, offers a natural altered state of consciousness where such divine encounters can occur. Empirical studies demonstrate that the phenomenology of these experiences is shaped by an individual's intention, control, and interpretation. This chapter considers how cultural frameworks, spiritual practices, and personal belief systems inform dream encounters, and then situates our own qualitative exploration of lucid dream agency within this broader context. In particular, we provide two illustrative case studies of expert lucid dreamers' encounters with the divine, and further enumerate the broad range of supernatural agents generated within lucid dreams in our study. In doing so, we emphasize the enduring role of dreams as sites where cognition and religion meet, and where individuals make sense of the sacred through the creative landscapes of the dreaming mind.

DOI: 10.4324/9781003158189-7

Dreams Across Cultures and History: Divination, Meaning, and the Sacred

Throughout history and across cultures, dreaming has been a powerful medium for religious and spiritual experiences. One of the earliest recorded dreams dates to the third millennium BCE, attributed to the Sumerian King Dumuzi of Uruk (Hoffman, 2004). In the dream, symbols of loss, such as a seized lamb, a vanished crook, and an overturned milk churn, are interpreted by his sister as a warning of imminent danger, prompting him to flee. The interpretation of this dream, while recognizing its symbolic function, offers a glimpse into the Mesopotamian worldview and how Dumuzi likely saw his role within it (Bulkeley, 2001; Hoffman, 2004). It also demonstrates how dreams were often treated as authoritative messages from the divine, guiding Dumuzi to take action in his waking life as a response. Indeed, scholars suggest that dreams may have been among the earliest human experiences to evoke belief in a spiritual realm (McNamara, 2016, p. 3, 2018a; McNamara & Bulkeley, 2015; Nordin, 2024). Because they appear to offer messages beyond the limits of waking life, dreams were often regarded as compelling evidence for the existence of gods or a higher power. The religious role of dreaming, however, takes different forms. In some traditions, dreams direct individuals outward, toward a greater understanding of divine will or otherworldly beings. In others, dreams invite reflection inward, supporting self-knowledge and personal transformation. While impressive literature offers profound, comprehensive analyses of the role of dreams in specific religions, the scope of this section will be to compare the utility of dreams widely across different beliefs. Notably, the diverse application of dreams will be discussed in relation to the three Abrahamic religions, non-theistic beliefs, and Indigenous practices around the world.

Dreams to Orient Outward: Theistic Dreams

Dreams can deeply shape how individuals relate to their cultural and religious environments, particularly when they are perceived as messages from a higher power. In many strands of Christianity, Judaism, and Islam, dreams can be understood as spontaneous communications from the divine rather than experiences actively influenced or controlled by the dreamer. In this view, the dreamer functions largely as a receptive vessel, open to receiving prophecy, instruction, or reassurance. This outward orientation is well-reflected in the Hebrew Bible, where the word "dream" appears over one hundred times (Mota-Rolim et al., 2020). In the Old Testament, dreams are used both as symbolic communications that require interpretation and as direct messages from God. These dreams frequently convey prophecy or offer guidance (McNamara, 2018a). Jacob's ladder dream in the book of Genesis is a prominent example. After fleeing from his brother, Jacob dreams of a ladder reaching to heaven, with angels moving upon it. God appears and blesses him, affirming divine protection. When Jacob awakens, he declares, "surely the Lord is in this place; and I did not know it. How awesome is this place! This is none other than the house of God, and this is the gate of heaven" (Gen. 28:12–15, RSV; Metzger & Murphy, 1991). Although Jacob's dream offers reassurance of divine presence, other biblical dreams convey warnings, instructions, or revelations (McNamara, 2018a). The stories of Joseph and Daniel, two major figures in the biblical Old Testament, demonstrate the important role that dream interpretation held in these traditions. Joseph's own prophetic dreams and his ability to interpret the dreams of others reveal the credibility given to the practice. For example, he interprets the Pharaoh's dream of seven fat cows followed by seven thin ones as a sign of a coming famine. His foresight earns the Pharaoh's trust and leads to his appointment as second in command in Egypt, ultimately fulfilling God's prophecy (Gen. 41, RSV; Metzger & Murphy, 1991). Daniel likewise interprets King Nebuchadnezzar's dream of a statue destroyed by a stone as a prophecy concerning the rise and fall of kingdoms established by God (McNamara, 2018a; Mota-Rolim et al., 2020). Both Joseph and Daniel exemplify how dreams were not only personal experiences but also instruments that shaped religious and political outcomes (Mota-Rolim et al., 2020).

In Islamic tradition, dreams are also considered meaningful forms of divine communication. The Prophet Muhammad, believed to have received early revelations in dreams, teaches that dream interpretation is a fundamental practice that requires care and discernment (Mota-Rolim et al., 2020). Classical Islamic scholars classify dreams into three types: those sent by Allah (*rahmani*), those that arise from the self (*nafsani*) and those sent by Satan in the form of nightmares (*shaytani*) (Ibn Khaldūn, 2005). Dreamers are encouraged to increase the guidance in their dreams through the practice of *Istikhara*, or dream incubation (Edgar & Henig, 2010). The practice of *Istikhara* may involve reading passages from sacred texts and interpreting dream symbolism the following night (Edgar & Henig, 2010). In contrast, some traditions discourage the discussion of negative dreams, and direct the dreamer to prayer instead (Mota-Rolim et al., 2020). These differing approaches reflect the diversity within and across religious traditions in how dream content is engaged and given meaning.

Dreams to Orient Inward: Non-theistic Dreams

While some Abrahamic traditions emphasize dreaming as external communications from higher beings, other spiritual systems regard dreams as profound spaces for self-exploration and the transcendence of ordinary consciousness. Many non-theistic and Indigenous practices highlight the introspective potential of dreams, valuing them as tools for inner awareness and personal transformation. Within Hindu and Buddhist traditions, for example, dreams are often framed as opportunities to transcend ordinary states of consciousness and glimpse deeper spiritual truths. Hindu practices such as Yoga Nidra involve a meditative state in which the practitioner maintains a passive witnessing of the body and mind during the transition to sleep. While sharing some key elements with contemporary lucid dreaming induction (see Section, "Evidence from Lucid Dreaming" below), Yoga Nidra endorses a non-reactive observation to mental content allowing practitioners to disengage from egoic identity. This sustained observation is believed to lead to deeper self-realization and, ultimately, a pathway toward enlightenment (Mota-Rolim et al., 2020).

Dreams themselves are sometimes viewed as symbolically rich terrains that can have healing and prophetic properties. As such, some Hindu practitioners travel to pilgrimage centres for the purpose of dream incubation rituals, where dreams act as communication channels between humans and the divine (Morinis, 1982). The Taraknath Temple of Tarakeswar holds dream rituals termed *dharnā*, in hopes of relieving illness. The practitioner is instructed to perform a series of pre-sleep rituals prior to calling upon a deity to appear in their dream. If successful, most practitioners report receiving a dream message within four to five days in the temple, which may take the form of a direct cure, a diagnosis of illness, or instructions for treatment (Morinis, 1982). Interestingly, many of the actions instructed within the dream reflect the perceived quest to attest or affirm one's faith and devotion to the deity. By treating dreams and the temples in which they occur as liminal spaces within the Hindu cosmic order, *dharnā* creates a framework through which pilgrims may engage in dialogue and exchange with the divine (Morinis, 1982).

Tibetan Buddhism shares in the belief that both waking and dreaming are equally illusory states, and turns to dreams as a metaphor for the transient, unfixed nature of waking experience (Hsia, 2010; Khu & Khumairoh, 2024). Buddhism itself is believed by some to have important ties to dreaming, as the Buddha's enlightenment was foretold through his own dreams (Bautze-Picron, 2003), and the religion may have been first introduced to China through the dream of the Emperor Ming Han, where a golden statue in his dream was later interpreted as the Buddha (Hsia, 2010). Subsequent texts in Chinese Buddhism depict the importance of dream narratives in affirming their doctrine (Hsia, 2010). While the deep, dreamless sleep is also recognized as a valuable state for spiritual practice in Buddhism (Gillespie, 2002), here dreams, too, offer opportunities to engage with the divine and to transcend the self. For the Kadam Choeling Indonesian Buddhist community, the appearance of one's guru in their dream provides direct affirmation of successful spiritual practice (Khu & Khumairoh, 2024). Unlike divine figures in theistic dreams, the guru functions as both a physical human being with waking relationships to the dreamer, and as a powerful source capable of transcending the bounds of waking and sleeping life (Khu & Khumairoh, 2024). Thus, the guru's dream presence affirms the interpersonal connection with the individual, the benevolent nature of the teacher, and a successful sign of the dreamer's progression on a spiritual path. Whereas monasticism is restricted to only men in some traditions of Buddhism, laywomen can and do experience divine wisdom through dreams and visions. For example, Thai Theravada Buddhism gives significant value to the spiritual dreams of both monks and laypeople alike, and regards them as authoritative voices for communication with spiritual realms (Jackson, 2025). In this way, dreams act as unique, boundaryless spiritual spaces where anyone regardless of gender, age, class, or religious status is granted access to divine knowledge (Jackson, 2025).

Beyond the significant phenomenology of dreams and their communicative potential, practitioners of Tibetan Buddhism can work with the sleep and dreaming states to further align themselves with ultimate reality. The exercise of dream yoga encourages practitioners to stabilize awareness within dreams, intended to reveal the illusory nature of all phenomena including the self. The Dalai Lama teaches that dream yoga enables practitioners to access a "special dream state" in which the soul is untethered from the physical body (Mota-Rolim et al., 2020). This discipline involves cultivating lucidity—that is, awareness—within dreams and gradually gaining control over dream content. The framework of dream yoga bears semblance to lucid dream practice, where the dreamer is guided through the steps of recognizing the dream state, refining awareness, and manipulating or conjuring new phenomena in the dream (Sheehy, 2025). As an adjunct to secular lucid dreaming practices, dream yoga encourages the practitioner to carry the awareness of being in an illusory space into their waking life (Sheehy, 2025). In other words, if one can maintain awareness of the illusory nature of the dream state, a similar recognition of the illusory nature of the waking mind can develop. Lucidity, being an instrumental element of dream yoga, allows individuals to practice non-attachment to the unreal forms of dream content. Successful practice leads to a diminishment of dreaming, to experiences of deep dreamless sleep, waking non-attachment, and attainment of enlightenment.

Beyond Buddhist practices, other spiritual systems position dreams as privileged states for accessing knowledge and encountering guiding agents—notably spiritism. Spiritism is a belief system incorporating elements of Eastern religions with Western esoteric traditions, and is influenced in part by modern scientific principles (de Sá & Mota-Rolim, 2015). At its core, spiritism posits that the human soul exists separately from the human body. The agency of the soul does not depend on the consciousness of the person and can thus "detach" from the body during sleep, often without the dreamer's conscious intention or awareness (Gyimesi, 2016; Mota-Rolim et al., 2020). The soul is then free to commune with other souls and explore realms that are not confined to the physics of waking life. Allan Kardec, the founder of spiritism, describes dreams as the confused recollection of the spirit's nightly endeavors (Kardec, 1865). Times in which the individual has no dreams are not unusual, as they simply do not remember everything the spirit had seen. Spiritism has been tied to the phenomenon of out-of-body experiences (OBEs), the sensation of perceiving the world outside of one's physical body (de Sá & Mota-Rolim, 2015). OBEs can be experienced while awake, asleep, or dreaming, though they commonly occur within the context of a lucid dream (de Sá & Mota-Rolim, 2015). Oliver Fox, a pioneer in spiritism, believed that having experienced a lucid dream was necessary to induce an OBE. The characteristics of an OBE, including sensations of flying, witnessing one's own body, and recognizing the bizarre nature of the environment, indeed correspond with subjective lucid dream experiences (de Sá & Mota-Rolim, 2015).

Spiritism can provide an ontological framework for the practice of mediumship, or the purposeful communication between the living and spirit world. Espiritismo, a branch of spiritism, is practiced by many Afro-Cuban mediums, where dreams are significant vehicles for communication with the dead (*muerto*). (Espirito Santo, 2009). In Havana, dreams are held in high regard as spaces where knowledge, personhood, divinity, and destiny can be accessed through the diluted boundaries of the body (Espirito Santo, 2009). In addition to one's own soul separating from the body during sleep, practitioners (*espiritistas*) believe that they can take on the form of spirit guides or deceased loved ones during dreams, temporarily gaining access to a spirit's vision. The work of a medium is then to materialize the knowledge gained through a dream by communicating its message in waking life, treating the dream as sacred truth with real consequences for destiny (Espirito Santo, 2009).

Supernatural Agents in Dreams: Cognitive, Neurobiological, and Cultural Facets

Cognitive Facets

Mystical encounters between a dreamer and the gods, angels, deities, spirits, demons, and divine presences embedded within a dream are sometimes referred to as "numinous dreams," "Big dreams," or "significant dreams" (Bulkeley, 1996). These entities are broadly conceptualized in the literature as supernatural agents (SAs)—entities that are perceived to possess autonomy, intentions, and power beyond human capability (McNamara, 2018b; McNamara & Bulkeley, 2015). The defining feature of these figures is the sense of agency that is attributed to them. Agency refers to one's ability to intentionally exert an action that has an influence over oneself or the world around (McNamara, 2018b). Neurocognitively, agency can be understood in terms of predictive processing; the brain continuously forms predictions about how a chosen action will influence the external world; if the brain's predictions are correct, one can safely affirm that the action came from the self, and attributes self-agency to the action. If the predictions are incorrect, one is more likely to attribute the agency to an external cause (McNamara & Bulkeley, 2015).

It has been demonstrated that humans have a tendency to mis- or over-attribute agency to outside events or entities, a social adaptation that likely evolved to help humans detect the presence of others in ambiguous environments (Wood, 2012). This tendency can be related to a cognitive mechanism known as the Hyperactive Agency Detection Device (HADD) (Barrett, 2000). Individuals then rely on theory of mind, the capacity to attribute thoughts, desires, and intentions to others, to make sense of the agency of the external figure (Maij et al., 2017). From an evolutionary perspective, it was safer to (falsely) assume intentionality in another being than to miss a potential threat. Environments that are ambiguous, unpredictable, and threatening foster a greater reliance on the HADD, and thus result in greater externally attributed agency (Nordin, 2024). Some evidence suggests that individuals exhibit a heightened tendency to assign meaning to external or mystical agents to alleviate unease in times of social threat (Robertson et al., 2024). Seeking explanation through transcendental sources may increase one's sense of comfort and controllability, which is otherwise inaccessible in unpredictable or environments. While the latter examples demonstrate how over-attribution of "other" agency can provide comfort in times of stress, it is also often the case that reduced self-agency can be a distressing and impairing facet of mental illness. Paranoid delusions offer a striking example. These occur when the brain misinterprets the source of events, not recognizing them as self-generated. Instead, the changes in one's environment are perceived as coming from external agents, whether other people, objects, or SAs like God or the devil (Synofzik et al., 2010). This misattribution often fuels feelings of suspicion and persecution, making the environment increasingly frightening and confusing, and out of one's control.

While the HADD can contribute to maladaptive beliefs in some contexts, it also plays a powerful and often meaningful role in religious life, where relocated agency is experienced as emotionally resonant, guiding, or sacred. Nordin (2024) suggests that divination rituals serve as spaces where relinquished human agency opens the practitioner to receiving divinatory information. In Ouija board sessions, for example, users attempt to channel paranormal communication through a planchette pointed at letters of the alphabet. Users passively place their hands over the planchette but refrain from moving it themselves. Due to a relinquished sense of agency, any movement of the planchette is believed to be due to spiritual activity (Hughes & Gooding, 2025). In such cases, the uncertainty of the outcome allows cultural and personal beliefs about SAs to act as a framework of understanding, making ambiguous movements feel purposeful and significant (McNamara, 2018b; Nordin, 2024).

Perhaps the most pervasive and everyday context where agency is attributed to other entities occurs within dreaming. With the exception of lucid dreaming, REM-phase dreams are typically reported by the dreamer as low in personal agency, marked by diminished ability to control or influence the dream environment (McNamara, 2018a; 2018b; McNamara & Bulkeley, 2015; Nordin, 2024; Nordin & Bjälkebring, 2021). This already creates a heightened tendency to attribute ToM and relocate agency to external figures, though this alone is not sufficient to generate experiences of SAs. In other words, not all REM-phase dream characters are described as mystical or spiritual. For a dream character or entity to be perceived as meaningful within the dream, it should violate intuitive expectations in a way that is striking yet not so implausible as to be dismissed (McNamara & Bulkeley, 2015). The dreamer should also assign significance to the entity, often accompanied by strong emotional responses that reinforce and enhance the memory of the encounter. To illustrate, a demonic figure in a nightmare might produce feelings of terror and helplessness, whereas a god-like presence may evoke reverence and adoration; both are likely to be highly memorable experiences, classified as encounters with SAs (McNamara & Bulkeley, 2015).

Neurobiological Facets

The cognitive processes underlying encounters with the divine in dreams are likely tied to the unique neurobiological conditions of REM sleep. During this stage of sleep, the executive control network of the dorsolateral prefrontal cortex (dlPFC) is markedly deactivated, resulting in diminished self-monitoring, reflective awareness, and volitional control. In contrast, dopaminergic and cholinergic activity increases in limbic and paralimbic areas, including the amygdala and medial prefrontal cortex (mPFC), which are implicated in emotional arousal, memory retrieval, and internally generated imagery (McNamara, 2018a). This shift contributes to a heightened reliance on perceptual information and a greater tendency to imbue dream content with emotional or symbolic meaning (Peterson et al., 2002). Additionally, the reduction of serotonergic activity during REM may play a role in loosening cognitive boundaries, increasing suggestibility, and enhancing the salience of anomalous or spiritually charged experiences (McNamara, 2016; 2018a). Alterations in serotonin function have been demonstrated in other states known to induce mystical experiences. For example, classic psychedelic substances such as psilocybin and LSD primarily target 5-HT2A serotonergic receptors, a mechanism proposed to underlie the meaningful and transcendent qualities of these experiences (McNamara, 2016; 2018a). Furthermore, individual differences in serotonin receptor expression have been correlated with a greater propensity for self-transcendence, including dimensions of religious behavior, subjective experience, and individual worldview (Borg et al., 2003).

Taken together, these findings support the idea that mystical and divine experiences in dreams can be understood through the neurobiological mechanisms that shape REM cognition. Deactivation of the dlPFC impairs predictive models of cause and effect, while heightened limbic activation fosters emotionally charged and sensorily rich imagery. Concurrent neurochemical shifts promote cognitive flexibility and could facilitate the acceptance of improbable or symbolic dream content. Thus, the functional and neurochemical architecture of REM sleep may provide fertile ground for the emergence of mystical experiences and divine encounters.

Cultural Facets

Crucial to the development of shared cultural beliefs is the transmissibility of ideas across individuals and generations. Dreams have long served as sources of spiritual insight and religious meaning, yet not all dream content is equally likely to be remembered, shared, or integrated into cultural systems. The Content Affordance Relevance for Dream Divination (CARDD) theory proposes that experiences involving SAs are particularly well-suited for transmission because they possess a constellation of cognitive and emotional features that make them especially compelling and memorable (McNamara & Bulkeley, 2015; Nordin, 2024; Nordin & Bjälkebring, 2021). Specifically, dreams that possess high emotional intensity, low dreamer agency, bizarre imagery, and SAs that minimally violate intuitive assumptions are more likely to be communicated to others (Nordin, 2024). Dream sharing is a common and perhaps inherent practice in human beings, and has been shown to foster social bonding and empathy (Blagrove et al., 2019). Interestingly, the tendency to report supernatural dream experiences is not dependent upon one's religiosity. One study found that both religious and non-religious individuals were equally likely to report mystical dreams, even when the dream theme itself was perceived as religious (Nordin & Bjälkebring, 2021). With approximately half the population experiencing mystical dreams (Bulkeley, 2009a), it is possible that the motivation to communicate such dreams with others lies more in evolved dream-sharing practices and dream distinctiveness than in religious beliefs. The tendency to seek expert opinion on mystical dreams, however, is strongly correlated with one's religious beliefs (Nordin & Bjälkebring, 2021; Nordin, 2024). Interpretation of dreams through a religious expert may function to strengthen the relationship between dreams and religion. Mystical dream content encourages religious consultation, where religious authority validates the meaning of the dream through a theological lens (Nordin, 2021). In this way, dreams both draw from and build to the surrounding dominant cultural narrative.

Although few dreams today inspire new religions (McNamara, 2016), they frequently deepen existing faith or evoke curiosity about the divine. Dreams marked by strong "imagistic religiosity" can reinforce prior beliefs (Bulkeley, 2009a), while rare but emotionally charged dreams may serve as catalysts for psychological or spiritual growth (Bulkeley, 2009b). The continuity hypothesis, which emphasizes the close correspondence between waking life and dream content, further supports the notion that religious dreams typically mirror an individual's pre-existing beliefs (Bogzaran, 1991). Bulkeley (2009b) demonstrated that a person's religious affiliation could be reliably inferred from their dream reports alone. In a study of Chinese Buddhists, themes of revelation and prediction, as well as encounters with divine beings and teachers, appeared more frequently than in the dreams of non-religious participants (Zhang et al., 2018). The appearance of such mystical dreams seemed to correspond with the engagement in their practice, and were often accompanied by feelings of reverence. Similarly, another study found that 40% of all mystical dream reports contained direct references to Christianity, reflecting the predominantly Christian background of the sample (Bulkeley, 2009a). Even in the absence of explicit Christian imagery, many individuals reported dreams of a brilliant light, a universal symbol of divinity across multiple religious traditions. Personal conceptions of the divine often shape these experiences: those who envision the divine in personalized form may dream of figures such as Christ or Buddha, whereas individuals who view the divine as impersonal tend to encounter more abstract manifestations, such as a pervasive presence or energy (Bogzaran, 1991). Regardless of form, mystical dreams are typically sanctified either theistically, grounded in one's religious beliefs, or non-theistically, through their association with divine or transcendent qualities (Phillips & Pargament, 2002). Importantly, the human mind appears predisposed to generate SA concepts during dreaming, and such experiences are not fixedly tied to one religion over another (Bulkeley, 2007; McNamara & Bulkeley, 2015). Mystical dreams lend themselves to cultural transmission where they can be shared, remembered, and embedded within collective belief systems (Bulkeley, 2007; 2009b; Nordin, 2024).

Integrative Understanding of Supernatural Agents

Cognitive, neurobiological, and cultural facets provide a means to understand the seemingly ethereal phenomenon of supernatural agent encounters in dreams. Each religion or spirituality draws upon its own epistemology to support and explain such mystical dream experiences. The diverse perspectives of belief systems on supernatural dreams can be regarded as credible and meaningful forms of guidance to comprehend and interact with one's dream environment, often deriving from traditional knowledge sharing. While science brings epistemic value to the topic of mystical dream encounters, it ultimately cannot substantiate the existence or non-existence of SAs. The scientific view alone can be reductive, inflexible, and exert a Eurocentric perspective on a pervasive phenomenon that holds cultural weight. Ideally, neurocognitive, psychological, and religious viewpoints can be integrated into a broader framework of understanding, complementing one another and providing a more holistic reflection on mystical dream experiences. Bulkeley (1996) provides a compelling argument for the place of both science and religion on the topic of supernatural dreams, and argues that, contrary to the prevailing notion that science and religion are incompatible, the two approaches have historically frequently converged to shape our understanding of dreaming. For instance, it is largely accepted that dreams can access memories or information that is generally inaccessible to our waking consciousness. It is also accepted that the creativity, symbolism, and intense emotions accessed within dreams can give rise to powerful psychological and spiritual transformation in waking life (Bulkeley, 1996). Thus, from both scientific and religious standpoints, dreams represent rich environments from which we can draw valuable information about the mind, soul, or higher self.

Dream Guides and Supernatural Agency: Evidence from Lucid Dreaming

Much of the literature on mystical dreaming and SA encounters has emphasized dreaming as a state of reduced agency, which facilitates the attribution of "other" agency especially to dream figures. One framework highlights how REM neurobiological mechanisms generate the cognitive materials that cultures and individuals draw upon in perceiving SAs (McNamara, 2018b). However, this framework does not preclude more deliberate or controlled means of engaging with SAs; in fact the author notes that experiences of SAs both within waking and dreaming states often involve an interplay between effortful, intentional elicitation of SAs, and automatic cognitive processes such as those that generate dream content during REM sleep (McNamara, 2018). Indeed, this interplay is particularly evident in lucid dreams, which provide a compelling context for examining SA encounters. Lucid dreaming is understood as the experience of becoming aware that one is dreaming while actively in a dream (Baird et al., 2019). This awareness may occur spontaneously, often triggered by noticing anomalies in the dream environment, or through intentional induction methods. Spontaneous lucid dreaming occurs at least once in approximately 55% of individuals, though more frequent lucid dreaming (once a month or more) is less common (Tzioridou et al., 2025). Typically accompanying this awareness is an increased level of control and ability to intentionally modify the dream environment or narrative, that is, agency. Dreamers often report the capacity to fly, summon characters, revisit memories, or shift the dream's emotional tone through volitional effort. The act of lucid dreaming is overwhelmingly described as a positive experience, with emerging evidence suggesting that lucid dream practice could be applied to the treatment of nightmares, depression, and PTSD (Holzinger et al., 2020; Sackwild & Stumbrys, 2021). Notably, approximately 40% of lucid dreamers report using these experiences specifically for mental or physical healing (Sackwild & Stumbrys, 2021). The increased sense of agency may be attributed to transient increases in activity of prefrontal cortical regions (Baird et al., 2019). This phenomenon can be especially meaningful when directed toward personal or spiritual goals, such as confronting fears, exploring creativity, or receiving guidance. For many, these dreams are not just psychologically useful but deeply spiritual in nature, providing a sense of connection to higher powers, inner wisdom, or autonomous figures such as SAs. In this sense, lucid dreams may function as a hybrid state of consciousness, where intentionality manifests in positive, enjoyable experiences, while default processing of "other" agency allows for feelings of wonder or mystery projected into the dreamworld.

Contemporary Studies of Spiritual Lucid Dreaming

Aside from their growing utility as therapeutic tools for clinical indications, lucid dream practices are sometimes used for their ability to spark new spiritual experiences and personal growth. In one study, 42.9% of participants endorsed using lucid dreams specifically to seek spiritual encounters (Stumbrys & Erlacher, 2016). This public interest in tailoring lucid dream experiences toward transcendence has led some scholars to empirically explore the dream content, practices, and dreamer characteristics that give rise to spiritual dream phenomena. Bogzaran

(1991) and Stumbrys (2021) provide detailed examinations of the intersection between lucid dreaming and spirituality, emphasizing how intention and levels of control shape subjective encounters with SAs. In Bogzaran's early work, lucid dreamers who deliberately invoked a divine presence were often successful in eliciting an SA, while those who surrendered control tended to experience the divine more passively (Bogzaran, 1991). In other words, the approach taken to elicit the divine within the lucid dream played a significant role in determining the form and unfolding of the encounter. Consistent with the continuity between waking beliefs and dream content, Bogzaran (1991) found that the form of the SA closely reflected participants' prior conceptions of the divine. Among dreamers who held personified conceptions of God, 83% encountered an anthropomorphic figure, while 87% of those who envisioned the divine as impersonal experienced formless presences such as light or energy. Reports of luminous brilliance, geometric patterns, and multidimensional spaces are also common in spiritually oriented lucid dreams (Krippner et al., 2002, p. 38; Bulkeley, 2009a). Importantly, the subjective interpretation applied to these encounters, in addition to the actual dream content, plays a central role in whether dreamers perceive the experience as spiritually transcendent (Stumbrys, 2021). The meaning mined from these experiences, when integrated into waking life, can foster both psychological and spiritual growth. Whether grounded in theistic representations of the divine or personally resonant symbolism, these mystical experiences may deepen individuals' sense of connection with the relationships, environments, and forces that shape their world (Bulkeley, 2009a)

To further explore the dimensions that appear to play a role in spiritual and psychological well-being, Stumbrys (2021) examined specific factors of spirituality and their relation to mystical dream experiences. Results revealed that reporting more joyful transcendent experiences, and feeling more unity with all existence, were positively associated with lucid dream frequency (Stumbrys, 2021). Stumbrys posits that this factor may be highly influenced by the attitude of "otherness" that the dreamer holds toward dream characters. For instance, ego-logical attitudes recognize the dream outcomes and characters as stemming from their own heightened agency, where ego-logical attitudes accept characters as independent, autonomous figures (Stumbrys, 2021). It is possible that the heightened awareness of one's own control within lucid dreams precludes the connection or responsibility felt toward other dream characters.

Overall, recent research has established a connection between lucid dreams and spirituality. More evidence is being put forward to support the beneficial effects of transcendent dream experiences, with some participants reporting sustained psychospiritual impacts up to a year post-dream encounter (Esser, 2014). Building on this foundation, our study, detailed below, offers a qualitative exploration of deliberately elicited SAs within lucid dreams, attending to how their form, intentions surrounding their invocation, and agency attributed to them reflect the participants' waking beliefs and practices. By focusing on detailed dream reports, we aim to illustrate the ways in which spiritual encounters in lucidity are not only consistent with but also deepen the continuity between dreaming and waking spirituality.

Empirical Exploration of Lucid Dream Guides

In our recent research, we invited ten expert lucid dreamers to explore SA encounters in states of dream lucidity. Participants, who endorsed experiencing at least one lucid dream per week with high levels of dream control, were recruited to deliberately elicit and interact with their conception of an SA in lab and home settings. Specifically, participants spent four nights in the sleep laboratory with repeated awakenings for dream reports, and two weeks at home reporting dreams. Participants were instructed to become lucid and to set the intention of meeting their "dream guide," a supernatural agent that could provide information or direction within the dream. Participants represented a broad range of ages, genders, and belief orientations, including both theistic and non-theistic perspectives. The diversity of axioms allowed us to examine how waking world conceptions of the divine shaped the form and character of dream encounters. By documenting both the form these guides assumed and the dreamers' interpretations of their agency, we sought to illustrate how lucid dreams can serve as lived spaces where spiritual beliefs are actively enacted and explored. Presented below are the vignettes of two participants and their comparative experiences of eliciting and interacting with SAs in lucid dreams.

The first participant (Participant 1) is a 24-year-old agender individual with a high frequency and control of lucid dreams. They endorse a lifelong engagement in the Christian belief with strong faith and time spent daily with God. Through their dream experiences, both at home and in-lab, they practiced eliciting God as their dream guide, who appeared to them as a person, a presence, or an abstract representation. Particularly significant for them were instances in which God appeared in an abstract form, which they described as conveying a deeper spiritual connection.

In one instance of a lucid dream, they write:

> I then quickly remembered that God was supposed to appear in a perceivable form first. I tentatively asked, "God, can you appear in a perceivable form?" I think I expected something extravagant or a human-shaped figure, but then saw a white burst of light in front of me...floating towards me were spheres of what looked like white dandelion fluff, the kind you blow to make a wish... I felt immense joy and awe that this was the form that God chose to take. I felt humbled and thought of God appearing gently in a breath of wind. This is a reference to a Bible story when I think Elijah is on a mountain and is asking God to appear, and expects God to be something mighty and huge. There is a fire, but God was not in the fire. There was an earthquake, but God was not in the earthquake. There was a storm...but God was not in the storm. Then there was a light breath of wind, and that is where God was... I didn't have the words for all that in my dream, but knew that that was what I was referencing.
>
> *(Participant 1)*

Through this experience, the dreamer endorsed feeling a direct communication from God. The dream incubation process, used to practice inducing lucidity and to set the intention of meeting a dream guide, became itself a form of spiritual practice for the dreamer. To successfully elicit a spiritual experience, the individual often used verbal commands into the dream itself such as "subconscious, show yourself" or "God, can you appear in a perceivable form?" Once establishing an understanding of being in the presence of the dream guide, participants were instructed to ask an open-ended question to the guide or dream itself, designed to allow for creativity in the dream response. Participants were asked to take note of the question they chose and any answer they may have received within the dream. Continuing with the above dream report, the dreamer states:

> I then asked this cloud of dispersing fluff, "can I experience the creation of the universe?" and the fluff grew and turned into spheres, the one closest to me was the biggest. They then became purple and yellow flowers, with dense petals such that they remained perfect spheres floating in front of me. I felt an immense joy and delight that something was happening, and the flowers were breathtakingly beautiful. They were reminiscent of dahlias, my favourite flower… I had the complete sense that these floating flowers were how God chose to appear. Unexpected, intangible, plural, perceivable, beautiful, personal and relevant to me.
>
> *(Participant 1)*

As evidenced from their writing, the participant was able to receive an experience that reflected their conception of God and felt a true presence. Although God did not appear in human form, the description of the SA as dispersing dandelion fluff evoked qualities often associated with divinity, such as ephemerality, gentleness, and transcendence. The dreamer explicitly connected this imagery to the biblical story of Elijah, who discovers God not in dramatic forces of nature but in a quiet whisper (1 Kings 19:11–13, New International Version, 2011). In this way, the dream not only mirrored scripture familiar to the participant but also reinforced their waking faith, offering phenomenological support for the continuity hypothesis underlying religious cognition in dreams. When the participant asked, "can I experience the creation of the universe?", the unfolding imagery of vibrant, spherical flowers was experienced as a personal gift from God. This response, simultaneously intimate and transcendent, left the participant with a strengthened conviction in God's presence. Overall, the participant was successfully able to induce and engage meaningfully with their understanding of an SA in a lucid dream state.

The second participant (Participant 2) is a 29-year-old man of South American descent with over a decade of lucid dreaming practice. Raised Catholic but not deeply engaged in the church, his spirituality expanded alongside his lucid dreaming experiences, leading him to study and incorporate aspects of Vedic and Buddhist teachings as well as concepts from physics into his worldview. Unlike the first participant, who sought to elicit their personal conception of God grounded in the Christian faith, this individual's approach was framed around a "higher self" he referred to as the *Magical Personality*. For him, the lucid dream served as a site for direct inquiry into consciousness and multidimensional reality, where encounters with SAs became opportunities for exploration and guidance.

In one report, he describes:

> I still called, like, a guide. I said it in Spanish. I said, "I call upon the Magical Personality," which is how I've been referring to a guide lately. And once I did it, there was, like, a pair of hands that appeared from the ceiling...And I asked it the question, I said, "tell me something important" ... And then it was weird, because those hands stretched from the wall, and came and grabbed my hands.
>
> *(Participant 2)*

The imagery of hands reaching down and grasping his own may reflect his conceptualization of the SA as an extension of his own self rather than an external deity. This dream draws upon integrative spiritual motifs, including elements of embodiment, interconnectedness, and transcendence. The tactile nature of the encounter (the guide physically holding his hands) may also emphasize a relational, embodied dimension of agency, in which guidance is conveyed not through verbal or symbolic messages but through physical connection. The framing of the SA as the *Magical Personality* highlights how dream incubation can reflect pre-existing spiritual practices. In this case, the invocation was conducted in Spanish which underscores a personal ritual language and framed around a belief in multidimensional access points within consciousness. For the participant, the lucid dream is an arena in which to collaborate with an aspect of self that transcends waking limitations.

As he explained:

> Well, it was being in dialogue with the whole dream. I really felt a sense of unification with the whole dream. I felt as if I were intimately communicating with my subconscious, or whatever you'd call it...the creative spirit of the dream. But at the same time, this dialogue left room for surprises...Personally, I see it as the more meaningful the dream, the more it's like a dance between the dreamer and the dream.
>
> *(Participant 2)*

This reflection suggests that the participant may not have viewed lucidity primarily as a tool of control. Instead, his description points to a more co-creative understanding of the lucid dream, where the agency of the dream guide remained active. By describing the experience as a "dance between the dreamer and the dream," he implied that meaning emerged through a collaboration rather than a unilateral authorship. From this perspective, the SA could be interpreted less as a fixed figure and more as a dynamic presence that could both guide and surprise him.

The two vignettes outlined above demonstrate how pre-existing beliefs and practices shaped participants' experiences of elicited dream guides. While both participants approached lucidity as a means of engaging with an SA, their ontologies of the guide differed in ways that mirrored their waking-world spiritual orientations. For the first participant, whose Christian faith was central to their daily life, the dream encounters drew directly on biblical narratives and reinforced their devotional relationship to God. The appearance of the divine presence through subtle, ephemeral forms was interpreted through scriptural precedent. In this sense, the dream provided not only personal reassurance but also continuity with established religious imagery, aligning with accounts of dreams as spaces where scripture and faith may be confirmed or deepened. By contrast, the second participant's experiences were framed by an integration of spiritual and philosophical perspectives. His invocation of the *Magical Personality* reflects a belief in multidimensional consciousness and a higher aspect of self, cultivated through both lucid dream practice and meditation. Here, the SA was not interpreted as an external deity but as a dynamic presence emerging from within the dream itself.

Taken together, these accounts suggest that the phenomenology of spiritual lucid dreams cannot be understood apart from the dreamer's pre-existing frameworks of belief. Where one dreamer perceived divine affirmation consistent with Christian scripture, another perceived guidance in the form of an inner, multidimensional self. These findings lend support to the continuity hypothesis in the context of religious cognition, highlighting how personal theology and spiritual practice inform not only the content but also the perceived agency of dream figures. At the same time, they invite consideration of the ways in which lucidity itself introduces new dynamics of agency. Participants exercised volitional control in calling for the appearance of a dream guide and choosing how to interact with them meaningfully. Yet the forms, behaviors, and reactions of the SA were largely unexpected in our sample. As one participant reflected, the most meaningful encounters resembled a "dance between the dreamer and the dream," where deliberate intention met the dream's own creative spontaneity. The autonomous ability to shape the dreamscape, coupled with the element of surprise, makes lucid dreaming an attainable and alluring state for mystic encounters.

Conclusion

Dreaming, from the Mesopotamian era onward, has provided a framework through which individuals derive meaning about the self and their place within broader culture. Prophetic messages, warnings, and divine affirmations received through dreams have long contributed to the body of ontological beliefs, continually informing and being informed by the religious doctrines that shape one's worldview. This is evident across theistic traditions, where both Christianity and Islam highlight the power of dreams and dream messages in forming foundational religious narratives. Non-theistic traditions, including Hinduism, Buddhism, and Spiritism, have recognized the transformational utility of dreams in guiding individuals toward enlightenment. As such, dreams can be used as channels for accessing higher forms of knowledge not ordinarily available in waking life. The presence of otherworldly entities (e.g., gods, spirits, deities) that guide and shape meaningful dreams can be approached through the lenses of science and religion alike. The neurobiological mechanisms underlying dreaming support the cognitive processes possibly necessary for the perception of SAs. Much of the scientific basis for this understanding has emphasized the diminished sense of agency characteristic of REM dreaming. Lucid dreams, however, offer a more complex picture, where deliberate efforts to elicit SAs coexist with automatic processes that generate unexpected content (in line with McNamara, 2018). Future research would benefit from examining how these dual routes of agency interact, offering a fuller account of the mechanisms that support SAs within dreaming. Scholars note that dreams serve as a point of intersection between scientific and religious viewpoints, as both seek to account for the psychological and spiritual transformations that arise from these profound experiences. Lucid dreaming presents a unique context to deliberately seek out and interacting with SAs. Our study offers a qualitative account of two expert lucid dreamers' personalized encounters with the divine; analyses of the dream reports point to the continuity of religious life in dreams and the profound impact of these experiences. Ultimately, the reviewed literature and case reports reveal how the dream state serves as a bridge between personal belief systems and transcendent experiences, allowing individuals to encounter, interpret, and affirm the sacred in ways that shape both inner life and collective traditions.

References

Baird, B., Mota-Rolim, S. A., & Dresler, M. (2019). The cognitive neuroscience of lucid dreaming. *Neuroscience and Biobehavioral Reviews, 100*, 305–323. https://doi.org/10.1016/j.neubiorev.2019.03.008

Barrett, J. L. (2000). Exploring the natural foundations of religion. *Trends in Cognitive Sciences, 4*(1), 29–34. https://doi.org/10.1016/s1364-6613(99)01419-9

Bautze-Picron, C. (2003). The five Dreams of the Bodhisatta in the Murals of Pagan. *Berliner Indologische Studien, 15–17*, 341–368. https://hal.science/hal-00547441

Blagrove, M., Hale, S., Lockheart, J., Carr, M., Jones, A., & Valli, K. (2019). Testing the empathy theory of dreaming: The relationships between dream sharing and trait and state empathy. *Frontiers in Psychology, 10*, 1351. https://doi.org/10.3389/fpsyg.2019.01351

Bogzaran, F. (1991). Experiencing the divine in the lucid dream state. *Lucidity Letter, 10*(1/2), 1–10.

Borg, J., Andrée, B., Soderstrom, H., & Farde, L. (2003). The serotonin system and spiritual experiences. *The American Journal of Psychiatry, 160*(11), 1965–1969. https://doi.org/10.1176/appi.ajp.160.11.1965

Bulkeley, K. (1996). Dreaming as a spiritual practice. *Anthropology of Consciousness, 7*(2), 1–15. https://doi.org/10.1525/ac.1996.7.2.1

Bulkeley, K. (2001). Penelope as Dreamer. In: Bulkeley, K. (Ed.), *Dreams*. Palgrave Macmillan. https://doi.org/10.1007/978-1-137-08545-0_14

Bulkeley, K. (2007). Sacred sleep: Scientific contributions to the study of religiously significant dreaming. In: Barrett, D. & McNamara, P. (Eds.), *The new science of dreaming:*

Vol. 3. Cultural and theoretical perspectives (pp. 71–94). Praeger Publishers/Greenwood Publishing Group.

Bulkeley, K. (2009a). Mystical dreaming: Patterns in form, content, and meaning. *Dreaming, 19*(1), 30–41. https://doi.org/10.1037/a0014788

Bulkeley, K. (2009b). The religious content of dreams: A new scientific foundation. *Pastoral Psychology, 58*, 93–106. https://doi.org/10.1007/s11089-008-0180-8

de Sá, J. F. R., & Mota-Rolim, S. A. (2015). Out-of-body experiences: Historical and neuroscientific aspects. *Sciences & Cognition, 20*(1). Retrieved from https://revista.cienciasecognicao.org/index.php/cec/article/view/985

Edgar, I., & Henig, D. (2010). Istikhara: The guidance and practice of Islamic dream incubation through ethnographic comparison. *History and Anthropology, 21*(3), 251–262. https://doi.org/10.1080/02757206.2010.496781

Espirito Santo, D. (2009). Making dreams: Spirits, vision and the ontological effects of dream knowledge in Cuban espiritismo. *Suomen Antropologi: Journal of the Finnish Anthropological Society, 34*(3), 6–24. https://doi.org/10.30676/jfas.116541

Esser, T. (2014). Kundalini and non-duality in the lucid dreaming state. In: Hurd, R. & Bulkeley, K. (Eds.), *Lucid dreaming: New perspectives on consciousness in sleep: Science, psychology, and education; Religion, creativity, and culture* (pp. 233–263). Praeger.

Gillespie, G. (2002). Dreams and dreamless sleep. *Dreaming, 12*, 199–207. https://doi.org/10.1023/A:1021104527848

Gyimesi, J. (2016). Why 'spiritism'? *The International Journal of Psychoanalysis, 97*(2), 357–383. https://doi.org/10.1111/1745-8315.12364

Hoffman, C. (2004). Dumuzi's dream: Dream analysis in ancient Mesopotamia. *Dreaming, 14*(4), 240–251. https://doi.org/10.1037/1053-0797.14.4.240

Holzinger, B., Saletu, B., & Klösch, G. (2020). Cognitions in sleep: Lucid dreaming as an intervention for nightmares in patients with posttraumatic stress disorder. *Frontiers in Psychology, 11*, 1826. https://doi.org/10.3389/fpsyg.2020.01826

Hsia, R. P. C. (2010). Dreams and conversions: A comparative analysis of catholic and Buddhist dreams in Ming and Qing China. Part Two. *Journal of Religious History, 34*(2), 111–141. https://doi.org/10.1111/j.1467-9809.2010.00858.x

Hughes, G., & Gooding, P. L. T. (2025). ERP correlates of agency processing in joint action. *Social Cognitive and Affective Neuroscience, 20*(1), nsaf006. https://doi.org/10.1093/scan/nsaf006

Ibn Khaldūn., Rosenthal, F., Dawood, N. J., & Lawrence, B. B. (2005). *The Muqaddimah: An introduction to history*. 1st Princeton classic ed./with a new introduction by Bruce B. Lawrence. Princeton University Press.

Jackson, P. A. (2025). Buddhist visions, dreams, and possession trance: Spiritual authority, ritual diversity and religious innovation in Thailand. *South East Asia Research, 33*(3), 1–24. https://doi.org/10.1080/0967828X.2025.2532791

Kardec, A. (1865, July). Théorie des rêves. Revue Spirite – *Journal d'etudes psychologiques, 8(7)*, 207–210. Retrieved from https://kardecpedia.com/en/study-guide/899/spiritist-review-journal-of-psychological-studies-1865/5814/july/theory-about-dreams

Khu, S., & I. Khumairoh. (2024). "A dream of guru came to me": Meanings of dreaming about spiritual teacher for Chinese Indonesian Buddhists. *Ethos, 52*, 259–273. https://doi.org/10.1111/etho.12426

Krippner, S., Bogzaran, F., & de Carvalho, A.P. (2002). *Extraordinary dreams and how to work with them*. State University of New York Press. https://doi.org/10.1353/book4504

Maij, D. L. R., van Schie, H. T., & van Elk, M. (2017). The boundary conditions of the hypersensitive agency detection device: an empirical investigation of agency detection in threatening situations. *Religion, Brain & Behavior, 9*(1), 23–51. https://doi.org/10.1080/2153599X.2017.1362662

McNamara, P. (2016). *Dreams and visions: How religious ideas emerge in sleep and dreams.* Praeger.

McNamara, P. (2018a). The science and theology of dreams. *Theology and Science, 16*(4), 484–497. https://doi.org/10.1080/14746700.2018.1525227

McNamara, P. (2018b). Supernatural agent cognitions in dreams. *Journal of Cognition and Culture, 18*(3–4), 428–450. https://doi.org/10.1163/15685373-12340038

McNamara, P., & Bulkeley, K. (2015). Dreams as a source of supernatural agent concepts. *Frontiers in Psychology, 6*. https://doi.org/10.3389/fpsyg.2015.00283

Metzger, B. M., & Murphy, R. E. (eds). (1991). *The new (Oxford) annotated Bible with the Apocryphal/Deuterocanonical books: New revised standard version.* Oxford University Press.

Morinis, E. A. (1982). Levels of culture in Hinduism: A case study of dream incubation at a Bengali pilgrimage centre. *Contributions to Indian Sociology, 16*(2), 255–270. https://doi.org/10.1177/006996678201600205 (Original work published 1982)

Mota-Rolim, S. A., Bulkeley, K., Campanelli, S., Lobão-Soares, B., de Araujo, D. B., & Ribeiro, S. (2020). The dream of god: How do religion and science see lucid dreaming and other conscious states during sleep? *Frontiers in Psychology, 11*, 555731. https://doi.org/10.3389/fpsyg.2020.555731

New International Version. (2011). Biblica. (Original work published 1973). https://www.biblegateway.com/passage/?search=1%20Kings%2019%3A11-13&version=NIV

Nordin, A. (2024). Gauging oneiromancy - The cognition of dream content and cultural transmission of (supernatural) divination. *Religion, Brain & Behaviour, 14*(2), 161–182. https://doi.org/10.1080/2153599X.2023.2172068

Nordin, A., & Bjälkebring, P. (2021). The counterintuitiveness of supernatural dreams and religiosity. *Journal of Cognition and Culture, 21*(3–4), 309–330. https://doi.org/10.1163/15685373-12340114

Peters, F. (2021). The sense of supernatural agency. *Journal of Cognition and Culture, 21*(1–2), 1–24. https://doi.org/10.1163/15685373-12340094

Peterson, N. D. J, Henke, P. G., & Hayes, Z. (2002). Limbic system function and dream content in university students. *Journal of Neuropsychiatry and Clinical Neurosciences, 14*(3), 283–288. https://doi.org/10.1176/jnp.14.3.283

Phillips, R. E. III, & Pargament, K. I. (2002). The sanctification of dreams: Prevalence and implications. *Dreaming, 12*(3), 141–153. https://doi.org/10.1023/A:1020166208750

Robertson, K., Gold, I., Veissière, S., Robillard, R., & Solomonova, E. (2024). Delusional ideation is associated with social imagery: Felt presence, social anxiety, empathy and loneliness. *Psychiatry Research Communications, 4*(2). https://doi.org/10.1016/j.psycom.2024.100169

Sackwild, L., & Stumbrys, T. (2021). The healing and transformative potential of lucid dreaming for treating clinical depression. *International Journal of Dream Research, 14*(2), 296–308. https://doi.org/10.11588/ijodr.2021.2.81533 (Original work published October 31, 2021)

Sheehy, M. R. (2025). Dreaming oneself awake: Psychological flexibility, imaginal simulation, and somatic awareness in Tibetan Buddhist dream yoga. *Dreaming*. Advance online publication. https://doi.org/10.1037/drm0000302

Stumbrys, T. (2021). The luminous night of the soul: The relationship between lucid dreaming and spirituality. *International Journal of Transpersonal Studies, 40*(2), 64–74. https://doi.org/10.24972/ijts.2021.40.2.64

Stumbrys, T., & Erlacher, D. (2016). Applications of lucid dreams and their effects on the mood upon awakening. *International Journal of Dream Research, 9*(2), 146–150. https://doi.org/10.11588/ijodr.2016.2.33114

Synofzik, M., Thier, P., Leube, D. T., Schlotterbeck, P., & Lindner, A. (2010). Misattributions of agency in schizophrenia are based on imprecise predictions about the sensory consequences of one's actions. *Brain: A Journal of Neurology, 133*(Pt 1), 262–271. https://doi.org/10.1093/brain/awp291

Tzioridou, S., Campillo-Ferrer, T., Cañas-Martín, J., Schlüter, L., Torres-Platas, S. G., Gott, J. A., Soffer-Dudek, N., Stumbrys, T., & Dresler, M. (2025). The clinical neuroscience of lucid dreaming. *Neuroscience and Biobehavioral Reviews, 169*, 106011. https://doi.org/10.1016/j.neubiorev.2025.106011

Wood, G. (2012). Attributing agency: Fast and frugal or all things considered? In: Nagasawa, Y. (Ed.), *Scientific approaches to the philosophy of religion*. Palgrave Frontiers in Philosophy of Religion. Palgrave Macmillan. https://doi.org/10.1057/9781137026019_5

Zhang, D., Li, Q., Shen, H., Song, H., Xu, K., Liu, F., Wang, J., & Liu, D. (2018). The dreams of monks: Studies on Chinese Buddhists' dream content. *Dreaming, 28*(3), 235–244.

8

REM SLEEP CONTRIBUTES TO THE NEURAL BASIS OF RELIGIOUS AND SPIRITUAL EXPERIENCES

Patrick McNamara

Introduction

Dreams have always contributed to religious consciousness and religions have always, in turn, shaped dream content (McNamara, 2016; Lanternari, 1975). Many religions began as literally a dream or vision in the mind of the founder. In the holy scriptures of the three Abrahamic Faiths dreams abound, with perhaps the dream called "Jacob's ladder" being one of the most famous. The patriarch Jacob was traveling, when he came to a place that apparently had been a very ancient pagan dream incubation site. Jacob rested, fell asleep, and then dreamt of a ladder going up to heaven with angels descending and ascending on the ladder. When Jacob awakened, he renamed the site Bethel, and it continues to this day to be a holy pilgrimage site for people who use dreams as a portal to heaven. Another biblical patriarch called Joseph was in fact a specialist in dream interpretation, as was the prophet Daniel. Jesus's birth was announced via a dream. When Joseph discovers that Mary is pregnant, he plans to quietly divorce her. But then:

> Behold, an angel of the Lord appeared to him in a dream, saying: Joseph, son of David, do not be afraid to take Mary as your wife, for that which is conceived in her is of the Holy Spirit. She will bear a son, and you shall name him Jesus, for he will save his people from their sins.
>
> *Matthew 1:20–21*

It seems that for all of human history, dreams have carried messages from the gods to humans and these messages become the raw material for the generation of religious and spiritual experiences, practices, and ideas. Many anthropologists have documented the central role of dreams in generating religious imagery, languages,

DOI: 10.4324/9781003158189-8

doctrines, practices, and beliefs. A number of these ethnographers and anthropologists, such as Steward Lincoln (1935), Eggan (1949), Devereux (1951), Kilborne (1981), Kracke (1979), and Irwin (1994), have made dreams a central focus of their work. The role that dreams play in the generation of religious and cultural systems has also been very thoroughly documented and reviewed several times in the anthropological literature (see, e.g., Barnouw, 1963; Bourguignon, 1972; D'Andrade, 1961; Eggan, 1961; Grunebaum & Caillois, 1966; Irwin, 1994; Kennedy & Langness, 1981; Lohmann, 2003; Laughlin, 2011; Tedlock, 1987, 1992).

Despite this overwhelming evidence of the central role of dreams in the generation of religious traditions and experiences, cognitive and neuroscientists of religion (CNSR) virtually never even mention dreams as a source of religious cognition. Nor do neuroscientists study REM sleep and dreams as a source of religious and spiritual experiences. This situation is all the more lamentable given that so much has been learnt about REM sleep and dreams since the 1950s when REM sleep was first documented (Azerinsky & Kleitman, 1953). Most cognitive scientists and neuroscientists still hold prescientific views of dreams as "things" that either are just epiphenomena of the sleeping brain, or at best Freudian or Jungian reflections of some mysterious "unconscious." But decades of very careful research by sleep medicine specialists and psychologists who specialize in the study of dreams have demonstrated that dreams are more accurately seen as modulators of levels of daytime social behaviors and ultimately as strategic social acts that may have lasting effects on daytime social interactions. Their functional contributions to simulating social interactions make them an effective contributor to religious forms of experience and cognition, given that most religious ideologies involve a pantheon of characters or supernatural agents with whom the individual interacts. In addition, REM sleep neurobiology overlaps to a significant extent with those brain networks activated in neuroimaging studies of individuals performing religious/spiritual tasks like prayer or meditation. When REM intrudes into daytime consciousness (as in daydreams), we very reliably get more religious and spiritual imagery and experiences. In any case, let us review some basic facts of REM neurobiology relevant ultimately to religious experiences.

REM Sleep and Dreams

When measured electrophysiologically, sleep (in humans) is composed of four major brain states or stages. The first three (N1–N3) constitute NREM sleep, with electroencephalographic (EEG) measures indicating light sleep in N2 and deep slow-wave sleep (SWS) in N3. The fourth stage is not part of NREM sleep and is characterized by periodic or phasic bursts of rapid eye movements or REM under the closed eyelids. REM sleep is indicated by EEG data, electroculographic activity, and a reduction in electromyographic (EMG) activity. EMG electrodes are usually placed under the chin and indicate when the muscle paralysis characteristic of REM sleep occurs (Rechtschaffen & Kales, 1968).

REM and NREM sleep states alternate throughout the night in a period of about 90 minutes. Stage N1 is a transitional stage to N2 or light sleep. N3 is composed of SWS, which must be partially made up if lost due to sleep deprivation. That is, there is an increased amount of SWS after periods of sleep deprivation. NREM stages dominate the first third of the night, while REM dominates the last third (Carskadon & Rechtschaffen, 2000). A sleep cycle is defined as a period of NREM sleep followed by a period of REM sleep. During a single night, a person will progress through three or four NREM–REM sleep cycles, each lasting 90–110 minutes and becoming progressively longer through the night. Usually, the NREM period will last about 80 minutes or longer, followed by a REM period that can be as short as one minute in the early cycles. Toward the morning, REM periods can last as long as 45 minutes.

REM sleep accounts for about 22% of total sleep time in humans. Although the cortex is activated in REM, arousal thresholds are higher in REM than in the waking state (or in SWS, for that matter). The phasic aspects of REM, such as intermittent muscle twitching, autonomic nervous system (ANS) discharges, and REMs, occur in some mammals and likely in humans as well in association with bursts of ponto-geniculo-occipital (PGO) waves. These are essentially electrical spikes in the visual centers of the brain indicating that the animal is orienting toward some significant stimulus. Mammals also exhibit a theta rhythm in the hippocampal formation during REM. REM is also associated with ANS instabilities that become more extreme as the duration of REM episodes increases across the night.

REM's tonic characteristics are a desynchronized EEG, penile erections in males/clitoral engorgement in female, and atonia of the antigravity muscles. Its phasic characteristics include bursts of REMs under the closed eyelids, myoclonic twitches of the facial and limb muscle groups, increased variability in heart rate, respiration, and blood pressure (BP), and ANS discharges. Other correlates of REM include effects on the release of selected hormones—especially growth factors. Virtually all mammals (with some exceptions, e.g., certain sea mammals) exhibit both SWS and REM sleep. Most sleep scientists believe that animals who exhibit REM sleep also have something like the phenomenal experiences that we call dreams. When motor centers are lesioned in cats and they go into REM sleep, we can see them appear to hallucinate threats as they snarl and growl and scratch, and so on, or they hallucinate playing with captured prey, and so forth. When motor inhibition centers are lesioned in humans, associated with REM Behavior Disorder (RBD), they too hallucinate threats and later report that they were dreaming about intruders attacking them, and so on. But these dream enactment behaviors in humans can also become more elaborate and then we get reports of interactions with supernatural figures and other fantastic imagery.

Under healthy conditions, REM sleep "turns on" when activity levels of the biogenic amines (e.g., norepinephrine) decrease and activity levels of acetylcholine increase (Hobson, 2001).

The case of dopamine (DA) is complex as its activity levels in some regions likely decrease in REM but increase in other brain regions during REM. It is therefore not surprising to find that drugs that increase cholinergic or DA-ergic activity generally tend to increase REM sleep and dream recall. People on the nicotine patch often report that they are dreaming more and that their dreams have become vivid and intense.

Brain activation patterns are different in many ways for REM and NREM sleep, with REM sleep demonstrating high activation levels in limbic/amygdaloid sites and dopamine or DA-ergic and cholinergic circuits, and deactivation of dlPFC sites (Dang-Vu et al., 2007; Hobson, 2007; Hobson, Pace-Schott, Stickgold, & Kahn, 1998; Maquet & Franck, 1997; Maquet et al., 1996; Nofzinger, Mintun, Wiseman, Kupfer, & Moore, 1997), as well as cessation of activation in the noradrenergic locus coeruleus and the serotoninergic raphe nucleus. Perogamvros and Schwartz (2012) noted that dopaminergic limbic sites are activated in REM. In addition, midline anterior paralimbic areas that include both subcortical areas, such as basal forebrain, hypothalamus, ventral striatum, and hippocampus, and paralimbic cortices, such as insula, anterior cingulate, orbitofrontal cortex, and supplementary motor area, are all areas activated during REM. All of these areas participate in the so-called "social brain" areas and in processing experiences concerning the self in its social interactions and in the assignment and computation of value to experiences.

REM Intrusion and Daydreams

How do REM dreams influence waking cognitions and behaviors? There is now evidence that emotional memories are consolidated during REM (Murkar & De Koninck, 2018). In addition, as mentioned above, the neurobiology of REM regularly intrudes into waking consciousness in the forms of daydreams and "microsleeps." Daydreams and visionary and altered states of consciousness from a neurocognitive point of view are very likely, at least partially, generated by this REM intrusion phenomenon of (Bob & Louchakova, 2015; Vaitl et al., 2005). To the extent that daydreams reproduce the normal physiology of REM sleep, then dream-induced cognitions around religious ideas like supernatural agent or SAs will become available to waking consciousness. In addition, when full-blown REM physiology intrudes into daytime consciousness, as is the case with narcolepsy it inevitably creates a range of states of consciousness from reverie and daydreamy states to outright delusional states. Frequent daydreaming or mindwandering, is strongly associated with trait "absorption and imaginative involvement," a dissociative tendency for immersed awareness and involvement in fantasy. Mind wandering, in turn, has been shown to be strongly linked with DMN activity, paralimbic and midline neural networks, and sites such as the angular gyrus, mPFC, and posterior cingulate gyrus. There is overlap between REM sleep and mind-wandering, with activation of the DMN and decreased activation of the dlPFC. Indeed, some theories and reviews of brain activation patterns in REM suggest that it essentially involves activation and deactivation and active rewiring of DMN network (dlPFC; Fox et al., 2013; Dang-Vu et al., 2010; Domhoff & Fox, 2015).

It is well-established that sleep deprivation reliably produces compensatory attempts to enter REM throughout the day resulting in REM microsleeps as well as reports of dreamy states and dissociative symptoms (Limosani, D'Agostino, Manzone, & Scarone, 2011; Palagini & Rosenlicht, 2011). The role of sleep mechanisms in the generation of visual hallucinations is well-recognized in narcolepsy in the case of hypnagogic hallucinations, which are thought to derive from a REM-dissociation state in which dream imagery intrudes into wakefulness. Van de Kloet, Merckelbach, Giesbrecht, and Lynn (2012) and Mahowald, Cramer Bornemann, and Schenck (2011) review a range of evidence that demonstrates that dissociative symptoms such as absorption, derealization, and depersonalization and other symptoms associated with a range of psychiatric disturbances originate from REM. REM intrusion has been reported to contribute to symptoms and delusional states in schizophrenia (Cohrs, 2008; Gottesmann & Gottesman, 2007).

The typical REM dream contains between two and three characters in addition to the dreamer. These other characters are typically composed of familiars and unfamiliars. The familiar characters are people familiar to the dreamer—people like family members, emotionally significant friends, and acquaintances. The unfamiliar characters in a REM dream typically are just "known" to be strangers without many defining features at first. When the other characters are unknown to the dreamer (i.e., strangers), there is an increased chance that an SA will appear in the dream and that there will be aggression directed toward the dreamer thus indicating a transient loss in agency in the dreamer. It is an especially important fact for the dreams and religion hypothesis that about 50% of characters in dreams are strangers to the dreamer. These unfamiliar or undefined character lines in dreams very likely are the templates into which is written the development of SAs in a dream.

In some dream series, up to 80% of characters are unknown to the dreamer. Almost all supernatural monsters from nightmares morph into activity from strangers in dreams. Next to strangers in dreams, animals most often morph into SAs in dreams. Animals occur in about 10% of dreams overall, but the percentage rises dramatically in children's dreams. Upward 50% of children's dreams contain animals of one kind or another.

Virtually all dreams involve the self or are about the self interacting with other characters, in more or less familiar though intense ways. The dreamer's sense of self or his/her core experience of self fluctuates profoundly in dreams. The dreamer, for example, experiences a loss of agency in a significant number of REM dreams. Just as religious ideas are about transformations of the self, so too in dreams the self undergoes significant emotional transformations in interaction with other significant dream characters. Almost all of these self-transformations in dreams involve changes in the sense of agency as described later.

SAs appear in a significant percentage of REM dreams but certainly not in all REM dreams. My claim here is not that we will find SAs ready-made in all REM dreams—rather it is that the dreamwork constructs the cognitive images and representation or building blocks that characterize or make up SAs. Once dreams manufacture the primary building blocks for SAs, they become available by being stored in memory to waking consciousness, which then finishes the work of mentalizing SAs as real entities. Dreams do this by taking representations of normal everyday agents (i.e., embodied characters with no special powers) and then deconstructing them systematically so that constituent parts can be reused in the dream (via an investment of an unusual amount of agency or power in the character) or in waking life to cognize unusual agents. In other words, key attributes of ordinary agents get decoupled from one another and from context in the dream so that they can be used to construct SAs during waking life.

For example, the key attribute of mind or intentionality becomes decoupled from an ordinary human body and then later, either in a dream or in waking life, gets recombined with special bodies (e.g., animal bodies) so that you have a man's mind in a bear's body, and so on. These therianthropes of the upper Paleolithic might be good examples of this process. When minds are placed in unusual bodies in a dream, these new beings are also invested with unusual powers or abilities. They might have special mind-reading and other abilities and are interacted with in the dream as if they were real. A man's mind in a bear's body, for example, might lead to the idea that the composite being is especially strong, cunning, dangerous, and so on.

To complete these transpositions of mind or agency from one character to another in a dream, one needs placeholder empty characters who can receive attributions projected by the dreamer during a dream. Strangers (or unfamiliar characters) and animals fill the bill here. Because strangers are literally nonentities, they can be filled with anything the dreamer wishes to project onto them. Once a stranger is invested with special mental and physical attributes by the dreamer, he or she becomes a *special* character who drives the action of the dream forward. If the new attributes are really special and unusual, the new character will become a supernatural character. These on-the-fly dynamic character transformations (including loss of agency in the dreamer with subsequent over-attribution of agency and other abilities in a stranger character) using standard cognitive analyses of dream narratives themselves.

In short, an initial plausible hypothesis is that dreams give rise to SAs by reducing agency in the dreamer and transferring it several times over to another dream character (typically a stranger) who takes on supernatural powers and becomes a God or demon. REM's chemical environment of high-dopamine and low-serotonin activity promotes all of these steps by facilitation of the detection of unexpected events or anomalies and then preventing agency or power within the dreamer and plunging the dreamer into a liminal state almost akin to an LSD trip, though of course not quite as intense.

REM sleep neurophysiology is optimal for the production of the cognitive processes that give rise to SAs. During REM, the gamma rhythm centered around 40 Hz becomes uncoupled in the cortical areas, between the hippocampus and the cortex, and the intra-hippocampal gamma coherence is decreased. There is no resetting of the gamma rhythm by sensory stimulation during REM sleep. In every REM episode, there is an elevation in dopamine and acetylcholine activity and a reduction in serotonin and norepinephrine activity. In addition, there is increased activation in the amygdala, portions of the limbic system, and ventromedial cortex, and a reduction in the activation in parietal and dlPFCs. The reduction in dlPFC and in serotonin and norepinephrine activity promotes the reduction in agency experienced by the dreamer during the dream. The activation of ventromedial prefrontal cortex (vmPFC) supports theory-of-mind processing abilities and therefore likely promotes attribution of agency to other dream characters.

I believe the transfer-of-agency cognitive process occurs most reliably and most frequently in intense REM dreams and nightmares (see McNamara, 2008; McNamara, 2009; McNamara & Bulkeley, 2015). Phenomenologically, dreams and nightmares are characterized by an abundance of (McNamara, 2009, 2022) decentering elements such as loss of control, disorientation, fear, sense of effort, attempts at escape, and attempts at connection with other dream characters. These basic but fragmented experiential dream episodes might remain in short-term offline emotional memory circuits that then become the raw material for the construction of RSEs when the social context permits spiritual experiences in waking life.

I and colleagues (Balch et al., 2025) tested some of the ideas summarized above concerning the influence of dream content items such as dreamer agency on day-to-day changes in spiritual experiences. We assessed whether dream content could reliably influence daytime spiritual and religious experiences. In Study 1, we used computational linguistic tools to analyze supernatural content in a large dataset, which we gathered from participants across a two-week period in an intensive longitudinal design collecting data in the home using previously validated survey instruments, diaries, and the Dreem 3 Headband. We investigated the impacts of dream content and sleep architecture on waking God-concepts, "closeness to god ratings," and God images. After gathering and analyzing all of that data with linear mixed effects (LME) modeling of the data we used a simple, one-perceptron computational model or artificial neural network (ANN) with no activation function to mimic the mixed effects LMEs to assess the similarities and differences between LMEs and ANNs. The saliency maps of ANN showed that T-4 and T-3 dream-based content predictors influenced the model outputs more than the T-1 and T-2 inputs, demonstrating the importance of the time-lagged effects in daily closeness-to-God ratings.

Of particular note was that supernatural content in dreams was associated with dream content characterized by higher levels of strangeness, lack of control, and opacity, as well as negative emotionality when compared to dreams without supernatural content. Supernatural content in RSEs was associated with power and dominance but also associated with more positive semantic variables (friendliness, virtue, etc.). This indicates that a common feature of SAs in both dreams and RSEs may be their inability to be controlled by the subject or the dreamer, but that this operates very differently in each context. In dreams, SAs are thus distinguished by being more tangible (characterized by spatial and arousing dimensions) and more negative and bizarre. SA content in dreaming is therefore more likely to correspond to disruptions in personal agency, which may trigger updates in overall representations of supernatural agents in day-to-day life.

This analysis revealed that supernatural dreams have lower levels of dream agency, and are rated as more bizarre, strange, scary, and aggressive. We then assessed the impact of dream content variables and sleep architecture on two dimensions of God-images (closeness and authoritarianism). These studies demonstrated a significant effect of these dream content features on these SA dimensions with both concurrent and lagged effects, as well as a positive relationship between REM% and both dimensions of daily God rating outcomes.

The deep temporal neural network, TSANN, which we trained on data gathered in the two-week study confirmed the importance of the four-day lagged effect on closeness-to-god ratings. We used participant-stratified K-fold cross-validation procedures and ran repeated training replications on study two data, which revealed optimal values for closeness-to-God ratings after 500 to 1,250 learning epochs and precisely reproduced the four-day lagged effects of dream content variables like dreamer agency discovered in the two-week study. These results strongly suggest that lower agency in the dream and dream affect are causally influencing daytime closeness-to-God experiences.

Thus, across all three studies in this project, lower dreamer agency and negative dream affect both characterized dreams with supernatural content and impacted daily changes in closeness to God. These results therefore support our hypotheses and are consistent with McNamara (2016) and Nordin (2024a, 2024b). We suggest that the same cognitive processes (mentalizing, social simulation, relational thinking) that enable individuals to relate to SAs during the day are calibrated within and updated during dreams. Lower dream agency occurring in REM dreams sets up the cognitive conditions necessary for the dreaming mind/brain to simulate other dream characters who are invested with supernormal levels of agency and supernatural powers.

We suggest that the temporal lag effect documented here is broadly consistent with the now relatively abundant evidence (see Wagner, Gais, & Born, 2001) which demonstrates that the REM sleep and dream system functions as an emotional memory processing system. Our testing of different levels of the lags using the temporal ANN indicates that there is at least a two-to-three-day lag in the consolidation of dream events into both relational and conceptual schemas of God-images. This finding points to the need for future work to consider dream effects beyond the next morning.

To sum up: We now have both theory and empirical experimental evidence that dream content significantly influences religious ideas and spiritual experiences.

It is time for cognitive neuroscientists to take REM sleep and dreams into account when studying the brain bases of religious and spiritual experiences.

Bibliography

Abu-Akel, A. (2003). The neurochemical hypothesis of "theory of mind." *Medical Hypotheses, 60*(3), 382–386.

Abu-Akel, A., & Shamay-Tsoory, S. (2011). Neuroanatomical and neurochemical bases of theory of mind. *Neuropsychologia, 49*(11), 2971–2984.

Andreasen, N. C., Paradiso, S., & O'Leary, D. S. (1998). "Cognitive dysmetria" as an integrative theory of schizophrenia: A dysfunction in cortical-subcortical-cerebellar circuitry? *Schizophrenia Bulletin, 24*(2), 203–218.

Andrews-Hanna, J. R. (2012). The brain's default network and its adaptive role in internal mentation. *Neuroscientist, 18*(3), 251–270.

Antrobus, J. S. (1991). Dreaming: Cognitive processes during cortical activation and high afferent thresholds. *Psychological Review*, *98*, 96–121.

Azerinsky, E., & Kleitman, N. (1953). Regularly occurring periods of eye motility and concurrent phenomena during sleep. *Science*, *118*(3062), 273–274.

Badre, D., & D'esposito, M. (2007). Functional magnetic resonance imaging evidence of a hierarchical organization of the prefrontal cortex. *Journal of Cognitive Neuroscience, 19*(12), 2082–2099.

Balch, J., Hodulik, G., Raider, R., David, A., Reed, C., Wildman, W. J., ... & McNamara, P. (2025). Dream content influences daily spirituality. *Frontiers in Psychology, 16*, 1575174.

Balon, R. (1996). Bupropion and nightmares. *The American Journal of Psychiatry, 153*(4), 579–580.

Barnouw, V. (1963). *Culture and personality*. Homewood, IL: Dorsey Press.

Bayer, H. M, & Glimcher, P. W. (2005). Midbrain dopamine neurons encode a quantitative reward prediction error signal. *Neuron, 47*(1), 129–141.

Belicki, K. (1986). Recalling dreams: An examination of daily variation and individual differences. In J. Gackenbach (Ed.), *Sleep and dreams: A sourcebook* (pp. 187–206). New York: Garland.

Blagrove, M., Fouquet, N. C., Henley-Einion, J. A., Pace-Schott, E. F., Davies, A. C., Neuschaffer, J. L., & Turnbull, O. H. (2011). Assessing the dream-lag effects for REM and NREM Stage 2 dreams. *PLoS One*, *6*(10). doi: 10.1371/journal.pone.0026708

Blakemore, S. J., Frith, C. D., & Wolpert, D. M. (2001). The cerebellum is involved in predicting the sensory consequences of action. *Neuroreport, 12*(9), 1879–1884.

Bob, P., & Louchakova, O. (2015). Dissociative states in dreams and brain chaos: Implications for creative awareness. *Front Psychol*, *6*(1353). doi: 10.3389/fpsyg.2015.01353

Bonifay, E. (2002). L'Homme de Neandertal et L'Ours (Ursue Actos) dans la Grotte du Regourdou (Montingnac-Sur-Vezere, Dorgogne, France). In T. Tillet & L. Binford (Eds.), *L'Ours et l'Homme* (pp. 247–254). Liège: ERAUL.

Bourguignon, E. (1972). Dreams and altered states of consciousness in anthropological research. In F. L. K. Hsu (Ed.), *Psychological anthropology* (pp. 403–434). Cambridge, MA: Schenkman Publications.

Boyer, P. (2001). *Religion explained: The evolutionary origins of religious thought.* New York: Basic Books.

Boyer, P. (2002). *Religion explained: The human instincts that fashion gods, spirits, and ancestors.* New York: Random House.

Broughton, R. J. (1985). Three central issues concerning ultradian rhythms. In H. Schulz & P. Lavie (Eds.), *Ultradian rhythms in physiology and behaviour* (pp. 217–233). Verlag, Berlin, Heidelberg, New York, Tokyo: Springer.

Buchanan, T. W., & Lovallo, W. R. (2001). Enhanced memory for emotional material following stress-level cortisol treatment in humans. *Psychoneuroendocrinology, 26*(3), 307–317.

Buckner, R. L., Andrews-Hanna, J. R., & Schacter, D. L. (2008). The brain's default network. *Annals of the New York Academy of Sciences, 1124*(1), 1–38.

Bulkeley, K. (2006). Revision of the good fortune scale: A new tool for the study of "big dreams." *Dreaming, 16*(1), 11–21. doi: 10.1037/1053-0797.16.1.11

Bulkeley, K. (2007). Sacred sleep: Scientific contributions to the study of religiously significant dreaming. In D. Barrett & P. McNamara (Eds.), *The new science of dreaming* (pp. 71–94). Westport, CT: Praeger.

Bulkeley, K. (2008). *Dreaming in the world's religions: A comparative history.* New York: New York University Press.

Bunzeck, N., & Duzel, E. (2006). Absolute coding of stimulus novelty in the human substantia nigra/VTA. *Neuron, 51*(3), 369–379.

Burgess, P. W., Gilbert, S. J., & Dumontheil, I. (2007). Function and localization within rostral prefrontal cortex (Area 10). *Philosophical Transactions: Biological Sciences, 362*(1481), 887–899.

Cai, D. J., Mednick, S. A., Harrison, E. M., Kanady, J. C., & Mednick, S. C. (2009). REM, not incubation, improves creativity by priming associative networks. *Proceedings of the National Academy of Science of the United States of America, 106*(205), 10130–10134. doi: 10.1073/pnas.0900271106

Cantero, J. L., Atienza, M., Stickgold, R., Kahana, M. J., Madsen, J. R., & Kocsis, B. (2003). Sleep-dependent theta oscillations in the human hippocampus and neocortex. *The Journal of Neuroscience: Official Journal of the Society for Neuroscience, 23*(34), 10897–10903.

Carskadon, M. A., & Rechtschaffen, A. (2000). Monitoring and staging human sleep. *Perspectives on Psychological Science, 3*, 1197–1215.

Carter, M. E., Borg, J. S., & de Lecea, L. (2009). The brain hypocretins and their receptors: Mediators of allostatic arousal. *Current Opinion in Pharmacology, 9*(1), 39–45.

Cartwright R. (2010). *The twenty-four hour mind: The role of sleep and dreaming in our emotional lives*. Oxford: Oxford University Press.

Chauvet, J., Deschamps, E. B., & Hillaire, C. (1995). *Chauvet cave: The discovery of the world's oldest paintings.* London: Thames and Hudson.

Christoff, K., & Gabrieli, J. (2000). The frontopolar cortex and human cognition: Evidence for a rostrocaudal hierarchical organization within the human prefrontal cortex. *Psychobiology, 28*(2), 168–186.

Clemens, Z., Weiss, B., Szucs, A., Eross, L., Rasonyi, G., & Halasz, P. (2009). Phase coupling between rhythmic slow activity and gamma characterizes mesiotemporal rapid-eye-movement sleep in humans. *Neuroscience, 163*(1), 388–396.

Cohrs, S. (2008). Sleep disturbances in patients with schizophrenia: Impact and effect of antipsychotics. *CNS Drugs, 22*, 939–962. Review. doi: 10.2165/00023210-200822110-00004

Comeau, B. G. (1996). *Grizzly bear spiritual power and shamanism in native cultures of the Pacific slope of North America* (Unpublished doctoral dissertation). University of Ottawa, Canada.

Crescentini, C., Di Bucchianico, M., Fabbro, F., & Urgesi, C. (2015). Excitatory stimulation of the right inferior parietal cortex lessens implicit religiousness/spirituality. *Neuropsychologia, 70,* 71–79. doi: 10.1016/j.neuropsychologia.2015.02.016

D'Andrade, R. G. (1961). Anthropological studies of dreams. In F. L. K. Hsu (Ed.), *Psychological anthropology: Approaches to culture and personality* (pp. 296–332). Homewood, IL: Dorsey Press.

Dahan, L., Astier, B., Vautrelle, N., Urbain, N., Kocsis, B., & Chouvet, G. (2007). Prominent burst firing of dopaminergic neurons in the ventral tegmental area during paradoxical sleep. *Neuropsychopharmacology, 32*(6), 1232–1241.

Damasio, A. R., Everitt, B. J., & Bishop, D. (1996). The somatic marker hypothesis and the possible functions of the prefrontal cortex [and discussion]. *Philosophical Transactions of the Royal Society B, 351*(1346), 1413–1420. doi: 10.1098/rstb.1996.0125

Dang-Vu, T. T, Schabus, M., Desseilles, M., Sterpenich, V., Bonjean, M., & Maquet, P. (2010). Functional neuroimaging insights into the physiology of human sleep. *Sleep, 33*(12), 1589–1603. Review. PMID:21120121.

Dang-Vu, T. T., Desseilles, M., Petit, D., Mazza, S., Montplaisir, J., & Maquet, P. (2007). Neuroimaging in sleep medicine. *Sleep Medicine, 8*, 349–372. doi: 10.1016/j.sleep.2007.03.006

Darsuad, A., Wagner, U., Balteau, E., Desseilles, M., Sterpenich, V., Vandewalle, G., et al. (2011). Neural precursors of delayed insight. *Journal of Cognitive Neuroscience, 23*(8), 1900–1910. doi: 10.1162/jocn.2010.21550

Devereux, G. (1951). *Reality and dream: Psychotherapy of a Plains Indian.* New York: International Universities Press.

Dixon, B. R. (1908). Notes on the Achomawi and Atsugewi Indians of Northern California. *American Anthropologist, 10*, 208–220.

Doblin, R. (1991). Pahnke's "Good Friday Experiment": A long-term follow-up and methodological critique. *Journal of Transpersonal Psychology, 23*(1), 1–28.

Domhoff, G. W. (2002). Using content analysis to study dreams: Applications and implications for the humanities. In K. Bulkeley (Ed.), *Dreams: A reader on the religious, cultural, and psychological dimensions of dreaming* (pp. 307–319). New York: Palgrave.

Domhoff, G. W. (2003). *The scientific study of dreams: Neural networks, cognitive development, and content analysis*. Washington, DC: American Psychological Association.

Domhoff, G. W. (2003). *The scientific study of dreams: Neural networks, cognitive development, and content analysis*. Washington, DC: American Psychological Association.

Domhoff, G. W. (2005). The content of dreams: Methodologic and theoretical implications. In M. H. Kryger, T. Roth, & W. C. Dement (Eds.), *Principles and practice of sleep medicine* (4th ed., pp. 522–534). Philadelphia, PA: W. B. Saunders.

Domhoff, G. W. (2011). The neural substrate for dreaming: Is it a subsystem of the default network? *Consciousness and Cognition, 20*(4), 1163–1174. doi: 10.1016/j.concog.2011.03.001

Domhoff, G. W., & Fox, K. C. (2015). Dreaming and the default network: A review, synthesis, and counterintuitive research proposal. *Consciousness and Cognition, 33*, 342–353.

Eggan, D. (1949). The significance of dreams for anthropological research. *American Anthropology, 51*(2), 177–198.

Eggan, D. (1961). Dream analysis. In B. Kaplan (Ed.), *Studying personality cross-culturally* (pp. 551–577). New York: Harper and Row.

Fantini, M. I., Corona, A., Clerici, S., & Ferini-Strambi, L. (2005). Aggressive dream content without daytime aggressiveness in REM sleep behavior disorder. *Neurology, 65*(7), 1010–1015.

Farrer, C., & Frith, C. D. (2002). Experiencing oneself vs another person as being the cause of an action: The neural correlates of the experience of agency. *NeuroImage, 15*(3), 596–603.

Farrer, C., Franck, N., Georgieff, N., Frith, C. D., Decety, J., & Jeannerod, M. (2003). Modulating the experience of agency: A positron emission tomography study. *NeuroImage, 18*(2), 324–333.

Faulkner, W. (1942). *Go down, Moses*. New York: Vintage, 1990.

Fincher, C. L., Thornhill, R. (2008). Assortative sociality, limited dispersal, infectious disease and the genesis of the global pattern of religion diversity. *Proceedings of the Royal Society B: Biological Sciences, 275*(1651), 2587–2594. doi: 10.1098/rspb.2008.0688

Fisher, C., Byrne, J., Edwards, A., & Kahn, E. (1970). A psychophysiological study of nightmares. *Journal of the American Psychoanalytic Association, 18*, 747–782.

Fletcher, P. C., & Frith, C. D. (2009). Perceiving is believing: A Bayesian approach to explaining the positive symptoms of schizophrenia. *Nature Reviews Neuroscience, 10*(1), 48–58. doi: 10.1038/nrn2536

Foster, M. G. (1944). A summary of Yuki culture. *University of California Anthropological Records, 5*, 155–244.

Foulkes, D. (1985). *Dreaming: A cognitive-psychological analysis*. Hillsdale, NJ: Lawrence Erlbaum Associates.

Foulkes, W. D. (1962). Dream reports from different stages of sleep. *Journal of Abnormal and Social Psychology, 65*(1), 14–25.

Fox, K. C., Nijeboer, S., Solomonova, E., Domhoff, G. W., & Christoff, K. (2013). Dreaming as mind wandering: Evidence from functional neuroimaging and first-person content reports. Frontiers in Human Neuroscience, 7, 412.

Freud, S. (1913). *Totem and taboo*. London: WW Norton.

Friston, K. (2009). The free-energy principle: A rough guide to the brain? *Trends in Cognitive Science, 13*(7), 293–301.

Friston, K., Adams, R. A., Perritnet, L., & Breakspear, M. (2012). Perceptions as hypotheses: Saccades as experiments. *Frontiers in Psychology, 3*(151), 1–20.

Fuster, J. M. (2004). Upper processing stages of the perception-action cycle. *Trends in Cognitive Sciences, 8*(4), 143–145.

Fuster, J. M. (2008). *The prefrontal cortex* (4th ed.). New York: Academic Press.

Gayton, H. A. (1948). Yokuts and Western mono ethnography: I. *University of California Anthropological Records, 10*, 1–141.

Gayton, H. A. (1948). Yokuts and Western mono ethnography: II. *University of California Anthropological Records, 10*, 142–302.

Geshwind, N. (1979). Behavioural changes in temporal lobe epilepsy. *Psychol Medicine, 9*(2), 217–219.

Goodenough, D. (1991). Dream recall: History and current status of the field. In S. Ellman & J. S. Antrobus (Eds.), *The mind in sleep* (2nd ed., pp. 143–171). New York: Wiley Interscience.

Gottesmann, C., & Gottesman, I. (2007). The neurobiological characteristics of rapid eye movement (REM) sleep are candidate endophenotypes of depression, schizophrenia, mental retardation and dementia. *Progress in Neurobiology, 81*, 237–250. doi: 10.1016/j.pneurobio.2007.01.004

Grace, A. A., Floresco, S. B., Goto, Y., & Lodge, D. J. (2007). Review regulation of firing of dopaminergic neurons and control of goal-directed behaviors. *Trends in Neurosciences, 30*(5), 220–227.

Green, C., Garety, P. A., Freeman, D., Fowler, D., Bebbington, P., Dunn, G., & Kuipers, E. (2006). Content and affect in persecutory delusions. *British Journal of Clinical Psychology, 45*, 561–577. doi: 10.1348/014466506X98768

Griffiths, R. R., Johnson, M. W., Richards, W. A., Richard, B. D., McCann, U., & Jesse, R. (2011). Psilocybin occasioned mystical-type experiences: Immediate and persisting dose-related effects. *Psychopharmacology, 218*(4), 649–665. doi: 10.1007/s00213-011-2358-5

Griffiths, R., Richards, W., McCann, U., & Jesse, R. (2006). Psilocybin can occasion mystical-type experiences having substantial and sustained personal meaning and spiritual significance. *Psychopharmacology, 187*(3), 268–283. doi: 10.1007/s00213-006-0457-5

Grunebaum, G. E., & Caillois, R. (Eds.). (1966). *The dream and human societies* (No. 4). University of California Press.

Hall, C. (1963). Strangers in dreams: An empirical confirmation of the Oedipus complex. *Journal of Personality, 31*, 336–345.

Hallowell, A. I. (1926). Bear ceremonialism in the Northern Hemisphere. *American Anthropologist, 28*, 1–175. doi: 10.1525/aa.1926.28.1.02a00020

Hartmann, E. (1996). Outline for a theory on the nature and functions of dreaming. *Dreaming, 6*(2), 147–170. doi: 10.1037/h0094452

Hartmann, E. (1998). *Dreams and nightmares: The new theory on the origin and meaning of dreams.* New York: Plenum.

Hayden, B. (2003). *Shamans, sorcerers and saints: A prehistory of religion.* Washington, DC: Smithsonian.

Hobson, A. J., Pace-Schott, E. F., Stickgold, R., & Kahn, D. (1998). To dream or not to dream? Relevant data from new neuroimaging and electrophysiological studies. *Current Opinion in Neurobiology, 8*, 239–244. doi: 10.1016/S0959-4388(98)80146-3

Hobson, J. A. (2001). *The dream drug store.* Cambridge: MIT Press.

Hobson, J. A. (2007). Wake up or dream on? Six questions for Turnbull and Solms. *Cortex, 43*, 1113–1115, discussion 1116–1121. doi: 10.1016/S0010-9452(08)70717-2

Hobson, J. A., & Friston, K. J. (2012). Waking and dreaming consciousness: Neurobiological and functional considerations. *Progress in Neurobiology, 98*(1), 82–98. doi: 10.1016/j.pneurobio.2012.05.003

Hobson, J. A., Pace-Schott, E. F., & Stickgold, R. (2000). Dreaming and the brain: Toward a cognitive neuroscience of conscious states. *Behavioral and Brain Sciences, 23*(6), 793–842; discussion 904–1121.

Hollan, D. (1996). Cultural and experiential aspects of spirit beliefs among the Toraja. In J. Mageo & A. Howard (Eds.), *Spirits in culture, history, and mind* (pp. 213–236). New York: Routledge Press.

Hollan, D. (2003). The cultural and intersubjective context of dream remembrance and reporting: Dreams, aging, and the anthropological encounter in Toraja, Indonesia. In R. I. Lohmann (Ed.), *Dream travelers: Sleep experiences and culture in the Western Pacific* (pp. 169–187). New York: Palgrave Macmillan.

Horvitz, J. C. (2002). Dopamine gating of glutamatergic sensorimotor and incentive motivational input signals to the striatum. B*ehavioural Brain Research, 137*, 65–74.

Hu, P., Stylos-Allan, M., & Walker, M. P. (2006). Sleep facilitates consolidation of emotionally arousing declarative memory. *Psychological Science, 17*(10), 891–898.

Huguelet, P., Mohr, S., Borras, L., Gillieron, C., & Brandt, P. Y. (2006). Spirituality and religious practices among outpatients with schizophrenia and their clinicians. *Psychiatric Services, 57*, 366–372. doi: 10.1176/appi.ps.57.3.366

Hultkrantz, A. (1970). Attitudes to animals in Shoshoni Indian Religion. *Studies in Comparative Religion, 4*, 70–79.

Hultkrantz, A. (1987). *Native religions of North America: The power of visions and fertility.* New York: Harper and Row.

Irwin, L. (1994). *The dream seekers: Native American visionary traditions of the Great Plains*. Norman: University of Oklahoma Press.

Jeannerod, M., & Pacherie, E. (2004). Agency, simulation, and self-identification. *Mind Lang, 19*(2), 113–146.

Jedrej, M. C., & Shaw, R. (Eds.). (1992). *Dreaming, religion, and society in Africa*. Leiden: E. J. Brill.

Johnson D. D. P., & Krüger O. (2004). The good of wrath: Supernatural punishment and the evolution of cooperation. *Political Theology, 5*(2), 159–176. doi: 10.1558/poth.2004.5.2.159

Johnson, S. C., Baxter, L. C., Wilder, L. S., Pipe, J. G., Heiserman, J. E., & Prigatano, G. P. (2002). Neural correlates of self-reflection. *Brain, 125*, 1808–1814.

Kahan, T., & LaBerge, S. (2011). Dreaming and waking: Similarities and differences revisited. *Consciousness and Cognition, 20*, 494–519.

Kahn, D., & Hobson, J. A. (2005). Theory of mind and dreaming: Awareness of feelings and thoughts of others in dreams. *Dreaming, 15*, 48–57.

Kahn, D., Stickgold, R., Pace-Schott, E. F., & Hobson, J. A. (2000). Dreaming and waking consciousness: A character recognition study. *Journal of Sleep Research, 9*(4), 317–325.

Kapur, S. (2003). Psychosis as a state of aberrant salience: A framework linking biology, phenomenology, and pharmacology in schizophrenia. *American Journal of Psychiatry, 160*(1), 13–23.

Kelley, W. M., Macrae, C. N., Wyland, C. L., Caglar, S., Inati, S., & Heatherton, T. F. (2002). Finding the self? An event-related fMRI study. *Journal of Cognitive Neuroscience, 14*(5), 785–794.

Kelly, M. H., & Keil, F. C. (1985). The more things change: Metamorphoses and conceptual structure. *Cognitive Science, 9*, 403–416.

Kelly, T. I. (1932). Ethnography of the surprise valley Paiute. *University of California Publications in American Archaeology and Ethnology, 31*, 66–210.

Kennedy, J. G., & Langness, L. L. (1981). Introduction. *AnthroSource, 9*(4), 249–257.

Kilborne, B. J. (1981). Moroccan dream interpretation and culturally constituted defense mechanisms. *Ethos, 9*(4), 294–312.

Kilroe, P. (2000). The dream as text, the dream as narrative. *Dreaming, 10*(3), 125–137.

Kimhy, D., Goetz, R., Yale, S., Corcoran, C., & Malaspina, D. (2005). Delusions in individuals with schizophrenia: Factor structure, clinical correlates, and putative neurobiology. *Psychopathology, 38*, 338–344.

Kirkpatrick, L. A. (2005). *Attachment, evolution, and the psychology of religion*. New York: Guilford Press.

Kleitman, N. (1982). Basic rest-activity cycle—22 years later. *Sleep, 5*(4), 311–317.

Koechlin, E., & Summerfield, C. (2007). An information theoretical approach to prefrontal executive function. *Trends in Cognitive Sciences, 11*(6), 229–235.

Kracke, W. (1979). Dreaming in Kagwahiv: Dream beliefs and their psychic uses in Amazonian culture. *Psychoanalytical Study of Society, 8*, 119–171.

Kramer M. (1993). The selective mood regulatory function of dreaming: An update and revision. In A. Moffitt, M. Kramer, & R. Hoffman (Eds.), *The functions of dreaming* (pp. 139–196). Albany: State University of New York Press.

Krebs, R. M., Heipertz, D., Schuetze, H., & Duzel, E. (2011). Novelty increases the mesolimbic functional connectivity of the substantia nigra/ventral tegmental area (SN/VTA) during reward anticipation: Evidence from high-resolution fMRI. *NeuroImage, 58*(2), 647–655. doi: 10.1016/j.neuroimage.2011.06.038

Krippner, S., Bogzaran, F., & de Carvalho, A. P. (2002). *Extraordinary dreams and how to work with them*. Albany: State University of New York Press.

Kuiken, D., & Sikora, S. (1993). The impact of dreams on waking thoughts and feelings. In A. Moffitt, M. Kramer, & R. Hoffmann (Eds.), *The functions of dreaming* (pp. 419–475). Albany: State University of New York Press.

Lajoux, J. D. (2002). Les Donnees Ethnologiques du Culte de L'Ours. In T. Tiller & L. Binford (Eds.), *L'Ours et l'Homme* (pp. 229–234). Liège: ERAUL.

Lakoff, G. (1993). How metaphor structures dreams: The theory of conceptual metaphor applied to dream analysis. *Dreaming, 3*(2), 77–98. doi: 10.1037/h0094373

Lanternari, V. (1975). Dreams as charismatic significance: Their bearing on the rise of new religious movements. In T. R. Williams (Ed.), *Psychological anthropology* (pp. 221–236). Paris: Mouton.

Larson-Prior, L. J., Zempel, J. M., Nolan, T. S., Prior, F. W., Snyder, A. Z., & Raichle, M. E. (2009). Cortical network functional connectivity in the descent to sleep. *Proceedings of the National Academy of Sciences of the United States of America, 106*(11), 4489–4494. doi: 10.1073/pnas.0900924106

Laughlin, C. D. (2011). *Communing with the gods: Consciousness, culture, and the dreaming brain*. Brisbane: Daily Grail.

Leube, D. T., Knoblich, G., Erb, M., & Kircher, T.T.J. (2003). Observing one's hand become anarchic: An fMRI study of action identification. *Consciousness and Cognition, 12*, 597–608. doi: 10.1016/S1053-8100(03)00079-5

Levin, R., & Nielsen, T. (2009). Nightmares, bad dreams, and emotion dysregulation: A review and new neurocognitive model of dreaming. *Current Direction in Psychological Science, 18*(2), 84–88. doi: 10.1111/j.1467-8721.2009.01614

Lewis-Williams, J. D. (2002). *The mind in the cave: Consciousness and the origins of art*. London: Thames & Hudson.

Limosani, I., D'Agostino, A., Manzone, M. L., & Scarone, S. (2011). The dreaming brain/mind, consciousness and psychosis. *Consciousness and Cognition*, 987–992. doi: 10.1016/j.concog.2010.11.014

Lincoln, J. S. (1935). *The dream in primitive cultures*. Oxford: Cresset Press.

Littlewood, R. (2004). On from elsewhere: Prophetic visions and dreams among the people of the earth. *Dreaming, 14*(2–3), 94–106. doi:10.1037/1053-0797.14.2-3.9

Lohmann, R. (2003). *Dream travellers sleep experiences and culture in the Western Pacific*. New York: MacMillan Palgrave.

Macrae, C. N., Moran, J. M., Heatherton, T. F., Banfield, J. F., & Kelley, W. M. (2004). Medial prefrontal activity predicts memory for self. *Cerebral Cortex, 14*(6), 647–654. doi: 10.1093/cercor/bhh025

Mageo, J. M. (2006). Figurative dream analysis and U.S. traveling identities. *Ethos, 34*(4), 456–487.

Mahowald, M. W., Cramer Bornemann, M. A., & Schenck, C. H. (2011). State dissociation, human behavior, and consciousness. *Current Topics in Medicinal Chemistry, 11*, 2392–2402. Review.

Maia, T. V, & Frank, M. J. (2011). From reinforcement learning models to psychiatric and neurological disorders. *Nature Neuroscience, 14*(2), 154–162. doi: 10.1038/nn.2723

Maia, T. V. (2009). Reinforcement learning, conditioning, and the brain: Successes and challenges. *Cognitive, Affective and Behavioral Neuroscience, 9*(4), 343–364. doi: 10.3758/CABN.9.4.343

Maid of Heaven. (2016, February 13). Retrieved February 27, 2016, from https://en.wikipedia.org/wiki/Maid_of_Heaven

Malmgren, J. (1994, November 27). The Good Friday Marsh Chapel Experiment THEN—Rev. Mike Young—NOW "TUNE IN, TURN ON, GET WELL?" *St. Petersburg Times.*

Maloney, K. J., Mainville, L., & Jones, B. E. (2002). c-Fos expression of dopaminergic and GABAergic neurons of the ventral mesencephallic tegmentum and paradoxical sleep deprivation and recovery. *European Journal of Neuroscience, 15*(4), 774–778. doi: 10.1046/j.1460-9568.2002.01907.x

Maquet, P., & Franck, G. (1997). REM sleep and amygdala. *Molecular Psychiatry, 2*(3), 195–196. doi: 10.1038/sj.mp.4000239

Maquet, P., & Ruby, P. (2004). Psychology: Insight and the sleep committee. *Nature, 427*(6972), 304–305. doi: 10.1038/427304a

Maquet, P., Peters, J. -M., Aerts, J., Delfiore, G., Degueldre, C., Luxen, A., & Frank, G. (1996). Functional neuroanatomy of human rapid-eye-movement sleep and dreaming. *Nature, 383*, 163–166.

McDougall, I., Brown, F. H., & Fleagle, J. G. (2005). Stratigraphic placement and age of modern humans from Kibish, Ethiopia. *Nature, 433*(7027), 733–736.

McNamara, P. (2000). Counterfactual thought in dreams. *Dreaming, 10*(4), 237–246.

McNamara, P. (2004). *An evolutionary psychology of sleep and dreams*. Westport, CT: Praeger.

McNamara, P. (2008). *Nightmares: The science and solution of those frightening visions during sleep.* Westport, CT: Praeger Perspectives.

McNamara, P. (2009). *A neuroscience of religious experience*. Cambridge: Cambridge University Press.

McNamara, P. (2016). Dreams and visions: How religious ideas emerge in sleep and dreams. Bloomsbury Publishing USA.

McNamara, P. (2022). The cognitive neuroscience of religious experience: Decentering and the self. Cambridge University Press.

McNamara, P., & Bulkeley, K. (2015). Dreams as a source of supernatural agent concepts. *Frontiers in Psychology, 6*, 1–8.

McNamara, P., Johnson, P., McLaren, D., Harris, E., Beauharnais, C., & Auerbach, S. (2010). REM and NREM sleep mentation. *International Review of Neurobiology, 92*, 69–86.

McNamara, P., McLaren, D., Kowalczyk, S., & Pace-Schott, E. F. (2007). "Theory of mind" in REM and NREM dreams. In D. Barrett & P. McNamara (Eds.), *The new science of dreaming: Vol. 1. Biological aspects* (pp. 201–220). Westport, CT: Praeger.

McNamara, P., McLaren, D., Smith, D., Brown, A., & Stickgold, R. (2005). A "Jekyll and Hyde" within: Aggressive versus friendly social interactions in REM and NREM dreams. *Psychological Science, 16*(2), 130–136.

Melges, F. T., Tinklenberg, J. R., Hollister, L. E., & Gillespie, H. K. (1970). Temporal disintegration and depersonalization during marihuana intoxication. *Arch Gen Psychiatry, 23*(3), 204–210. doi: 10.1001/archpsyc.1970.01750030012003

Mellars, P. (2005). The impossible coincidence. A single-species model for the origins of modern human behavior in Europe. *Evolutionary Anthropology, 14*(1), 12–27.

Menon, V., & Uddin, L. Q. (2010). Saliency, switching, attention and control: A network model of insula function. *Brain Structure and Function, 214*(5–6), 655–667. doi: 10.1007/s00429-010-0262-0

Metzner, R. (Ed.). (2004). *Teonanacatl: Sacred mushrooms of visions*. Sonoma, CA: Green Earth Foundation.

Mitchell, J. P., Banaji, M. R., & Macrae, C. N. (2005). The link between social cognition and self- referential thought in the medical prefrontal cortex. *Journal of Cognitive Neuroscience, 17*(8), 1306–1315. doi: 10.1162/0898929055002418

Mohr, S., Borras, L., Betrisey, C., Pierre-Yves, B., Gilliéron, C., & Huguelet, P. (2010). Delusions with religious content in patients with psychosis: How they interact with spiritual coping. *Psychiatry: Interpersonal and Biological Processes, 73*, 158–172. doi: 10.1521/psyc.2010.73.2.158

Montangero, J. (2012). Dreams are narrative simulations of autobiographical episodes, not stories or scripts: A review. *Dreaming, 22*(3), 157–172.

Murkar, A. L., & De Koninck, J. (2018). Consolidative mechanisms of emotional processing in REM sleep and PTSD. *Sleep Medicine Reviews, 41*, 173–184.

Nielsen, T. A. (1991). Reality dreams and their effects on spiritual belief: A revision of animism theory. In J. Gackenbach & A. A. Sheikh (Eds.), *Dream images: A call to mental arms* (pp. 233–264). Amityville, NY: Baywood Publishing.

Nielsen, T. A., & Powell, R. A. (1992). The day-residue and dream-lag effects: A literature review and limited replication of two temporal effects in dream formation. *Dreaming, 2*(2), 67–77.

Nishida, M., Pearsall, J., Buckner, R. L., & Walker, M. P. (2009). REM sleep, prefrontal theta, and the consolidation of human emotional memory. *Cerebral Cortex, 19*(5), 1158–1166.

Nofzinger, E. A., Buysse, D. J., Germain, A., Price, J. C., Miewald, J. M., & Kupfer, D. J. (2004). Functional neuroimaging evidence for hyperarousal in insomnia. *American Journal of Psychiatry, 161*, 2126–2128. doi: 10.1176/appi.ajp.161.11.2126

Nofzinger, E. A., Mintun, M. A., Wiseman, M. B., Kupfer, D. J., & Moore, R. Y. (1997). Forebrain activation in REM sleep: An FDG PET study. *Brain Research, 770*, 192–201.

Norenzayan, A., Gervais, W. M., & Trzesniewski, K. H. (2012). Mentalizing deficits constrain belief in a personal God. *PLoS One, 7*(5). doi: 10.1371/journal.pone.0036880

Nordin, A. (2024a). Gauging oneiromancy—the cognition of dream content and cultural transmission of (supernatural) divination. Religion, Brain & Behavior, 14(2), 161–182.

Nordin, A. (2024b). Imagery of ritual actions in religious dreaming: steps toward a theory and method of the cognition of dreamt ritual interaction. Religion, 54(2), 271–296.

Northhoff, G., & Bermpohl, F. (2004). Cortical midline structures and the self. *Trends in Cognitive Sciences, 8*(3), 102–107. doi: 10.1016/j.tics.2004.01.004

Northhoff, G., Heinzel, A., de Greck, M., Bermpohl, F., Dobrowolny, H., & Panksepp, J. (2006). Self-referential processing in our brain—a meta-analysis of imaging studies on the self. *NeuroImage, 31*(1), 440–457.

Oades, R. D., & Halliday, G. M. (1987). Ventral tegmental (A10) system: Neurobiology. 1. Anatomy and connectivity. *Brain Research, 434*(2), 117–165.

Offenkrantz, W., & Rechtschaffen, A. (1963). Clinical studies of sequential dreams. I. A patient in psychotherapy. *Archives in General Psychiatry, 8*, 497–508.

Opler, H. M. (1941). A Colorado Ute bear dance. *Southwestern Lore, 7*, 21–30.

Owen, A. D., Hayward, R. D., Koenig, H. G., Steffens, D. C., & Payne, M. E. (2011). Religious factors and hippocampal atrophy in late life. *PloS One, 6*(3), e17006. doi: 10.1371/journal.pone.0017006

Pace-Schott, E. F. (2001). "Theory of mind": Social cognition and dreaming. *SRS Bulletin, 7*, 33–36.

Pace-Schott, E. F. (2012). Prefrontal cortex in dreaming. In Patrick. McNamara and Dierdre Barrett (Eds.), *Encyclopedia of sleep and dreams: The evolution, function, nature, and mysteries of slumber* (Vol. 2, pp. 513–518). Santa Barbara, CA: Greenwood, an imprint of ABC-CLIO, LLC.

Pace-Schott, E. F. (2013). Dreaming as a story-telling instinct. *Frontiers in Psychology, 4*, 159. doi: 10.3389/fpsyg.2013.00159

Pace-Schott, E. F., & Hobson, J. A. (2002). The neurobiology of sleep: Genetics, cellular physiology and subcortical networks. *Nature Reviews, 3*(8): 591–605.

Pace-Schott, E., Johnson, P., & McNamara, P. (2012). Sleep, dreams and personality. In D. Barrett & P. McNamara (Eds.), *Encyclopedia of sleep and dreams* (pp. 652–654). Santa Barbara, CA: Greenwood Press.

Pagel, J. (2014). *Dream science: Exploring the forms of consciousness.* Waltham, MA: Academic Press.

Pahnke, W. N. (1963). *Drugs and mysticism: An analysis of the relationship between psychedelic drugs and the mystical consciousness* (Unpublished doctoral dissertation). Harvard University, Cambridge.

Pahnke, W. N. (1967). LSD and religious experience. In R. C. Debold & R. C. Leaf (Eds.), *LSD, man & society* (pp. 60–85). Middletown, CT: Wesleyan University Press.

Palagini, L., & Rosenlicht, N. (2011). Sleep, dreaming, and mental health: A review of historical and neurobiological perspectives. *Sleep Medicine Reviews, 15*(3), 179–186. doi:10.1016/j.smrv.2010.07.003

Park, Z. W. (1934). Paviotso shamanism. *American Anthropologist, 36*, 98–113.

Payne, J. D. (2010). Memory consolidation, the diurnal rhythm of cortisol, and the nature of dreams: A new hypothesis. In A. Clow, & P. McNamara (Eds.), *International review of neurobiology: Dreams and dreaming* (pp. 103–134). London: Elsevier.

Peluso, D. M. (2004). "That which I dream is true": Dream narratives in an Amazonian community. *Dreaming, 14*(2–3), 107–119.

Perogamvros, L., & Schwartz, S. (2012). The roles of the reward system in sleep and dreaming. *Neuroscience & Biobehavioral Reviews, 36*, 1934–1951. doi: 10.1016/j.neubiorev.2012.05.010

Pinter, M., Pogarell, O., & Oertel, W. (1999). Efficacy, safety, and tolerance of the non-ergoline dopamine agonist pramipexole in the treatment of advanced Parkinson's disease: A double blind, placebo controlled, randomized, multicentre study. *Journal of Neurology, Neurosurgery, & Psychiatry, 66*(4), 436–441.

Plihal, W., & Born, J. (1997). Effects of early and late nocturnal sleep on declarative and procedural memory. *Journal of Cognitive Neuroscience, 9*(4), 534–547.

Popa, D., Duvarci, S., Popescu, A. T., Lena, C., & Pare, D. (2010). Coherent amygdalocortical theta promotes fear memory consolidation during paradoxical sleep. *Proceedings of the National Academy of Sciences of the United States of America, 107*(14), 6516–6519. doi: 10.1073/pnas.0913016107

Presti, D. E., & Nichols, D. E. (2004). Biochemistry and neuropharmacology of psilocybin mushrooms. In R. Metzner (Ed.), *Teonanacatl: Sacred mushrooms of visions* (pp. 89–108). Sonoma, CA: Green Earth Foundation.

Ramnani, N., & Owen, A. M. (2004). Anterior prefrontal cortex: Insights into function from anatomy and neuroimaging. *Nature Reviews Neuroscience, 5*, 184–194. doi: 10.1038/nrn1343

Randerson, J. (2008, August 11). Clinical trials test potential of hallucinogenic drugs to help patients with terminal illness. *The Guardian*, p. 11.

Rangel, A., Camerer, C., & Montague P. R. (2008). Neuroeconomics: The neurobiology of value-based decision-making. *Nature Reviews Neuroscience, 9*(7), 545–556. doi: 10.1038/nrn2357

Rechtschaffen, A., & Kales, A. (1968). *A manual of standardized terminology, techniques and scoring system for sleep stages of human subjects*. US Department of Health, Education, and Welfare Public Health Service—NIH/NIND.

Redgrave, P., & Gurney, K. (2006). The short-latency dopamine signal: A role in discovering novel actions? *Nature Reviews Neuroscience, 7*, 967–975. doi: 10.1038/nrn2022

Redgrave, P., Gurney, K., & Reynolds, J. (2008). What is reinforced by phasic dopamine signals? *Brain Research Reviews, 58*(2), 322–339.

Rittenhouse, C., Stickgold, R., & Hobson, J. A. (1994). Constraint on the transformation of characters, objects and settings in dream reports. *Consciousness and Cognition, 3*, 100–113.

Samejima, K., & Doya, K. (2007). Multiple representations of belief states and action values in corticobasal ganglia loops. *Annals of the New York Academy of Sciences, 1104*, 213–228. doi: 10.1196/annals.1390.024

Schmitz, T. W., Kawahara-Baccus, T. N., & Johnson, S. C. (2004). Metacognitive evaluation, self-relevance, and the right prefrontal cortex. *NeuroImage, 22*, 941–947.

Schultz, W., & Dickinson, A. (2000). Neuronal coding of prediction errors. *Annual Review of Neuroscience, 23*, 474–500.

Schultz, W., Dayan, P., & Montague, P. R. (1997). A neural substrate of prediction and reward. *Science, 275*(5306), 1593–1599.

Schweickert, R. (1993). A multinomial processing tree model for degradation and redintegration in immediate recall. *Memory & Cognition, 21*(2), 168–175.

Schweickert, R., & Xi, Z. (2011). Theory of mind and metamorphoses in dreams: *Dr. Jekyll and Mr. Hyde* and *The metamorphosis.* In P. Leverage, H. Mancing, R. Schweickert, & J. William (Eds.), *Theory of mind and literature* (pp. 219–228). West Lafayette, IN: Purdue University Press.

Seeley, W. W., Menon, V., Schatzberg, A. F., Keller, J., Glover, G. H., Kenna, H., Reiss, A. L., & Greicius, M. D. (2007). Dissociable intrinsic connectivity networks for salience processing and executive control. *Journal of Neuroscience, 27*(9), 2349–2356.

Semendeferi, K., Damasio, H., Frank, R., & Van Hoesen, G. W. (1997). The evolution of the frontal lobes: A volumetric analysis based on three-dimensional reconstructions of magnetic resonance scans of human and ape brains. *Journal of Human Evolution, 32*(4), 375–388.

Semendeferi, K., Lu, A., Schenker, N., & Damasio, H. (2002). Humans and great apes share a large frontal cortex. *Natural Neuroscience, 5*(3), 272–276.

Shepard, P., & Sanders, B. (1985). *The sacred paw: The bear in nature, myth and literature.* New York: Penguin Arkana Press.

Siddle, R., Haddock, G., Tarrier, N., & Faragher, E. B. (2002). Religious delusions in patients admitted to hospital with schizophrenia. *Social Psychiatry and Psychiatric Epidemiology, 37*, 130–138. doi: 10.1007/s001270200005

Smith, A., Li, M., Becker, S., & Kapur, S. (2006). Dopamine, prediction error and associative learning: A model-based account. *Network, 17*(1), 61–84.

Smith, C. (2004). Consolidation enhancement: Which stages for which tasks? *Behav. Behavioral and Brain Sciences, 28*, 83–84. doi: 10.1017/S0140525X0541002X

Spencer, W. B., & Gillen, F. (1899; 1968). *The native tribes of central Australia.* New York: Dover.

Stamets, P. (1996). *Psilocybin mushrooms of the world.* Berkeley, CA: Ten Speed Press.

Stanton B., & David A. (2000). First-person accounts of delusions. *Psychiatr Bulletin, 24*, 333–336. doi: 10.1192/pb.24.9.333

States, B. O. (1993). *Dreaming and storytelling.* Ithaca, NY, and London: Cornell UP.

Stefanakis, H. (1995). Speaking of dreams: A social constructionist account of dream sharing. *Dreaming, 5*(2), 95–104.

Stepansky, R., Holzinger, B., Schmeiser-Rieder, A., Saletu, B., Kunze, M., & Zeitlhofer, J. (1998). Austrian dream behavior: Results of a representative population survey. *Dreaming, 8*, 23–30. doi: 10.1023/B:DREM.0000005912.77493.d6

Stickgold, R., & Walker, M. (2004). To sleep, perchance to gain creative insight? *Trends in Cognitive Sciences, 8*(5), 191–192. doi: 10.1016/j.tics.2004.03.003

Stickgold, R., & Walker, M. P. (2013). Sleep-dependent memory triage: Evolving generalization through selective processing. *Nature Neuroscience, 16*, 139–145.

Stickgold, R., Scott, L., Rittenhouse, C., & Hobson, J. A. (1999). Sleep-induced changes in associative memory. *Journal of Cognitive Neuroscience, 11*(2), 182–193. doi: 10.1162/089892999563319

Strauch, I., & Meier, B. (1996). *In search of dreams: Results of experimental dream research*. New York: SUNY Press.

Sutton, R. S., & Barto, A. G. (1998). *Reinforcement learning: An introduction*. Cambridge, MA: MIT Press/Bradford Books.

Tattersall, I. (1995). *The Last Neanderthal: The rise, success, and mysterious extinction of our closest human relatives* (New York: Macmillan, pp. 208, ISBN 0-02-860813-5).

Tedlock, B. (1987). Dreaming and dream research. In B. Tedlock (Ed.), *Dreaming: Anthropological and psychological interpretations* (pp. 1–30). Cambridge: Cambridge University Press.

Tedlock, B. (1992). *Dreaming: Anthropological and psychological interpretations*. New Mexico: School of America Research Press.

Thalbourne, M. A., & Delin, P. S. (1999). Transliminality: Its relation to dream life, religiosity and mystical experience. *The International Journal for the Psychology of Religion, 9*, 45–61.

Thompson, D. F., & Pierce, D. R. (1999). Drug-induced nightmares. *Annals of Pharmacotherapy, 33*(1), 93–98.

Turner, V. W. (1969). *The ritual process: Structure and anti-structure*. Chicago, IL: Aldine Pub.

Tylor, E. B. (1873). *Primitive cultures*. (Vols. 1–2). London: Murray.

Uddin, L. Q., Supekar, K. S., Ryali, S., & Menon, V. (2011). Dynamic reconfiguration of structural and functional connectivity across core neurocognitive brain networks with development. *Journal of Neuroscience, 31*, 18578–18589. doi: 10.1523/JNEUROSCI.4465-11.2011

Urgesi, C., Aglioti, S. M., Skrap, M., & Fabbro, F. (2010). The spiritual brain: Selective cortical lesions modulate human self-transcendence. *Neuron, 65*(3), 309–319.

Vail, K. E., Arndt, J., & Abdollahi, A. (2012). Exploring the existential function of religion and supernatural agent beliefs among Christians, Muslims, atheists, and agnostics. *Personality and Social Psychology Bulletin, 38*(10), 1288–1300.

Vaitl, D., Birbaumer, N., Gruzelier, J., Jamieson, G. A., Kotchoubey, B., Kübler, A., … & Weiss, T. (2005). Psychobiology of altered states of consciousness. *Psychol Bulletin, 131*(1), 98–127.

Van de Kloet, D., Merckelbach, H., Giesbrecht, T., & Lynn, S. J. (2012). Fragmented sleep, fragmented mind: The role of sleep in dissociative symptoms. *Perspectives on Psychological Science, 7*(2), 159–175. doi: 10.1177/1745691612437597

van den Heuvel, M. P., Stam, C. J., Kahn, R. S., & Hulshoff Pol, H. E. (2009). Efficiency of functional brain networks and intellectual performance. *Journal of Neuroscience, 29*(23), 7619–7624.

Vann, B., & Alperstein, N. (2000). Dream sharing as social interaction. *Dreaming, 10*(2), 111–119. doi: 10.1023/A:1009452822669

Verdone, P. (1965). Temporal reference of manifest dream content. *Perceptual and Motor Skills, 20,* 1253–1268. doi: 10.2466/pms.1965.20.3c.1253

Voorn, P., Vanderschruen, L. J., Groenwegen, H. J., Robbins, T. W., & Pennartz, C. M. (2004). Putting a spin on the dorsal-ventral divide of the striatum. *Trends in Neurosciences, 27*(8), 468–474.

Wagner, U., Gais, S., & Born, J. (2001). Emotional memory formation is enhanced across sleep intervals with high amounts of rapid eye movement sleep. *Learning and Memory, 8*(2), 112–129.

Wagner, U., Gais, S., Haider, H., Verleger, R., & Born, J. (2004). Sleep inspires insight. *Nature, 427,* 352–355. doi: 10.1038/nature02223

Walker, M. P. (2009). REM, dreams and emotional brain homeostasis. *Front. Neuroscience, 3*(3), 442–443.

Walker, M. P., & Stickgold, R. (2006). Sleep, memory and plasticity. *Annual Review of Psychology, 10,* 139–166.

Walker, M. P., & Van der Helm, E. (2009). Overnight therapy? The role of sleep in emotional brain processing. *Psychological Bulletin, 135*(5), 731–748. doi: 10.1037/a0016570

Walker, M. P., Liston, C., Hobson, J. A., & Stickgold, R. (2002). Cognitive flexibility across the sleep-wake cycle: REM-sleep enhancement of anagram problem solving. *Cognitive Brain Research, 14*(3), 317–324. doi: 10.1016/S0926-6410(02)00134-9

Walsh, R. (2010). Dreaming and narrative theory. In F. L. Aldama et al. (Eds.), *Toward a cognitive theory of narrative acts* (pp. 141–157). Austin: U of Texas P.

Wamsley, E. J., & Stickgold, R. (2010). Dreaming and offline memory processing. *Current Biology, 20*(23), R1010–R1013.

Wasson, R. G., Kramrisch, S., Ruck, C., & Ott, J. (1992). *Persephone's quest: Entheogens and the origins of religion.* New Haven, CT: Yale University Press.

Weeden, J., Cohen, A. B., & Kenrick, D. T. (2008). Religious attendance as reproductive support. *Evolution and Human Behavior, 29,* 327–334.

Wilson, D. S. (2002). *Darwin's cathedral: Evolution, religion and the nature of society.* Chicago, IL: University of Chicago Press.

Winkelman, M., & Baker, J. (2008). *Supernatural as natural: A biocultural theory of religion.* New Jersey: Prentice Hall.

Winson, J. (1972). Interspecies differences in the occurrence of theta. *Behavioral Biology, 7*(4), 479–487. doi: 10.1016/S0091-6773(72)80210-4

Wittmann, B. C., Bunzeck, N., Dolan, R. J., & Düzel, E. (2007). Anticipation of novelty recruits reward system and hippocampus while promoting recollection. *NeuroImage, 38*(1–9), 194–202. doi: 10.1016/j.neuroimage.2007.06.038

9

EMBODIED REPRESENTATION OF THE DIVINE

Irene Cristofori, Sara Di Marco, Gabriella Cucuzza, Guillaume Lio, Salvatore Aglioti, and Angela Sirigu

The Brain and the Belief in God

Belief in a deity is a fascinating aspect of the human mind. How does our brain construct and maintain vivid representations of God despite the absence of any actual personal experience or direct evidence? Studies on the neural basis of religious beliefs have begun to make their way into the neuroscience field (McNamara, 2009; McNamara and Butler 2014). Neuroimaging and lesion studies have already investigated the neural substrate of religious beliefs, highlighting shared networks between religious beliefs and social cognition (Urgesi et al. 2010; Schjoedt et al. 2011; Beauregard and Paquette 2006; Cristofori et al. 2016) converging on the key role played by the mPFC, inferior frontal gyrus, and temporoparietal junction, areas also involved in theory of mind (ToM), empathy, and emotion regulation. When Christian believers pray, for example, they often report a sense of engaging in a reciprocal, communicative relationship with God. Functional neuroimaging confirms that such practices activate a network involved in social interaction and personal memory, including the mPFC, precuneus, and temporopolar cortex (Kapogiannis et al. 2014; Schjoedt et al. 2009). Moreover, emotional and reward-related structures such as the anterior insula, amygdala, and vmPFC are also recruited during religious experiences (Kapogiannis et al. 2009; Schjødt et al. 2008). These findings support the argument that faith is a mental construct fundamentally rooted in affective processes, memory, and social-cognitive functioning. Converging evidence from ERPs, neuroimaging, and lesion studies (Urgesi et al. 2010; Schjoedt et al. 2011; Beauregard and Paquette 2006; Cristofori et al. 2016) shows that the anterior frontal and temporal cortex have a prominent role in the storage of key aspects of religious beliefs

DOI: 10.4324/9781003158189-9

and in the sensory experience of supernatural beliefs. Brain networks involved in social cognition, including ToM regions including the mPFC, inferior frontal gyrus (IFG), temporoparietal junction, as well as regions important for emotion regulation (dorsomedial, ventrolateral prefrontal cortices), play a role in rationalizing God's intent and emotions. A first study to examine ToM in the context of religious cognition was Kapogiannis et al. (2009). Multidimensional scaling analysis of religious beliefs revealed three main dimensions: Perceived level of God involvement, perceived God emotion, and doctrinal/experiential religious knowledge [see also (Modestino, O'Toole, and Reinhofer 2016)]. A follow-up study (Kapogiannis et al. 2014) found a pathway in which the dorsomedial prefrontal cortex (dmPFC) and precuneus, involved in episodic memory and bodily self-processing, were modulated by the right IFG, a key ToM-related brain region found activated when believers checked statements about God's involvement in their daily life.

Research with highly religious individuals while praying has revealed that ToM regions are involved in experiencing a relationship with God during prayer. Schjoedt et al. (2009) reported that praying recruited a cortical network involved in social cognition, including the temporopolar region, precuneus, and mPFC, and suggested that praying to God is similar to non-religious human interpersonal communication since, in prayer, God can be seen as an intentional agent with reciprocity capacity. Recall of religious beliefs stored in memory can also induce the emotional state of belief reflected by activation of the anterior insula, amygdala, and related emotional structures (Harris, Sheth, and Cohen 2008; Harris et al. 2009)· Also, reward-related brain regions like the vmPFC, striatum, and nucleus accumbens compute the enhanced valuation and reinforcement of established or newly acquired religious beliefs (Zhong et al. 2017; Schjødt et al. 2008). Finally, the dlPFC plays an important role in down-regulating supernatural or magical interpretations of unusual religious or other experiences (Schjoedt et al. 2011; Andersen et al. 2019) through cognitive control and executive functions.

Thus, religious thoughts seem to depend upon a variety of cognitive and emotional processes mediated by distinct brain networks (Seitz, Paloutzian, and Angel 2018). While studies to date have focused on the neural underpinnings of religious beliefs, religion is also a matter of overall bodily experience, involving different sensory modalities (touch, hearing, olfaction, vision). In this respect, beliefs are embedded in these bodily acts of worship. Hence, religious behavior is not solely an act of faith but also a practice, whereby one engages in some form of interior communication with one's God, through prayer or meditation. This raises little-studied questions about (1) the nature of the mental representation of God and (2) the internal conditions that give rise to and mediate this interaction. In this review, we will discuss how religious representations and feelings are embodied and how they engage low-level and associative brain structures involved in sensory/perceptual processing.

Representing God: The Face of the Divine

Most research has focused on the relationship between a believer's personality or cognitive profile and the strength of his/her faith, but surprisingly little is known about how believers build internal representations of divine sensory attributes and how sensory brain areas are associated with this process. The fMRI studies have identified several cortical areas that appear to represent the core of the adult face processing system. These are the inferior occipital gyrus ("OFA," occipital face area), the middle fusiform gyrus (FFA, Fusiform Face Area), the anterior temporal region (ATFA, anterior temporal face area) (Guntupalli, Wheeler, and Gobbini 2017; Foster et al. 2022), and the superior temporal sulcus (STS) (Haxby, Hoffman, and Gobbini 2000). The current dominant neural models suggest that these structures are divided along two neural pathways of face processing. The ventral pathway includes the FFA, which is implicated in the treatment of facial traits, that is, invariant features defining gender, age, and identity, and the ATFA which is a small face-sensitive region that contains information that goes beyond perceptual features of faces to include semantic information about a person's identity (Collins, Koski, and Olson 2016). In contrast, the STS pathway is more specialized in processing the face-state, that is, changeable facial-related processes such as speech, implied motion, emotional expressions, attention, and intentions (Schobert et al. 2018). This pathway is also considered the gateway to an extended system dedicated to social perception, encompassing the orbitofrontal cortex and the amygdala (Allison, Puce, and McCarthy 2000). In a recent study using high-density electroencephalography coupled with multivariate pattern classification and group blind source separation methods, Lio and collaborators isolated a late face signal in the STS peaking at 240ms after face-stimulus onset (Lio et al. 2025). The power of this evoked signal varied depending on the face region observed, being strong when the eye region fell on the fovea to decreasing in regions further away and outside the stimulus face. This suggests that cortical face-processing mechanisms in the STS show selective responses to eye gaze, which serves as a crucial cue for inferring others' attentional state, emotions, and intentions. What is the weight of visual processes when thinking of God? How specific is such an image, and how similar is this internal representation among believers? A recent behavioral study found that American Christians pictured the face of God as young, Caucasian, and kind, but perceptions varied depending on political ideology and the physical appearance of believers (Jackson, Hester, and Gray 2018). This confirms that believers humanize their image of God and endow it with specific facial features. However, in this study, the neural activity was not recorded and only Christians were tested. It would have been interesting to examine visual representations in different cultures and faiths. Islam forbids pictorial representations of Allah or the Prophet. Judaism also believes in an invisible God and refuses all representation of divine entities. What impact might this have on how the followers of these faiths conjure up an image of God and on its corresponding representation along the occipitotemporal and superior temporal streams? We propose that, in believers, any representation of God's image preferentially activates the face-selective regions within the ventral occipitotemporal cortex. We might expect this activity to be modulated by the reported vividness of the God image, strength of faith, and attachment to God. Antagonistic activity between the ventral-occipito-temporal pathway and the superior temporal stream could be found depending on the type of faith, permitting or prohibiting the pictorial representation of God. Future research should explore whether visualizing God activates the brain's face-processing network similarly to imagining a parent or friend. Particularly interesting would be the understanding of differences across religious traditions. For example, Islam and Judaism typically discourage visual representations of God, whereas Christianity permits and even promotes them.

Faith in the Body: Interoception and Spiritual Perception

Religious practice is often enacted through the body: kneeling in prayer, fasting, chanting, or meditating. These rituals not only express devotion but engage visceral processes—heartbeat, breath, gut feelings—that inform one's sense of spiritual presence. Neuroscientific research suggests that interoception—the perception of internal bodily states—is deeply tied to emotional and self-related processing (Craig 2002; Critchley et al. 2004).

One key vehicle for transmitting interoceptive information is the vagus nerve. The vagus nerve carries somatic and visceral efferents and afferents distributed throughout the central nervous system, either monosynaptically or via the nucleus of the solitary tract (Rutecki 1990). Vagal nerve fibers carry afferent information, modulating activity in the brainstem, thalamus, amygdala, hippocampus, and cerebral cortex. Corazzol and collaborators have recently shown that vagus nerve stimulation (VNS) enhances body awareness and consciousness by modulating a local circuit within the parietal regions (Corazzol et al. 2017). Interestingly, prayer has been shown to induce mystical sensations and an internal state of meditation related to activity in the frontoparietal cortex (Schjødt et al. 2008). Thus, we might expect that VNS could enhance religious cognition, including visual awareness and saliency of religious pictorial representations.

It would be interesting to use transcutaneous vagus nerve stimulation (tVNS) to non-invasively enhance interoceptive signals. This technique can influence awareness, emotion, and attention by stimulating afferent vagal fibers that project to brain areas such as the brainstem, thalamus, and insula (Frangos, Ellrich, and Komisaruk, 2015).

This would suggest that bodily states modulate the perceptual salience of religious stimuli, potentially making spiritual representations more vivid or emotionally compelling. It also aligns with findings that prayer or religious context can attenuate pain perception and alter sensory thresholds (Wiech et al., 2008; Schjødt et al., 2008).

Recent evidence further supports the impact of vagal modulation on autonomic and interoceptive processes that are relevant to spiritual experiences. The tVNS has been consistently shown to reduce resting heart rate and increase heart rate variability (HRV), markers of enhanced parasympathetic activity and improved autonomic regulation (Badran et al., 2018; Clancy et al., 2014; Bretherton et al., 2019). These physiological shifts foster a more balanced internal milieu, which may underline altered states of consciousness often reported during spiritual or meditative practices. Moreover, tVNS has been demonstrated to enhance heartbeat-evoked potentials (HEPs), a neurophysiological index of cardiac interoception, and to improve accuracy in heartbeat detection tasks, indicating a heightened bodily awareness (Villani et al., 2019; Villani, Tsakiris, and Azevedo, 2019).

In line with these autonomic and interoceptive effects, Finisguerra et al. (2019) explored how tVNS modulates spiritual self-representations. Their findings reveal that active tVNS selectively reduces the implicit association between the self and spirituality, without altering explicit spiritual or religious self-concepts. This suggests that vagal afferent stimulation can influence unconscious, embodied aspects of spirituality, possibly by altering the integration of interoceptive signals within subcortical and medial cortical networks.

Together, these data highlight the vagus nerve as a crucial neurophysiological bridge linking visceral bodily states and implicit spiritual experiences, thus providing a promising avenue for investigating the somatic basis of spirituality.

Conclusions

Whether representations of God are grounded in the sensory brain, are there common patterns across faiths, and how can we modulate these experiences? Future studies should better understand how human neural architecture makes such beliefs possible and persuasive. Face-selective areas of the visual cortex may be recruited when believers picture God's image, and interoceptive networks may be engaged during prayer and connection with the divine.

Funding

This work was supported by Cognitive Neuroscience of Religious Cognition (CNRC).

References

Allison, Truett, Aina Puce, and Gregory McCarthy. 2000. "Social perception from visual cues: Role of the STS region." *Trends in Cognitive Sciences*, 4 (7): 267–278.

Andersen, Marc, Thies Pfeiffer, Sebastian Müller, and Uffe Schjoedt. 2019. "Agency detection in predictive minds: A virtual reality study." *Religion, Brain & Behavior*, 9 (1): 52–64. https://doi.org/10.1080/2153599X.2017.1378709.

Badran, B. Badran, Andrew B. Yu, David Adair, Gregory Mappin, William H. DeVries, Donald D. Jenkins, and Mark George. (2018). "Short trains of transcutaneous auricular vagus nerve stimulation (taVNS) have parameter-specific effects on heart rate." *Brain Stimulation*, 11 (4): 699–708. https://doi.org/10.1016/j.brs.2018.04.004.

Beauregard, Mario, and Vincent Paquette. 2006. "Neural correlates of a mystical experience in carmelite nuns." *Neuroscience Letters*, 405 (3): 186–190. https://doi.org/10.1016/j.neulet.2006.06.060.

Bretherton, Beatrice, Lucy Atkinson, Aaron Murray, Jennifer Clancy, Susan Deuchars, and Jim Deuchars. 2019 July 30. Effects of transcutaneous vagus nerve stimulation in individuals aged 55 years or above: Potential benefits of daily stimulation. *Aging*, 11 (14): 4836–4857. https://doi.org/10.18632/aging.102074.

Clancy, Jennifer A., David A. Mary, Klaus K. Witte, John P. Greenwood, Susan A. Deuchars, and Jim Deuchars. 2014 Nov-Dec. "Non-invasive vagus nerve stimulation in healthy humans reduces sympathetic nerve activity." *Brain Stimulation*, 7 (6): 871–877. https://doi.org/10.1016/j.brs.2014.07.031. Epub 2014 Jul 16. PMID: 25164906.

Collins, Jessica A., Jessica E. Koski, and Ingrid R. Olson. 2016. "More Than Meets the Eye: The Merging of Perceptual and Conceptual Knowledge in the Anterior Temporal Face Area." *Frontiers in Human Neuroscience*, 10. https://www.frontiersin.org/article/10.3389/fnhum.2016.00189.

Corazzol, Martina, Guillaume Lio, Arthur Lefevre, Gianluca Deiana, Laurence Tell, Nathalie André-Obadia, and Pierre Bourdillon, et al. 2017. "Restoring consciousness with vagus nerve stimulation." *Current Biology: CB*, 27 (18): R994–R996. https://doi.org/10.1016/j.cub.2017.07.060.

Craig, Arthur D. 2002. "How do you feel? Interoception: The sense of the physiological condition of the body." *Nature Reviews Neuroscience*, 3 (8): 655–666. https://doi.org/10.1038/nrn894.

Cristofori, Irene, Joseph Bulbulia, John H. Shaver, Marc Wilson, Frank Krueger, and Jordan Grafman. 2016. "Neural correlates of mystical experience." *Neuropsychologia*, 80 (January): 212–220. https://doi.org/10.1016/j.neuropsychologia.2015.11.021.

Critchley, Hugo D., Stefan Wiens, Pia Rotshtein, Arne Öhman, and Raymond J. Dolan. 2004. "Neural systems supporting interoceptive awareness." *Nature Neuroscience*, 7 (2): 189–195. https://doi.org/10.1038/nn1176.

Finisguerra, Andrea, Alessandro D'Agostino, Valeria Mazzola, Andrea Benvenuto, Salvatore M. Aglioti, and Valentina Moro. 2019. "Transcutaneous vagus nerve stimulation affects implicit spiritual self-representations." *Consciousness and Cognition*, 73: 102774 https://doi.org/10.1016/j.neuroscience.2019.05.059

Foster, Celia, Mintao Zhao, Timo Bolkart, Michael J. Black, Andreas Bartels, and Isabelle Bülthoff. 2022. "The neural coding of face and body orientation in occipitotemporal cortex." *NeuroImage*, 246 (February): 118783. https://doi.org/10.1016/j.neuroimage.2021.118783.

Frangos, Eleni, Jens Ellrich, and Barry R. Komisaruk. 2015. "Non-invasive access to the vagus nerve central projections via electrical stimulation of the external Ear: fMRI evidence in humans." *Brain Stimulation*, 8 (3): 624–636. https://doi.org/10.1016/j.brs.2014.11.018.

Guntupalli, J. Swaroop, Galit Kelsey, Kevin Wheeler, and M. Ida Gobbini. 2017. "Disentangling the representation of identity from head view along the human face processing pathway." *Cerebral Cortex*, 27 (1): 46–53. https://doi.org/10.1093/cercor/bhw344.

Harris, Sam, Jonas T. Kaplan, Ashley Curiel, Susan Y. Bookheimer, Marco Iacoboni, and Mark S. Cohen. 2009. "The neural correlates of religious and nonreligious belief." *PLoS One*, 4 (10): e7272. https://doi.org/10.1371/journal.pone.0007272.

Harris, Sam, Sameer A. Sheth, and Mark S. Cohen. 2008. "Functional neuroimaging of belief, disbelief, and uncertainty." *Annals of Neurology*, 63 (2): 141–147. https://doi.org/10.1002/ana.21301.

Haxby, James V., Elizabeth A. Hoffman, and M. Ida Gobbini. 2000. "The distributed human neural system for face perception." *Trends in Cognitive Sciences*, 4 (6): 223–233. https://doi.org/10.1016/s1364-6613(00)01482-0.

Jackson, Joshua Conrad, Neil Hester, and Kurt Gray. 2018. "The faces of god in America: Revealing religious diversity across people and politics." *PLoS One*, 13 (6): e0198745. https://doi.org/10.1371/journal.pone.0198745.

Kapogiannis, Dimitrios, Aron K. Barbey, Michael Su, Giovanna Zamboni, Frank Krueger, and Jordan Grafman. 2009. "Cognitive and neural foundations of religious belief." *Proceedings of the National Academy of Sciences*, 106 (12): 4876–4881. https://doi.org/10.1073/pnas.0811717106.

Kapogiannis, Dimitrios, Gopikrishna Deshpande, Frank Krueger, Matthew P. Thornburg, and Jordan Henry Grafman. 2014. "Brain networks shaping religious belief." *Brain Connectivity*, 4 (1): 70–79. https://doi.org/10.1089/brain.2013.0172.

Lio, Guillaume, Martina Corazzol, Roberta Fadda, Giuseppe Doneddu, and Angela Sirigu. 2025. "A neuronal marker of eye contact spontaneously activated in neurotypical subjects but not in autistic spectrum disorders." *Cortex*, 183 (February): 87–104. https://doi.org/10.1016/j.cortex.2024.10.022.

McNamara, Patrick. 2009. *The neuroscience of religious experience*. Cambridge: Cambridge University Press. https://doi.org/10.1017/CBO9780511605529.

McNamara, Patrick, and P.M. Butler. 2014. "The neuropsychology of religious experience." In *The Handbook of the psychology of religion*, 2nd ed. Vol. Raymond F. Paloutzian and Crystal L. Park (Eds.). New York: The Guilford Press.

Modestino, Edward J., Partrick O'Toole, and AnnaMarie Reinhofer. 2016. "Experiential and doctrinal religious knowledge categorization in Parkinson's disease: Behavioral and brain correlates." *Frontiers in Human Neuroscience*, 10. https://doi.org/10.3389/fnhum.2016.00113.

Rutecki, Paul. 1990. "Anatomical, physiological, and theoretical basis for the antiepileptic effect of vagus nerve stimulation." *Epilepsia*, 31 Suppl 2: S1–S6. https://doi.org/10.1111/j.1528-1157.1990.tb05843.x.

Schjødt, Uffe, Hans Stødkilde-Jørgensen, Armin W. Geertz, and Andreas Roepstorff. 2008. "Rewarding prayers." *Neuroscience Letters*, 443 (3): 165–168. https://doi.org/10.1016/j.neulet.2008.07.068.

Schjoedt, Uffe, Hans Stødkilde-Jørgensen, Armin W. Geertz, and Andreas Roepstorff. 2009. "Highly religious participants recruit areas of social cognition in personal prayer." *Social Cognitive and Affective Neuroscience*, 4 (2): 199–207. https://doi.org/10.1093/scan/nsn050.

Schjoedt, Uffe, Hans Stødkilde-Jørgensen, Armin W. Geertz, Torben E. Lund, and Andreas Roepstorff. 2011. "The power of charisma—perceived charisma inhibits the frontal executive network of believers in intercessory prayer." *Social Cognitive and Affective Neuroscience*, 6 (1): 119. https://doi.org/10.1093/scan/nsq023.

Schobert, Anne-Kathrin, Corrado Corradi-Dell'Acqua, Sascha Frühholz, Wietske van der Zwaag, and Patrik Vuilleumier. 2018. "Functional organization of face processing in the human superior temporal sulcus: A 7T high-resolution fMRI study." *Social Cognitive and Affective Neuroscience*, 13 (1): 102–113. https://doi.org/10.1093/scan/nsx119.

Seitz, Rüdiger J., Raymond F. Paloutzian, and Hans-Ferdinand Angel. 2018. "From believing to belief: A general theoretical model." *Journal of Cognitive Neuroscience*, 30 (9): 1254–1264. https://doi.org/10.1162/jocn_a_01292.

Urgesi, Cosimo, Salvatore M. Aglioti, Miran Skrap, and Franco Fabbro. 2010. "The spiritual brain: Selective cortical lesions modulate human self-transcendence." *Neuron*, 65 (3): 309–319. https://doi.org/10.1016/j.neuron.2010.01.026.

Villani, Valentina, Alistair W. De Borst, and Rui T. Azevedo. 2019. "Transcutaneous vagus nerve stimulation (tVNS) enhances cardiac interoception." *Neuropsychologia*, 135, 107233. https://doi.org/10.1016/j.neuropsychologia.2019.107201

Villani, Valentina, Manos Tsakiris, Rui T. Azevedo. 2019 Nov. "Transcutaneous vagus nerve stimulation improves interoceptive accuracy." *Neuropsychologia*, 134: 107201. https://doi.org/10.1016/j.neuropsychologia.2019.107201. Epub 2019 Sep 25. PMID: 31562863.

Wiech, Katja, Miguel Farias, Guy Kahane, Nicholas Shackel, Wiebke Tiede, and Irene Tracey. 2008. "An fMRI study measuring analgesia enhanced by religion as a belief system." *Pain*, 139 (2): 467–476. https://doi.org/10.1016/j.pain.2008.07.030.

Zhong, Wanting, Irene Cristofori, Joseph Bulbulia, Frank Krueger, and Jordan Grafman. 2017. "Biological and cognitive underpinnings of religious fundamentalism." *Neuropsychologia*, 100 (June): 18–25. https://doi.org/10.1016/j.neuropsychologia.2017.04.009.

APPENDIX

Abbreviation

mPFC	Medial prefrontal cortex
vmPFC	Ventromedial prefrontal cortex
dlPFC	Dorsolateral prefrontal cortex
dmPFC	Dorsomedial prefrontal cortex
IFG	Inferior frontal gyrus
FFA	Fusiform face area
OFA	Occipital face area
ATFA	Anterior temporal face area
STS	Superior temporal sulcus
ERP	Event-related potential
ToM	Theory of mind
fMRI	Functional magnetic resonance imaging
tVNS	Transcutaneous vagus nerve stimulation
VNS	Vagus nerve stimulation

INDEX

Note: **Bold** page numbers refer to tables and *italic* page numbers refer to figures.